LOWELL LECTURES.

THE

PROBLEM OF HUMAN DESTINY;

OR,

THE END OF PROVIDENCE IN THE WORLD AND MAN.

BY

REV. ORVILLE DEWEY, D.D.

SECOND EDITION.

NEW YORK:
PUBLISHED BY JAMES MILLER
(SUCCESSOR TO C. S. FRANCIS AND COMPANY),
522 BROADWAY.
1864.

JOHN F. TROW,
PRINTER, STEREOTYPER, AND ELECTROTYPER,
46, 48, & 50 Greene Street,
New York.

PREFACE.

No person, with any comprehension of what he is doing would publish a book on the Problem of Human Destiny, without wishing to put into the title of it, some such phrase as "humble attempt" at a solution of, or "approximation" thereto. Herder denominates his great work, "IDEEN—*Ideas*, on the History of Humanity." I would have entitled this volume of Lectures, "Hints on the Problem of Human Destiny," but that the word "hints" did not seem to befit a Course of Lectures. Nor could I very well say, "Outlines of the Problem;" for the work does not pretend to be so much. In short, I do not see but I must let the title stand in its appalling nakedness and vastness; presuming that the reader will expect nothing on such a subject, but approximations, hints, and outlines.

I would say, however, very explicitly, that here are no abstruse discussions, such as might be looked for, perhaps, from the title of this volume; that, as I was to address a popular audience, my discourse has been conformed to that intention; that I undertook to speak for those who were to hear me, and not for philosophers; and that all I attempted, was to offer for the consideration of my hearers, certain views of life, of the human condition, and of the scene of the world, that might help them better to understand their nature, lot, and destiny.

I am sensible that I am putting forth this work at a time when the public mind is absorbed with questions, not of philosophy, but of awful fact; when we are pressed to solve, not the problem of the world, but the problem of our own national stability and honor. But although the first shock of the crisis seemed almost to unseat all our theories and thoughts of life, yet as the struggle has gone on, I confess that it has driven me, more and more, to the great principles and resorts of my faith in Providence and Humanity; and it has seemed to me, therefore, that the discussions proposed have some pertinence to the time.

SHEFFIELD, *April*, 1864.

TABLE OF CONTENTS.

LECTURE I.

LECTURE II.

LECTURE III.

LECTURE IV.

LECTURE V.

LECTURE VI.

LECTURE VII.

LECTURE VIII.

LECTURE IX.

LECTURE X.

LECTURE XI.

LECTURE XII.

ON THE PROBLEM OF HUMAN DESTINY.

LECTURE I.

ON THE CHARACTER, FITNESS, HISTORY, AND CLAIMS OF THE INQUIRY.

Have we any right to ask—is it natural and fit that a human being should ask, such questions as these—"Why do I exist? Why am I here? Why am I such as I am? Why was the world made and arranged as it is? This dread mystery of nature and life—what does it mean?"

If it *is* proper to ask such questions, then is there such a subject for legitimate discussion, as the problem of human destiny. This is the subject on which I am to enter this evening, with a view to some preliminary statement of its character, of the propriety of discussing it, of its history as a subject of thought, and of the natural interest that belongs to it.

Let me say a word or two of the title by which I have announced it; both for the vindication of the title, and the explanation of my purpose.

My theme, then, is *not* natural theology, nor, indeed, any other theology; it lies in the more general domain of philosophy. Theology, as a science, is the study of the Supreme Nature; and *natural* theology is the study of it, in what *exists*, in distinction from what is supernaturally *revealed*. The results of this theology I take for granted. I believe in God, in his perfection and providence. But having found the Divinity, I seek to find the humanity, in nature and life—to find, that is, its place, its function, its vocation, its destiny. That is to say—having found the divine nature, I seek to understand its intent and end in human nature; and by consequence in the material creation as ministering to it. After the problem of the Divinity, comes by natural and logical sequence the problem of humanity; in fact, it *has* followed in historical development. The Divinity was the question of the old Oriental sytems; the humanity has been that upon which the Hebrew and Christian, have fixed attention.

Again, the title "philosophy of history" would not suit my purpose; because history deals with nations, and my subject embraces, not only national, but social, domestic, and individual life. I might call it "the problem of existence;" but that would seem to indicate a more speculative theme; as, for instance, *how* things *came* into existence, or under what *view* existence is to be conceived of; and besides, though it is the problem of all earthly existence that is in my mind, yet it centres in humanity; and therefore I say, the problem of *human* destiny.

If I should say that "the problem of *evil in the world*" is my theme, I should come nearer to the matter in hand; but then I should only point to the *cause* naturally and immediately prompting inquiry, not to the whole compass of it, nor to its ultimate aim. The aim is to learn what this scene of human affairs meaneth; the compass of the inquiry is the whole mingled good and evil of the human lot; and the existence of evil, obviously, is only a part of the theme. But doubtless it is evil especially that raises the question, that drives us upon it. If all were bright and happy in this world, if the steps of men and generations were ever onward and upward, were free and buoyant, then there would be no problem to try, but only contemplation to delight us. The great wisdom that reigns over the world, would, indeed, *then*, as it must forever, invite our thoughts, but there would be no difficulty, no darkness, no doubt concerning the human condition. If man had been perfectly happy and pure, he would never have questioned his lot, nor struggled for the solution of its mysteries. But how is it now? The steps of humanity have been slow and heavy, and apparently backward at times; stumbling and weariness and sorrow have been in the path; dark clouds have hung over the way of generations, and men and nations have struggled with one another in the darkness; and the experience of every thoughtful human being, has pressed home upon him the question, What means this troubled scene of things? In other words, what is the reigning and ultimate aim that lies behind it?

What, then, *is* the reigning and ultimate aim that lies behind? This is our question. Is there any presumption in seeking to know what it is? Observe, that it does not answer our question to say that *infinite love* is the principle from which all things have sprung. What does that love aim to accomplish? I say, again, may we not humbly ask? There is a sort of mock modesty, mixed with philosophic pride, in comparing man seeking to comprehend the moral system of the world, to a fly upon a great wheel, seeking to know why it revolves, and for what end. The profession of ignorance may be prouder than the profession of knowledge. It is evident, I think, that Socrates himself felt more pride than humility, in professing to know nothing. For my part, I do not claim to be one of the philosophers, and am so unpretending as to profess that I do know something about our nature and condition, and what they mean. It would be strange, I think, if to the grandest and most importunate questioning of intelligent natures, there were no answer. In the humblest manufactory, a man could not live his *day's* life, but in misery and distraction, if he did not know what was going on there. And can he live this life, of vaster breadth and wider relations—this life, that "is sounding on its dim and perilous way" through the years of time, and consent to know nothing of the sublime processes that are going on here?—nothing of that great plan, that binding unity amidst boundless diversity, which alone makes of the universe an intelligent order and a goodly system?

My belief is, that this great and irresistible impulse of our nature to inquire into these things, is not given to be balked by heaven, nor scorned by man. My belief is, that this high questioning does admit of some answer. The celebrated statesman and Oriental scholar, William Humboldt, has said, "the world-history is not without an intelligible world-government." And this declaration is placed as a motto at the head of a philosophy of history, commonly thought to be sufficiently sceptical; I mean the German Hegel's. And sceptical enough it is. But while Hegel recognizes only an impersonal Reason as ruling in the world, nothing is more remarkable in his work, than to see how he traces everywhere in the history of the world, the thread of a design and a destiny, as distinct and determinate, as if it were everywhere drawn and held fast by a personal Will,—a hint, by the bye, of what is often confirmed by the study of philosophy,—that seeming atheism in the contemplation of the world, is often obliged to deny itself and to acknowledge a providence.

Our problem, then, is the world-problem; in short, it really *is* the problem of human destiny. I confess that I still feel some objection to this description of my theme; it is a more sounding title than I like. Not, however, that it is presumptuous; because presumption, surely, must be out of the question *here;* modesty, I think, is to be taken for granted on such a subject; the very greatness of the problem—the vastness of the treasure-house to which we resort, is an argument, nay, and a kind of warrant, at once for earnestness and humility. Everybody may go to the mines of California for gold, because they are so vast and exhaustless; and yet, for the same reason, nobody expects to get more than a small share of it. And so in the field of our inquiry—if one may pick up a few of the golden sands on this shore of boundless and mysterious wealth, it is well; and well may it engage his attention.

I have adopted the title *problem of human destiny*, then, for the simple reason that it better expresses and sets forth, than any other which has occurred to me, the object I have in view. A problem is something proposed, laid down—thrown out, as we familiarly say,—for examination. The Greek root from which it comes, προβάλλω, from βάλλω, to throw, suggests, in fact, the very figure. A problem is a ball thrown out, to be unwound, unravelled. And the subject which is presented in this kind of investigation, is the strangely mingled web of human destiny. It is, indeed, if I may say so, this ball of earth, around which ages have wound their many-colored tissues, tissues of savage and civilized life, of political institutions and social usages, of literature and art, of law, science, and religion; tissues woven out of human hearts, and steeped in all the bright and all the sombre dyes of human experience; tissues which have clothed the earth, bare and naked at first, with countless memories, traditions, histories, associations, sentiments, affections—which have, in fact, given the term *world* a *human* sense, which have made it mean a very different thing from the bare word, earth; tissues, in fine, broken and torn by outbreak, revolution, war, violence, or bound and knotted fast by despotism, caste, serfdom, slavery,—and intermingled and intertwisted in a thousand ways; and yet in which there is not one thread, laid by the Divine hand, that has not, as I believe, been drawing on to a sublime destiny.

To a sublime destiny, I say: and what is that? And where is it to be looked for? Is it in the original *nucleus* of the world, the mere material ball of earth? Is it in the sea, with its waves, or in the land, with its harvests—the dust beneath our feet? Is it in the ever-returning circuits of the seasons? Can you take any product of nature—flower or diamond, Andes or India—and say, "To form this, and such as this, was the end of all things"? No; instantly, intuitively, we say, no; where there is a destiny, there must be an experience, a consciousness of it; in our humanity only is the problem of this world's existence solved; in our humanity alone is there end or explanation; *man* is the world, and the world is man.

But let us look into this matter a little more closely, with a view to state more fully what is proposed as the subject of these Lectures, and more fully to legitimate this kind of inquiry.

You will remember, many of you, the opening observation of Dr. Paley in his Natural Theology, in which he supposes a man, in crossing a heath, to find a watch. He argues that the finder, on examining the mechanism, and discovering the purpose which it was designed to answer, would say, "somebody made it." He applies this reasoning to the world, which exhibits more design by far than a watch; and argues from effect to Cause, from design to a Designer, from the intelligence displayed in the universe to an intelligent Creator. And it seems to me that the argument would have been stronger if it had not taken the form of argument at all; *statement* here *is* argument; because design not merely *proves*, but *implies* a designer; just as action implies an actor, or a thing's being made implies a maker. You cannot say, "here is a design," without including in your thought, "here is a designer," any more than you can conceive of speech without a speaker. The world, the universe, is the utterance, the word, the expression of a mind.

There has manifested itself of late, in some quarters, a disposition to discredit this argument from design. In Germany has been revived the old theory of Plotinus and Iamblicus—for it is far older than Berkeley—that the world does not exist at all, but in our thought. Our inborn ideas, says Fichte, projected into space, are the universe. The world is but an idea; the world-creator is the mind. But this, if it were true, would only bring the argument from design *out* of nature into *humanity*—into this more astonishing realm of creative thought. Did this wonderful mind —world-creating, as they say it is—did this mind then create itself? Others have said, that the creation, not being *infinite*, cannot prove an infinite Creator. But if the Creator of this world or of the solar system, were imagined to be a finite and dependent creature, who, then, created *him?* The steps of *this* preposterous scepticism, alike lead us back to an infinite and independent Cause.

This is not the place for any elaborate discussion of the question, how it is that we come to be possessed with this great conviction of the existence of a God; whether by arguments drawn from within, or from without us; or whether by no argument,—the conviction being the impress upon our very nature, of the great hand that formed it. I will only say that if any instructed man can look upon himself or upon the universe around him; if he can ascend and dwell in thought amidst the countless millions of stars, or if he can take into his scope but the breadth of a summer's day, from the time when it touches the eastern hills with fire, to its soft and fading close; all its loveliness, its wealth and wonder of beauty, its domain crowded with thousand-fold life,—life clothing the mountain side, springing in the valley, singing and making melody though all the round of earth, and air, and waters; or if he can take any little plot of ground by his side, and study all its vegetable growth and insect life, and all that it drinks in from fostering nature around, all that it borrows from the ocean deep, and from the pavilion of the sun, to deck its flowery margin; if, in a word, any instructed man can read the handwriting that is written all over the great tablet of the universe, and not feel that it expresses a Mind—an Intelligence, a Wisdom, a love unbounded and unspeakable, he it is *not* to whom I speak: and well may I judge that there is no such man here, nor anywhere. Why, if one found inscribed upon some Rosetta stone, or upon the ribbed rocks of a desert mountain, but five such sentences as I am now uttering, he would say, without any doubt, "Some intelligent being has done this; some *mind* placed these words thus, one after another." And does the infinite volume of the universe give less assurance of a devising Intelligence? Good heaven! I am tempted to say, what sort of stupid mystification is it, that leads any man to deny that such a universe as this, expresses a Mind, and a Purpose?

But there being manifest design in the universe, and therefore a designing Mind, the question arises, What *is* this design? In other words, what is the *end* proposed in the creation? What may we believe that the infinite Creator intended to accomplish by the creation of this world, and of the beings and things upon it? And this question arises naturally and irresistibly; we cannot help asking it. Thus —to adopt the manner of Dr. Paley in the passage just referred to—if I were to bring here and place before you a lump of clay or a piece of marble, no inquiry might arise in your minds concerning it, unless it were the general question, why I had brought it here? But if I should bring and place before you an exquisite and beautiful piece of mechanism, that kind of vague question would not suffice, but you would especially and immediately ask, concerning this mechanism, what is it for? Is it to plane wood, or to print books, or to generate light and heat? What is it made for? And when this question was answered, you would as irresistibly ask, how does it *accomplish* its purpose? If it were a very complex instrument, you would have many questions to ask; as how this wheel, or that lever, this pulley, or that weight, helps on the general design.

Now, the frame of the world, the frame of our body, the frame of the soul, in other words, the whole system of nature and life and moral agency, is such a mechanism?

I do not suppose it is necessary to say anything to prove this point. The phrases in constant use—system of nature, system of the world, order of the universe, plan of the creation—recognize the doctrine and allow us to take it for granted. Every step in science opens a deeper insight into the wonderful and beautiful order of nature; the scientific explorer sees in the world a vast manufactory, filled with instruments and agencies, far more complicated and exquisite than the wheels and levers, the bands and pulleys, that weave the most splendid fabrics of human art. But every man who sees how this vast vegetable growth that covers the earth, ministers to innumerable living creatures, including the human race, sees a sublime order in nature. The earth, he cannot but see, is a bountiful table, spread and evermore replenished, by day and by night, for countless tribes of creatures. They come and go; they sleep and wake, without care; "they toil not, neither do they spin; they sow not, neither do they reap, nor gather into barns;" unbounded millions of creatures, with incessant wants, and no intelligence in themselves to supply those wants; but what then? *There is an intelligence* that provides for them. There is a bounty that feeds them. Each one finds his place and his position in the boundless feast. Each one has a set of organs, an apparatus, to assimilate the food to his nature, and convert it to his growth; a mouth to break it up, to grind it like a mill; the stomach to digest, *i. e.*, to amalgamate it with elements of animal life, and other organs to modify the supply—to dissolve and refine it, to bolt it, as it were, and cast away the chaff, while the pure nourishment is conveyed by ducts and channels innumerable, to every part of the system. Whoever knows this, knows that there is order in nature. It is true that we are less sensible of it, because we grow up amidst it; and many of its processes, too, are out of sight. I suppose, if there were machines in nature to make bones and build skeletons, and then, if there were other machines—gins to spin the hollow arteries and veins, and looms to weave the muscular fibre and the corded nerves, and founderies to mould the beating heart and the breathing lungs; and other contrivances still, for putting all the parts together, for setting up the frame and laying in the engines and the pipes, and putting on the integuments, and finishing off the man, like a statue—I suppose, I say, that many would be more impressed by all this visible mechanism. But it would be all coarse and clumsy compared with that which now exists, and would be far less indicative of an order and plan in the world.

But now, when we say there is order, there is a plan in the world, what precisely do we mean by that? We mean precisely that there is an arrangement of parts with a view to an end. An end, and means to an end—these are the two component elements of what we mean by intelligent order. I say intelligent order. A child or an idiot may place a hundred sticks parallel to each other, and this would be a sort of order. But in the order of nature we see the parts, the means, *i. e.*, conspiring to an end.

The end and the means, then—these are the points which we are brought to inquire into; these are the proper subjects of all high philosophy of our humanity, of history, and of the world, as the sphere of their development.

Our present inquiry is for the end. Let us look into this order of nature, then, and see if it does not, by very plain indications, lead us to a result—to a conclusion, that is to say, on the point which we have before us. We see subordinate aims in nature; let us see if they do not conduct us to an ultimate aim.

Herder commences his celebrated work on the "Philosophy of Humanity," by considering the world which we inhabit, in its primitive nature and relations. He devotes several chapters to such propositions as these: that the earth is one of the heavenly bodies; that it is a planet; that it passed through many revolutions before it came to its present form and condition; that it turns on its axis; that it is enveloped with an atmosphere, &c. He then proceeds to consider the geographical relations of the earth, and especially of its plains and mountain ranges, to human development. Other writers have followed in the same track. It would seem that philosophy, like Antæus, must touch the *earth*, to be strong.

I do not think it necessary, with my present view, to go back so far, or to take so wide a compass; something of this

I reserve for future consideration, especially the geographical relation. For the present, I wish to direct your attention to the simple point of organic growth in the world, and see to what it will lead us. You must allow me to do this in as few words as possible.

The basis of all is the soil. If the earth were a ball of solid iron or granite, there would be no soil, and no growth. It is formed of other materials, of other materials, *i. e.*, combined with these; and this, plainly, for an end: to produce trees, groves, the cedar of Lebanon, the hyssop that springeth by the wall, the herb yielding seed, the waving harvest —the whole vegetable growth of the world, a harvest for innumerable creatures. And this is the purpose answered by the soil. There is much to be said, and which we shall find occasion to say, of this basis and beginning of all growth and life on earth, this vast bed of raw material for all the varied fabric and workmanship of nature.

But look now a moment at this workmanship. Inlaid in every vegetable structure, air-cells and sap-vessels, to nourish its growth, and to produce fibre, flower, and seed; varied forms of structure—the wheat straw hollow, because for a given amount of material that form is strongest; the tree *not* hollow, because then it could not be used for timber, nor be as valuable for fuel; the fruit-bearing shrubs, like the blackberry, commonly provided with prickles, to defend them, or with small tough leaves, like the huckleberry, which do not invite the browsing herd; the esculent shrubs, herbs, and grasses, *not* so armed, because that would be fatal to the end; the orchard, the garden, the meadow, the pasture, the shady grove,—what is all this but a ministration of food and refreshment and beauty to the whole animal and human creation?

Observe, next, the animal creation. I do not say that it was made solely for man. It existed before man. It has an end proper to itself; a certain amount of enjoyment which, though lower, is more unalloyed than that of the human race.

Still, we see that it is mainly subservient to man. It furnishes him with food and raiment; it relieves his labor, and ministers to his pleasure. Some animals were evidently designed to be domesticated by man and to do him kindly and patient service--the horse, the ox, the camel, the dog. But of what use to him, it may be said, are the lion and tiger? I answer, of none, perhaps; but they are, at least, subject and subordinate to him in this sense, that where man comes, they disappear. They occupy, by the bounty of the Creator, a space which man does not want; a space which, perhaps, as in the instance of the deserts of Africa, he never will want; but whenever he does need the domain of these creatures, wild, untamable, and useless to him, their claim yields to his. They are made to live for him, or to perish for him, as he has occasion.

To man, then, we come at last in the ascending scale, and there is nothing higher; of this earthly creation, that is to say, he is the head. But in man, again, we see a double nature—a material frame, and something that is *not* material. To the material frame the lower creation directly ministers as *cause.* The vegetable and animal creation, that is to say, supplies to it *food,* without which it could not grow nor live. But is the body the end, the crowning glory of the world? Evidently it is not. Evidently it ministers to the soul. Its senses, appetites, and passions are all engaged in this ministry. To show this fully will require indeed some larger discourse. At present I am indicating only the steps of the ascent. But look a moment at the five senses in this view. Suppose a body in its general frame like that which we now possess, but without the senses, and the soul imprisoned in that body. What, then, do we see? What is done for it? Why it is *let out*—if I may say so—through touch, taste, smell, sight, hearing. For what end? Plainly for its delight, its culture, its growing knowledge. The senses are the specific organs of the soul. Their office is finer than that of the stomach, the liver, the lungs. These are but laborers in the comparison. The senses are artists. And as their office is finer, it is they that must have repose and relief. It is they only that *sleep.* The stomach, the lungs, the heart, do not sleep; they *labor on*, without pause or rest. These are servants. They keep the house of life in order and repair, that the inhabitant within, may have leisure and freedom to do his own proper work—to think, to meditate, to gaze upon the glories of the creation; to build up systems of science, philosophy, and art; to build up himself in that culture which is the end of all.

Nor does it conflict with this conclusion to say, that at every step, correlative ends are accomplished for their own sake. Nature is filled with lavish beauty and enjoyment; but still it points to an end. The stream overflows on every hand, but still there is a stream. Thus, in human life, I see a thousand gratuitous enjoyments; but I see, too, a higher and sublimer purpose. Thus the human body is a machine for work; but it is also a shrine for indwelling wisdom and devotion.

The Greek word for man, *ἄνθρωπος*, is composed of two words (*ἀνὰ ϑορέω*), which signify to *look upward.* Man is made to look upward. The ultimate end of all things on earth, is to form a being, filled with all nobleness and beauty, filled with virtue, wisdom, piety. The world-system is a pyramid of which humanity is the top. The broad earth, the vast substructure of soil, is the base. On it repose the layers and rounds, many and beautiful, of the vegetable creation. Next rise the orders of animal life. Above all, humanity, with its various component parts—some lower, some higher:—the digestive or building apparatus and the sentient organs; perception, memory, imagination, that gathers and moulds the stores of cognate facts; judgment that compares them, and the consequent grasp of general truth; and, above all, and ministered to by all, the spiritualized soul, the divine reason—that united intelligence and love, which gathers strength from all that is below, to rise to all that is above; which communes with heaven, with eternity, with God!

In this comparison, let it be observed that I describe the system of the world as it actually exists; as a system of relations, dependencies, connections running through the whole. If it were otherwise; if the vegetable kingdom stood completely distinct from the animal, and the animal from the human, then we might say that each one was made for ends proper, peculiar, limited to itself. But when we trace, throughout the system of the world, a connection and dependency as manifest as in any human machinery, as in that, for instance, by which wool is carded for the spindle, and spun for the loom, and woven for the fuller and dyer, to *make cloth*—we see in both alike an ultimate end. In the world-system, man is the end; and the highest in man is the ultimate end; that is, his virtue, his sanctity, his likeness to God.

Let me offer an observation in passing, upon the comparison which I have just used. There are some things in that process of making cloth, which, taken by themselves, not seen in their relations, seem very little to contribute to the desired result. They seem, in fact, to hinder and thwart the end. The material that is to be woven into a firm texture is, in the process of fabrication, rudely dealt with—pulled, and strained, and torn in pieces. A pure and shining fabric is to be made, fit for the array of princes; but soil, and damage, and discoloration, are a part of the process. So may the shining robes of virtue be fashioned. So may human affections be torn and riven. So may there be, in human life, many a hard struggle and strain, in order to come to the end.

Conceive now, on the whole, and yet more distinctly, of the highest thing in our humanity—what it is. It is not comfort, nor ease, nor pleasure; it is not birth, nor station, nor magnificent fortunes; it is not nobility, nor kingship, nor imperial sway. It is something more noble, *in the mind;* more kingly, more imperial, than all this. Conceive of a human being; what he is, and how it is with him, when he challenges your purest admiration; when unbidden tears start from your eyes as you think of him; when you, with all mankind, unite to consecrate and canonize his worth. Is earthly splendor or fortune, or is mere earthly happiness, any part of his claim? So far from that, it is when he stands alone, in the majesty of self-subsistent virtue; it is when he suffers for principle, and sinks and goes down with the last plank that honor has left him; it is when he wears himself out in unshared labors of philanthropy; it is when he dies for his country or for mankind—ay, rent and torn in pieces on the rack and the scaffold; it is then that he is noblest in your eyes. This highest in man, *all* that is highest and holiest, I believe, is the end of Providence; and it is my aim in these lectures to show how it is that Providence is ever promoting this end.

I have thus explained my design, and endeavored to justify it—to legitimate this kind of inquiry.

I cannot doubt that this is a subject of immense interest to all reflecting persons. The history of thought itself on this subject, would be one of immense interest. In the early ages of the world, indeed, there may have been but little thought about it; as we see there is but little now, in the earlier stages of our own life. And yet I cannot help believing, that in the mysterious depths of our humanity, this inquiry has always been dimly shadowed forth, even amidst barbarian ignorance; that the man who turned from the glare of day to his shaded Scythian tent or Bactrian hut, smitten down by the bitter strife of passion or sorrow, sometimes said with himself, "Wherefore is all this? Why am I made thus, and to what end?" But doubtless this inquiry has slowly developed itself with the progress of the world; and the history of it would be found to mark the steps of all human progress. It arose dimly in the old Hindoo, Chinese, and Persian systems of religion and philosophy. It struck far deeper roots into the Hebrew spiritualism. It occupied the thoughts of the Grecian and Roman sages. It has revealed itself in modern times in the more distinct forms of a philosophy of history, and a philosophy of humanity. It has swelled and deepened its channel through all the fields of human thought; history, philosophy, science, literature, are all more and more occupied with the question, what do all things mean? No question, I believe, has sunk so deeply into the cultivated mind of the modern world. And when, some twenty or thirty years ago, the Rev. and Earl of Bridgewater left a bequest of £8,000 as a prize for the best work on this subject, I believe it was widely felt that the sum was worthily bestowed, and that this specific direction of it, had touched the very theme of the age. It has been well said, I think, by one of the eloquent philosophers of France, Jouffroi, that this point of destiny, this object and end of being, is the very point about which all true poetry, philosophy, and religion have revolved—poetry, with its lofty sadness, with its visions and dreams of moral beauty, with its longings for better times on earth, and blessed regions in heaven; philosophy, with its profound and painful inquiries after the all-embracing, all-harmonizing result of human weal and woe; and religion, as it stands on the heights of the world, and speaks with authority from God, and faith in eternity.

It may be said, what need we more, since we *have* such a revelation? I answer, our having a Bible does not preclude us from preaching about it; our having a faith does not forbid our inquiring into it, and seeking for its confirmation; our receiving the facts of a revelation rather *inclines* us to study the philosophy of those facts. I may believe, as I do believe, that all the conditions of this life are designed and arranged to advance in us the highest culture; but how they fulfil their mission is a wide question, and into this question I propose thoughtfully and reverently to enter.

But let us go back a moment to the history of this great inquiry.

All the religions in the world have recognized this grand problem of human destiny. They have contemplated man as *having* a destiny beyond the little round of his daily pursuits; beyond earthly weal and woe, beyond the sphere of this world's kingdoms and empires. They have lifted up the dark curtain of time, on which the shows and glories, the battles and disasters of this world, are pictured, and pointed the busy actors to a solemn audit beyond. Everlasting repose, Elysian fields, or fair hunting grounds, have awaited them; or Tartarus, Tophet, Gehenna, and blackness of darkness.

The old Egyptian Sacerdotalism had an institution connected with the burial of the dead, which brought out this fact of a spiritual destination for men, into visible and impressive significance. The disposal of the body with the Egyptians, let it be remembered, was closely connected with the final state of the soul. They embalmed the body in the belief that the soul would return to it, after a wandering or metempsychosis of three thousand years. The institution to which I refer was this. On the banks of the lake Acherusia, sat a tribunal of forty-two judges, to examine into the life of all who were brought for burial in the great cemetery on the other side. In this examination no regard was to be paid to the rank or riches of the deceased, but only to his character, to his virtues or vices. If the result was favorable, his remains were conveyed in a boat to the *Elisout* or place of rest; if otherwise, they were cast into a deep trench, called *Tartar*—place of lamentations. Transferred to the Greek mythology, we find all this in Charon, his ferry-boat, Tartarus and the Elysian fields.

In the religious system of the Persians, among whom Hegel traces a development entitling them in his opinion to be called the earliest historical people—in the Zend-avesta of Zoroaster, that is to say, we find the mind of the author and the age, laboring with the problem of evil, and striving to meet it. Evil is in the world; how came it here? From the All-good, nothing but good could come;

2

whence came the evil? Two principles, teaches the Zend-avesta, reign over the world: Ormuzd, Light; and Ahriman, Darkness. From the accursed Ahriman comes all evil; not physical evil alone, as "winter and vermin," but "reprehensible doubt, and magic, and the false worship of Peris, and that which poisons men's hearts." Ormuzd, however, is the more powerful principle; and in twelve thousand years shall gain the victory." *

In the Hebrew Religion we find deeper traces of this great inquiry. The book of Ecclesiastes is a remarkable account of the questionings and strugglings of the mind upon this point. Throughout the largest portion of the work, the wise man of Israel appears as a sceptic and a satirist; he sees *no* high end for man; he sees no fitness in the conditions of life, to promote such an end; wealth and poverty, honor and shame, nay, science and ignorance, wisdom and folly, seem alike purposeless and useless: "vanity of vanities, all is vanity," is the burden of the teaching; and man is commended to eating and drinking and enjoying himself as he may; seemingly after a very reckless fashion. Then again the high and righteous aim is set before him, and God's favor and help are promised to him as his security and strength. So that to explain the book, the learned Eichhorn was led to adopt the theory that it is a dialogue, in which the sceptic and the believer are brought forward by the writer, to express their conflicting views; though there certainly are no marks of dialogue in the work, and it seems unnecessary to suppose in the case anything more than the strugglings of a single mind, after some clue to this maze of human passions and pursuits. Every man's thought is a dialogue.

In our Christian writings there is one book, Paul's Epistle to the Romans, which distinctly brings forward the same question. First, the great and universal fact of human imperfection, of human misery, is laid down; next the mis-

* Zendavesta, quoted by Heeren, Appendix I., in the 2d vol. on Asiatic Nations.

sion of Christ to a weak and wandering and sin-burthened race. These subjects, with some digressions, occupy the first six chapters. In the next chapter, Paul enters more particularly into the distress of the case, describes the struggle with sin and sorrow, and ends with the exclamation, "Oh wretched man that I am! who shall deliver me?" In the ninth chapter he speaks in encouraging and even exulting terms of a triumph. Man, it is true, "is subject to vanity," *i. e.* to dissatisfaction, weariness and pain; not willingly—life's burthens he would fain escape—but at the will of Him who hath subjected the same in hope. That is, for a good end, the Supreme Will hath placed him here; the case is hopeful; the destiny is noble, though fraught with elements of trial, strife and sorrow. *Through* strife and sorrow, the victory is to be gained. Man is "saved by hope." His state is one not of attainment, but of expectation, of progress. The great futurity forever draws him on. He does not see all that he seeks for. He struggles on through imperfection, uncertainty, darkness, error. Only by these, only by a battle does he gain the victory. This is the theory of his condition.

The thread of our inquiry, which runs through the whole course of philosophy, I have not time now to trace. Plato took it up again and again, and Aristotle; and after them, Zeno, and Epicurus, and even Pyrrho, the doubter—each after his own fashion. The new Platonic school in the third century, seems to me to have framed its theories with distinct, if not ultimate reference to this question. Plotinus, Jamblicus and Proclus cast scorn upon the present life and all its objects; and as the true end for man, strove to live above it, in a certain divine contemplation and ecstasy. In the early part of the eighteenth century, John Baptiste Vico of Naples, in his "Nuova Scienza," first expounded as a new science, the philosophy of history. Herder, Fichte and Hegel in Germany have labored in the same field. In France, Auguste Comte, in his great work, entitled "Philosophie Positive," has undertaken the herculean, task of an appreciation of the whole course and progress of human thought and history.

Mr. Buckle's Introductory Volumes on "the History of Civilization in England" have been added to the works I have mentioned—in some respects the most remarkable of them all. Failing on the moral side—denying freedom to the mind, and of course denying all proper moral influence in human affairs, it is at the same time such an account of the intellectual, scientific, political and material causes of human development and progress, that I know of nothing comparable to it, in the treatment of that branch of the subject. It is the more strange, that Mr. Buckle should have ignored the moral element—it is positively a phenomenon in literature—because his own mind was full of the very force that he denied; hardly anywhere is to be found a keener indignation at wrong, or a more eloquent espousal of human rights, or urging of human duties. In America, we have—still more recently—one most creditable contribution to the same general subject, in Dr. Draper's work on the Intellectual Development in Europe; in which the author seeks to show, though the point is sometimes almost lost sight of in the admirable and splendid array of facts, that this development is never uncertain or fortuitous in the causes or processes that lead to it, but always strictly dependent on law.

This brief allusion to the history of our theme, shows that it has been encompassed with doubt and difficulty. There are two lines in our great dramatist, that express the feeling of the sceptic and the scorner with almost terrific point and energy. Life, he says,

"Life is a tale,
Told by an idiot; full of sound and fury,
Signifying nothing."

There is a sound of the wayward and mad world sometimes in our ears, that seems to answer to that description. There are spectacles of failure, defeat, moral disaster, and miserable degradation, that sorely try the better faith.

Alas! we say, perhaps, is there *any* end for man—for man, the victim of absurd institutions, the sport of untoward circumstances, the burden-bearer, the slave; for man, baffled, thwarted, worn down with tasks, beguiled by illusions, wandering after phantoms,—is there any end for man? Was he made for anything high, great, ultimate? *Is* there a power above that guides him, and that has appointed such an end for him, and the means to that end? Is there any contemplation of our sin-stricken humanity, in which all that composes its mysterious frame and fortunes can find a mission and a destiny? Life is a bewildering scene; is there any clue to it? It is a changeful and often tragic drama; is there any tendency, any plan, any plot in it? It is a tale of strange things: has it any moral?

This is no idle or curious question. It is vital, and it is imperative. It is not given to us to choose whether we shall *be*, and shall be such as we are. Suppose a man is angry with his lot—angry with the world and with himself --with his nature, his freedom, his remorse, his life-long struggle, and says he does not care, and will not yield. What then? Down upon him, and upon his very frame and fate, sink the silent and everlasting laws: and there is no escape. Still the question of destiny presses upon him, and there is no discharge from the great bond of his nature and condition.

It is *experience* that is involved in this question. It is the life-experiment of every human being. The issue of the experiment is not merely future and everlasting, but now, day by day, it comes out—out from every event, exigency, situation, pursuit, engagement—the absolute, distilled essence of good or ill for us. Can it come to good? Was it meant for that?

It is a wide-reaching experiment; it embraces everything; can it *all* come to good?

> "The whips and scorns of time,
> The oppressor's wrong, the proud man's contumely,
> The pangs of despised love, the law's delay,

> The insolence of office, and the spurns
> That patient merit of the unworthy takes,"—

is it all to be reckoned in the good account?

It is a diversified experiment; it seems often strange, confused and purposeless; there are doubtless high traits in it, but it seems often poor, paltry and low. What conflicting elements mingle in it!—melancholy and gladness, laughter and tears, solemn intent and wayward levity! Can any lines be descried, stretching through this field, apparently of wide waste and disorder, and pointing to a happy issue? In all its diversified states—of youth, of manhood, and of old age, of sex, parentage, childhood, home, neighborhood, community—is it good?

It is an experiment of depth and reality—enough, far enough, from being indifferent to any who knows it. Stern, inexorable, overwhelming at times, is the lot of our being, take it as we will. Beneath the smooth surface of life, under the mask of pride or politeness, how many a fierce battle is fought, or bitter sorrow endured! What raging passion, dark intrigue, brooding discontent, despite, shame, sorrow! Like the black cloud beneath a smiling sky, like the lightning in that cloud, so oftentimes is the heart of man. Oh, could we say that "with like beneficent effect," sorrow gathers and broods, and passion darts its fires!

Could I but see that life is a school—all of it, altogether, and always; that all the homes of life are full of divine instruction; full, not of petty details alone, but of sublime instrumentalities; that eating and drinking and waking and sleeping, are not accidents but ordinances; that labor and weariness, and the tending of infancy, and the sports of childhood, and the voice of singing, and the making merry, and the feeling sad and low and heavy-hearted, are all ministrations to an end, and are actually doing something to bring it about—*that* would be an optimism, which would clear up to me the troubled brow of life, would renovate the face of the world.

But I must not pursue this subject any farther at

present. In my next Lecture I must consider the dread problem of evil; whence it sprang, or in what light it is to be regarded: for this lies at the foundation of my whole theory of life.

One word more let me say in close: The advocate before a jury, or the speaker in a deliberative assembly, has one great and singular advantage, in that he addresses those who, in common with himself, have something to do; who must share his labor, to come to a decision. Most other assemblies are full of passive hearers, content if they are entertained. Indeed in our popular lyceums, and in our popular literature too, entertainment is the thing so especially, if not exclusively demanded, that the speaker, the writer, is led to select the most salient points, and often to pass over topics and details less attractive, but of the utmost importance to his subject. Now I do not want such passive hearers; and I cannot pursue any such holiday course. I must descend to humble, pains-taking details, when the subject requires it. Indeed, Gentlemen and Ladies, I am afraid I must weary you sometimes, for your profit. In short, if you will permit me to say so, I desire to establish between you and me for the time, the friendly compact of persons giving their minds to a common task; together seeking to understand a vast and momentous subject, on which the stability, peace and happiness of all thinking minds do much depend.

I am not sorry that the place and occasion require me to make this a popular theme. I am to speak, not for phisophers, but for the people. I wish to meet the questions which arise in all minds, that have awaked to any degree of reflection upon their nature and being, and upon the collective being of their race. I have hoped that I should escape the charge of presumption, by the humbleness of my attempt—the attempt, that is to say, to popularize a theme which has hitherto been the domain of scholars.

LECTURE II.

THE PROBLEM OF EVIL. THE CASE PRESENTED, THE THEORY OFFERED, AND THE BEARING OF IT CONSIDERED.

I FOREWARN you that this is the longest, and perhaps the least entertaining Lecture that I have to deliver to you. I have to grapple with a hard problem, and I ask your close and careful attention. We shall go on more easily when we get through with this.

I am to consider, in this Lecture, the problem of evil in the world. In doing this, I shall first state the case; next propound the theory which I have to offer, and thirdly consider the bearing of this theory upon our future inquiries,—or the principles by which, under this theory, we must abide.

First. I am to state the case; what the problem is; what is the degree, extent, and pressure of evil.

It is often said that this life is a mystery, that this world is a mystery; and I confess that I am so sensible of a feeling of this kind, that I am so haunted with it, and as it seems to me sometimes, so strangely and inexplicably haunted with it through all my life, and especially through all my hours of more abstract meditation and soliloquy, that I am often tempted to question myself on this point, and to say, "Well, what is so mysterious? what *is* it? Something certainly there is that is *not* mysterious; much there is that is intelligible." And it is pertinent and important to the investigation before us that we should draw the line of distinction here, though it be a very simple thing to do so, and should say plainly—the line is clearly between what can be known, and what cannot be known. There is a veil which we cannot penetrate; but all things do not lie in its shadow. Something we can know; much, I believe. In short, mystery has its place, but manifestation also has its place in all things.

I feel the mystery; I am overshadowed by it; but there is light upon the edges of the great shadow, and there are openings of light into it; these I may humbly explore. I feel the mystery. Infinitude, eternity, the immeasurable plan; life, being, and the Being of all being—God; depth beyond depth is here, unfathomable, unsearchable. Nay, the common scene around us, doubtless, and our own life in it, are full of mysteries; only our familiarity cheats us out of the natural wonder. If on some bright summer's day you had found yourself standing here in the street or in the field, amidst all this moving throng of men and things—if you had found yourself standing here, without one precedent step, with no memory of the past; your eye, your ear, your sense and soul suddenly opened to all the sights and sounds of the living universe—sun and sky overhead, and waving trees around, and "men as trees walking," you would have asked, with uncontrollable astonishment, what is all this? And whence and what am I that behold it? But it is no less a real wonder for being familiar; and there are moments, in dreams of the mind, when we lose our intense self-consciousness and almost our personality, in which all this appears the wonder and mystery that it is.

But when we wake from this bemazing wonder into knowledge and inquiry, when we begin to understand what our life is, and to study the life of the world, then the mystery becomes profound difficulty, and seeming contradiction; our very knowledge confounds us. For we know that we suffer; that the world suffers. *That* needs not to be insisted on; we know it too well. And we know that God is *good.* Instinctively we say, the Author of this fair universe and of this human nature, must be good: to Him the happiness of his creatures must be desirable, nay infinitely precious. Why, even our human paternity feels unspeakable longings for the good and happy life of its offspring; this same world is filled with such yearning, ay, and sacrifice, even unto death. And yet—I say it with reverential awe, and I say it too with perfect trust—here is Almighty power, here is Infinite love; and the world is its creation and care; and yet, in spite of faith and humility, we cannot but exclaim, what a world is it!

Very dark it is. But not all dark—let us make up our account of it carefully—not all darkness, not all misery, not all evil; not, in the aggregate and mass of its experience, a hateful and miserable world; but nevertheless, such an amount of evil, both physical and moral, as bewilders all calculation; such an amount of hardship, disaster, sickness, sorrow, injustice, bloodshed, brutality and bitter sufferance, as must fill every thoughtful beholder with mingled horror and indignation. And yet, I repeat, this is a part of the domain of Infinite Benevolence. And I humbly venture to think that I can understand, in some degree, the problem of its sins and sorrows. But it is an awful problem. From the beginning, says the great Expositor of Christianity to the nations, "this creation groaneth and travaileth in pain until now." For sixty centuries, says another, the human race has been travelling on in quest of repose, and has not found it. And history tells the same sad tale. Whole races of men, like the Tartars and Africans, wandering in darkness and barbarism; whole empires torn and rent in pieces, or dying out by slow decay; whole armies mown down on ten thousand bloody fields; cities sacked, towns and towers whelmed in ruin; thousands and tens of thousands of human beings sighing away their lives in prisons and dungeons, which no sunlight nor blessed breath of heaven's air ever visits; the foot of man set upon the neck of his brother to crush him down to agony and despair—such things, oh! and many such things, of more indescribable horror, have had their place in the history of the world. As it was before man dwelt on the earth; it passed through ages of material convulsions, through the thunder of earthquakes, through the smoke and fire of volcanoes; so, in its moral history, there have been volcanoes and earthquakes, thunders of war, and fires of human wrath, and the smoke and smouldering of widespread and mournful desolations.

And yet, if we would make out a fair statement of the case, which we are now attempting, in the first place, we must not forget that there is something *besides evil* in the world. We must not pass by the observation, however familiar, that history, as it has been usually written, is likely very much to mislead us. It deals with what is palpable and public, and not with what is private and unseen—with the tragedy, and not with the comedy of life—with the camp and court, rather than with households and homes. Suppose the history of Europe in Napoleon Bonaparte's time to be read twenty centuries hence; and that, of all the literature that might illustrate its social character, only a few fragments should remain—that almost the only record left, were one of murderous wars and of court intrigues and vices. Why, the men of that distant day would doubtless look back upon the French Revolution and the years succeeding, as a barbarous and bloody time; and they might say of Europe, then, with as much emphasis as we do of the world at large—what traces are there upon it but of war, and havoc, and misery? They would see over all the horizon but the one black cloud. The millions of happy homes beneath it; the cultivated fields which spread far and wide on each side of the track of armies—ay, fields which *fed* those armies, and all Europe beside; the quiet abodes that were scattered over hundreds of valleys and mountains, and the virtues and charities that flourished in them—these, the observers, looking through the glass of history, would not see.

And it is worthy of special notice that the *farther* we are removed from the field of observation, the more are we exposed to mistake the facts. Thus the terms Arab, Egyptian, Assyrian, and Hindoo, carry to most minds nothing but ideas of barbarism. We think of the multitudes of Asia in past times, as but more intelligent hordes of animals. Our useful arts and profound sciences not known to them, we conclude that they have known nothing. Their customs, costumes, ways of life, mode of being, so different from ours, we hardly bring them within the range of our common humanity. But if there is any clear proof of intellectual culture and refinement, it is in the language of a people. And by this rule of judging there must have been, and we know that there have been, periods of Asiatic culture exhibiting a very high order of attainments. The Sanscrit, the old Hindoo language, with its fifty letters, is, in its alphabet, the most perfect language in the world; and it has an extant literature of which only ignorance can profess to think lightly.* The old Persian and Arabic are not uncultivated tongues; they have many affinities with our English and with German speech; so much so, that Leibnitz said, that a German could understand, at sight, whole Persian verses. Nay, and we know that those languages have bodied forth, in philosophy and in fiction, some of the finest conceptions of human thought. We know that the regal halls of Arabia and Persia have not shone with barbaric splendor only, but have listened to some of the loftiest and sweetest strains of poetry. I can hardly instance anything in our literature more admirable than the prayer of the Persian poet, Sadi, "O God, have mercy upon the wicked; for thou hast done everything for the good in having made them good!" And I know not that a scene of greater moral beauty can be produced from all our works of imagination than that of an Arabian romance, in which the monarch calls to his pres-

* Dr. Draper, in his admirable book on the Intellectual Development of Europe, says that the works of Gotama, the great expounder of Buddhism, consist of 800 large volumes. I cannot help thinking they must be very small in the amount of matter contained in each; but even then, the fact is remarkable enough. (See Dr. Draper, p. 53.)

ence the youthful poet, and placing him in the midst of his court, points him to all the luxuries and splendors which he had brought to decorate his royal halls, and, in the pride of his heart, bids him describe the scene; when the poet, severe in youthful virtue and full of the inspiration of genius, bursts forth into admiration of the surrounding magnificence, and at the conclusion says: "Long live the king under the shadow of his mighty palaces!—but let him remember that all this lustre shall grow dim and fade away; and the eyes that see it shall grow dim, and darkness shall settle upon them; and these lofty palaces shall sink to the dust, and their mighty lord shall sink to the dust also:" then, when trembling courtiers interfered, and fawning sycophants grew bold in their displeasure, we read that the king bowed down, humble and in tears at the rebuke, and loaded the noble reprover with his approbation and his gifts. We have inherited a good measure of the Jewish contempt for heathens; but it may be doubted whether there are many *Christian* courts that would ever witness such a scene, or many Christian monarchs that would have shown such nobleness.

There is one further observation, of an entirely different character, to be made in this statement of the problem of evil in the world. It is this: that broad and vast and immense as that problem may appear, it is, after all, in actual experience, purely individual. Millions of beings lived in India, millions in China. In Assyria, in Egypt, in Greece, in the Roman Empire, in the whole world, millions upon millions untold have lived; but the question really does not turn upon some vast calculation of weal and woe, but upon the part which each individual man has had in them. We generalize this boundless mass of human existence, and are apt to regard it as if one being had experienced it all. But the truth is, nobody has experienced more of it, than you or I have, or might have experienced. With regard to all the intrinsic difficulties of the case, it is as if but one life had been lived in the world; and since no man has lived another's life, or any life but his own, there *has been*, to actual, individual consciousness, *but one life*, of thirty, seventy, or a hundred years, lived on earth. The problem really comes within that compass. In the questions which humanity asks concerning a providence, each one of the unnumbered millions of the human race stands apart and alone; as much so, as if they were separated from each other by an interval of a million years. It is enough for every being, in every world, satisfactorily to settle the questions that arise concerning his existence for himself; he has no occasion to go farther; perhaps he has no business to go farther; but certainly he has no occasion to go farther, *unless* he finds beings, the conditions and allotments of whose existence are different from his. If he does *not* find a differing lot, then, I say, settling the question for himself does settle it for all. If I can solve the problem of existence for myself, I have solved it for everybody; I have solved it for the human race. In other words, if I can see it to be right that one being should be created so, I can see it to be right that unnumbered millions should be.

Let us, then, analyze this vast aggregate of human existence into its separate and individual consciousness, if we would understand it, or the questions that arise from it—into that form, in fact, in which only it can be said to exist. Humanity, mankind, but as an abstraction, does not exist; *man* only *lives*. From the vast mass of what we call misery, mischance, and failure, let us single out this man. Did the man who lived in India, in Tartary, ages ago—did the man who walked in the train of an Assyrian court, or was marshalled in the hosts of Rome, or travelled down through the Middle Ages—did he enjoy and value his life? Were there pleasures and satisfactions amidst his strugglings and sorrows? And amidst his strugglings and sorrows, was any valuable experience developed? Did he learn anything worth learning? And does the man who stands in this modern world—do you and I, find anything in our life, that makes us prize it; anything that makes us feel that we had infinitely rather have it, than have it not? Doubtless we do, and other men do; all men do. I am satisfied that there is an almost universal overrating of the miseries of life as compared with its blessings; and that not one in a million of those whom we lament over as if their life was a misfortune, would thank us for our sympathy, or accept the conclusion that they had better not have existed at all.

II. And now, such being the *case* of the world's life, we come to inquire, in the next place, upon what theory this state of things is to be accounted for. In this system of the world, there is suffering and sin; there is suffering and sin in the individual heart. How, under the sway of a good and wise providence, are these things to be understood? How could these things be? In other words, we meet here with the long-vexed problem of "the origin of evil." Let me say here, that I do not like the phrase "origin of evil." Not whence is evil, nor how it came into the world, is my question; but the fact that evil exists; and what view is to be taken of it.

With regard to this problem, I know it is often said, that no theory ever offered, and none that ever can be offered, does, or will, throw any satisfactory light upon it; and that those only who do not understand the problem, will imagine that it can be relieved, in any degree, from its insurmountable difficulties. It may be that this is my own case; at any rate, I must risk the imputation, for I conceive that this problem does *not* defy all human efforts for relief or explanation. I do not believe that a point so essential to any reasonable comprehension of the lot of our life, is left to be a dark and terrible enigma. It would be strange, indeed, if the one thing that crushes me to the earth—*evil*, should be as unintelligible as if it were the blindest mischance; if the only word I can utter, when writhing with pain, or weighed down by affliction, is *mystery;* if the one great question which my nature asks,—"why is evil, erring, grief, sin, permitted in the world?"—is to strike me dumb, as an idiot. It is vain to think of keeping the human mind away from it. It *will ask* the question. It has been asking from the beginning.

I do not submit, then, to this lofty *caveat* against inquiry. I am satisfied that to this ever-pressing question about the reason why evil exists, there is an answer as to the *principle;* and that all the difficulty lies in *details*—*i. e.*, in the application of the principle. And this is the distinction which I should take in regard to an observation of Bayle, quoted with approbation by Leibnitz.* "Those who pretend," says Bayle, "that the conduct of God in regard to sin, and the consequences of sin, has nothing in it for which they cannot render a reason, deliver themselves up to the mercy of their adversary." I grant that this is true, or may be true, with regard to details, but *not* with regard to the principle. I do *not* pretend that there is *nothing* in the events of human life and history, for which I cannot render a reason. In the application of the principle there may be difficulty, though not a difficulty that has any tendency to disturb it. Leibnitz himself says the same thing in reference to his own theory. His theory—if that can be called a theory, which is nothing but an *assertion*—is this: that in the best possible system of things evil was an inevitable part; and when explanation is demanded by his antagonist, he says, "Mr. Bayle demands a little too much; he would have us show *how* evil is bound up with the best possible plan of the creation—which would be a perfect explanation of the phenomenon; but we do not undertake to give it, nor are we obliged to do so; it would be impossible in the present state; it is enough that it may be true, it may be inevitable"—(though, strangely to me, while hovering about this point throughout almost the entire Théodicée, he never once *says wherein* this inevitableness consists—) "it may be," he says, "that certain particular evils are bound up with what is best in general. This," he says, "is sufficient for an answer to objections; but not for a comprehension of the thing." †

* Théodicée, p. 55, edition of M. A. Jacques.

† Ib., p. 158.

But such difficulty, I repeat, about the *application* of principles, is common to all subjects; it attaches no peculiar mystery to the problem of evil. I may also say, that to go into this application—to go into details, is the very business of these lectures: we shall have perpetually to answer questions; our *present* concern is with the *theory*—with the principle upon which those questions are to be answered.

While I am upon this point—the difference, that is to say, between the principle and the details—let me make another distinction. It is often said that nothing but a future life can clear up the mysteries of the present. That is true, with regard to details. Why some particular series of calamities is permitted; why a paralyzing disease presses upon the whole of this life, perhaps nothing but a future life can tell. But the *principle* lying at the basis of the problem, I think we shall see, stands clear and manifest, here and now.

Or, to state the same thing in a more general way:—here is a world and a world system; here is man placed in it, with a particular constitution, mental and bodily; here is a story of human fortunes, running back into darkness and obscurity; a story full, doubtless, of strange things, to our human view—full, certainly, of complications hard to unravel—full of strugglings and sorrows. Now, why this *particular kind* of world and system and race, should have been chosen to occupy this particular space and time in the boundless domain of being; why our nature should be so weak, or why so strong, why so high or so low; or why *such* and *so great* evils should attend our human development, rather than others—manifestly it is altogether beyond us to say. I must pray you to attend to the distinction I am making, for I would not be thought guilty of the presumption and folly of saying that I can answer such questions. If this is what is meant by mystery in the creation, I admit it all, and a great deal more. And if any one should say, on some hearsay report of the lecturer's design this evening, "Oh! he proposed to solve the mystery of the world, and the mystery of all the evil in the world!" I answer that I propose no such thing! To Pope's line,

"All partial evil, universal good,"

Voltaire mockingly and bitterly says, "A singular notion of universal good—composed of the stone, of the gout, of all crimes, of all sufferings, of death, and damnation."* To any such one-sided or passionate reasonings about evil, I am not concerned at present to reply. *Be* it a mystery—something beyond our reach to comprehend—why this particular form of the creation is chosen, and therefore, why these special "ills that flesh is heir to," are put into the system; still, there is a principle lying at the bottom of all, and accounting for much, which is not mysterious, and which I may, without presumption, I think, offer for your consideration. Let us, then, proceed to state those inevitable laws of all being—of all being but God himself—which lead us irresistibly to that principle.

First, the system in which evil exists is a *creation*. It is not something self-existent, but something made, arranged, set in order by a Power above.

Secondly, to a created system limitation necessarily attaches. It could not be infinite, in magnitude nor in any other attribute. Created power cannot be omnipotent; created intelligence cannot be omniscient. Every created intelligence, every created moral nature, must have a beginning; and the law of its action is, and for aught that we can see must be, development, growth, progress. At any rate, limitation belongs of necessity to the whole system; to men and things alike.

Thirdly, limitation implies imperfection. Human knowledge is of necessity imperfect; the human will and conscience are of necessity imperfect; the material elements, too, air, earth, water, are necessarily imperfect. That is to say, they can have no absolute and infinite perfection, like the being of God. In other words, their perfection, such as

* La Raison par Alphabet; article *Tout est bien.*

it is, must be relative; *i. e.*, they answer the best purpose that they can, with reference to some end. Thus the air is the best element for the lungs to breathe; the lungs the best organ for imparting purity and vitality to the blood; the system of circulations the best for the growth of the body; the body the best organization for the soul; the powers of the soul the best for high culture and happiness: but there is no *absolute* best in them, no absolute perfection; there cannot be. Throughout and at every step, there is imperfection, liability to hurts, liability to go wrong. Thus again, every organ, every element is best for its specific purpose, but not for every other purpose. Nay more; that which *fits* it for one thing, *un*fits it for another. The whole human frame is good, is perfect for its purpose. For its purpose, it is required to be composed of delicate organs, and to be covered with a sensitive envelopment. It is perfect for its purpose; but it is not so good for fight; it is not clad in mail; it is not bullet-proof.

The question is, how comes evil to be in the world? Or, in other words, why was it not excluded from the system? Certainly it is not desirable for its own sake; infinitely otherwise; we feel it to be infinitely otherwise. How often does the vision rise before our minds, of a world without pain and without sin without one sorrow or wrong in all its blessed dwellings; and we say, with a tone perhaps, of something like complaint as well as heavy sighing, why could not this world have been such? Why, then, *was* it not such a world? And the answer that I give is, that it was in the nature of things impossible. This is my principle—that it was, in the nature of things, and by the inevitable conditions of the problem, impossible to exclude evil.

Before I attempt to show how and why it was impossible, let me provide, by a remark or two, against any preconceptions that may arise in your minds with regard to my design. I do not intend then, in the first place, to take up any questions in theology. According to the statutes of the Lowell Institute, and equally in accordance with my own views of propriety in such a course of lectures, I am required to avoid all polemic discussion. And indeed I do not see, but the question which I raise in this lecture, presses equally upon every theology. For if any one traces all the evil in the world to the sin of Adam, then the question would be, why was not Adam prevented from sinning? And my answer is, that he *could* not—being a free moral and imperfect creature—that he *could* not be prevented. If this is true, it must be a great relief to see it; for it must seem strange that he was not kept pure, if that was possible. It appears to me that we are bound to think that he and his posterity would have been kept in perfect innocence and bliss, if, in the nature of things, it had been possible.

Let me further say that the position which I take—viz., that evil could not be prevented—implies no limitation of the Divine power or goodness. This idea of power, I conceive, is to be put out of the case altogether. Yet it has very closely adhered both to ancient and modern reasonings upon evil. Lactantius, in his treatise on "The Wrath of God" (sec. 13), introduces the Epicureans as reasoning thus: "Either God wills to remove evil, and cannot; or he can, and will not; or he cannot, and will not; or he can, and will. If he wills, and cannot, that is weakness. If he can, and will not, that is malignity. If he will not, and cannot, that is a defect both of power and goodness. But if he can and will; then why is evil?" Or, to take a modern instance of the same kind of reasoning—in Samuel Rogers's "Table Talk," Mr. Rogers is quoted as saying, "The three acutest men with whom I was ever acquainted, James Mackintosh, Malthus, and Bobus Smith, were all agreed that the attributes of the Deity must be in some way limited, else there would be no sin and misery." And Leibnitz quotes Bayle to the same effect in his preface to the "Theodicèe." Mr. Rogers and his friends thought, as I know from more private sources, that, as the limitation could not be of wisdom or goodness, it must be of power, *i. e.*, of power to make the world otherwise. Now I must venture to say, that all this language, whether of Lactantius, or of Mr. Bayle, or of Mr. Rogers and his friends, very much surprises me. For the truth is, that power has nothing to do with the case. There are such things as inherent, intrinsic *natural impossibilities.* It is impossible, for instance, that matter should exist without occupying space; and it is not so proper to say that God cannot make it so, as that the thing cannot be. It *is* said, I know, that God *cannot* make two mountains without a valley, *i. e.*, a depression of land between them; but that I take to be only the strongest, popular expression of the utter impossibility of the thing. The idea of power, strictly speaking, or of more power or less, has no relevancy to the case. If I take two balls and lay them before me, and then add two more, the sum cannot be five balls; and as to power more or less to do that, why infinite power can no more make them five, than an infant's power. Again, the sum of the angles of every triangle is equal to two right angles—no more and no less—and it cannot be otherwise. And you might as well ask me why God could not make a triangle to include four or six right angles, as ask why He could not make an imperfect, moral and free nature without any liability to error or mistake.

If this were what the ancients meant by fate, they had meant rightly. But it is not to be represented as a power *above God.* For it is only saying that irreconcilable contradictions cannot meet in the same nature. It is only saying that a thing cannot be one thing, and a totally different thing from what it is, at the same time.

If now I have sufficiently guarded my proposition from mistake, let us proceed to examine it. The problem of evil, the question why is it?—this is the subject before us.

Evil is of two kinds, natural and moral. With regard to the latter, I think the case is very clear. But let us inquire for a moment concerning the former—*i. e.*, natural or physical evil.

The great and comprehensive form of natural evil is *pain.* And by pain I mean now, of course, physical suffering; or, the suffering that springs from a bodily organization. The question is, could such an organization be made, and made to answer its purposes to voluntary agents, without that liability? Or rather, here are two questions. Could it be made at all? That is one question. Was it possible to make an organ capable of pleasure, without its being liable to pain when hurt, broken, or torn in pieces? Look, for instance, at that sensitive vesture with which the human body is clothed, the skin; or at the corresponding membrane that lines the interior cavities of the structure, the mucous membrane. With soft and gentle touches applied to the body, with warm and balmy airs breathing upon it, or sweet odors inhaled, or healthful food received, this sensitive vesture, within and without, thrills with pleasure. Could it be—was it in the nature of things possible, that cold could freeze it, or the knife cut it, or baleful poison could enter in, or starving and death, without giving pain? *Could* the sense of touch, alive to all impressions, find every impression equally agreeable? In fact, would not such a perpetual monotony of impression, have been itself disagreeable? But *could* any sensitive integument be made to which it should be indifferent whether water bathed or fire burned it? Pleasure and pain *seem* to us necessarily correlative, necessarily bound together, in any organ that is capable of either.

I may doubt then, whether it was possible, in the nature of things, to exclude pain from the human or from any sensitive organization. But it is yet clearer, in the next place, that pain is necessary to the *purposes* which this organization was designed to answer. I suppose that it is universally conceded that there are such purposes; that the body was made for the mind, made to train, to educate the mind. But suppose it were made only for itself. Even then—even for the body's preservation, pain is as necessary as pleasure. The mind's prudence needs the salutary admonition of pain.

"The burnt child dreads the fire." But not the fire alone, every element around us, would prove fatal to the ignorance, inexperience, and impetuosity of childhood, if pain did not teach it prudence. The body itself would perish in a thousand ways, if caution and wisdom were not learnt from suffering. Then again—looking to higher purposes—what is it, as the primary impulse, that stirs the world to activity, to industry? What is it that prevents it from sinking into perpetual languor and sleep? It is the pain of hunger. Or why does man build his rude hut, or fashion his clothing of skins, but to protect himself against the pain which the elements would inflict? Or if we say, that sloth itself is irksome and painful, still it comes to the same thing. "Uneasiness," of some kind, as Mr. Locke teaches, "is the *universal* motive to action." But suppose, on the other hand, that there was no pain. Suppose that all sensation were pleasurable. How certainly would the human race sink into the fathomless gulf of sensualism? If excess never brought satiety nor suffering with it, how certain must it be, that it would never stop; and that the whole man, the whole nature, the whole world, would sink into utter moral perdition! Man, we say, is to be trained; his higher nature is to be developed and cultivated. To this end, the senses minister. To effect it, they have pleasures to offer. But they must have other means than pleasure at their disposal, or they could never fulfil their office.

Either in the nature of things, then, or in the purposes of things, or in both, we say, that physical evil, as far as we can see, was inevitable.

But let us now look at what is more material to the problem we are considering—at moral evil.

Was it possible to frame a nature, moral, finite and free, and to exclude from it all liability to error, to sin? I answer that by the very terms of the statement, it was just as impossible, as to make two mountains without a valley; or, to make the angles of a triangle to be equal to three or four right angles. The very statement of the case excludes the possibility.

Let us look at the case. Here is a being created with certain moral faculties. He is capable of loving the right. He is capable of loving the wrong. He is also perfectly free to do the one or the other, at his pleasure. If he pleases to do wrong, nothing can prevent him, that leaves him free. He is imperfect moreover, and is liable, from defect of knowledge, to go astray. He is endowed, too, with the love of happiness; he must be so—the very capability of happiness implies the love of it; and in his ignorance, he is liable to suppose that the evil way will make him happiest; that the indulgence of his appetites and passions, for instance, will yield him a fuller satisfaction than the culture of his higher nature. Aberration and failure, alas! are, more or less, the story of every human life. Aberration and failure, too, are grievous sins: for this being had power—had freedom, that is to say, to choose the better part. The fact is so; but the question is—was it possible to place him beyond the reach of this peril? If it were, then we are to find the origin of evil in the arbitrary and mysterious will of Heaven. But was it possible? Was it possible to make this being impeccable, incapable of evil, independent of temptation?

What is the only conceivable condition on which such a result can be secured? That man's will be bound, constrained, compelled to the right course. But then he is not free. Take away that perilous element, freedom, and then he may be safe; but *then* he is no longer a moral being. So long as he is imperfect and free, he must be liable to choose wrong. He need not, indeed, in a palpable case, choose wrong. He need not be guilty of positive malignity, of intentional sin—and the distinction is important—but he must be exposed to sins of inadvertence, exposed to slide into evil unawares. Nay, and in a *palpable case*, he must be free to go wrong, if he pleases; else he is not a moral being.

But what then *is* evil, in man, under this theory?—it may be asked; and I ought to pause here a moment to answer. Is evil a *mere mistake*, a mere confusion as to what is right, of a mind dazzled by worldly fascinations or clouded by sense and appetite? Far from it. There is indeed mistake about it, confusion of mind, blinding temptation. Still, when a man is drawn to evil, he commonly knows it to be evil. Why, but for this, is there any struggle in his mind about it? How is it, but for this knowing better, that the descent to gross vice, to falsehood, to dishonesty, is often achieved through strife, misgiving, and agony at every step? Nay, and it must not only be that he knows better, but that he can do better; else he could not blame himself. What, in fact, is the case presented to the tempted and falling? There, on the one hand, is some advantage—pleasure, lucre, distinction—*happiness*, the mind calls it. Here on the other hand, is purity, rectitude, virtue. Between these lies the question. Here is the crisis—the most tremendous that can *be*, in the nature of things. What does the man do? What does he choose? There *is* no compulsion. There is no compulsion to evil; and there is no compulsion to good. Power Almighty, that reaches to the infinite height above, and to the infinite deep below, and sways the boundless spheres around, touches not that solemn prerogative of choice. What does the man do? He chooses the wrong! What is the definition of that act? A violated conscience! It is the most awful fact in the history of humanity: a violated conscience! It is the breaking of the highest law in the universe, and of that which the offender feels and knows to be the highest—the manifested law of the infinite Rectitude. The consequences, indeed, are fearful; the most dreadful miseries in the world are the results of wrong-doing; but they stand in just and lawful accordance with the deed—not in any disproportion.

But suppose the man to choose right: let us consider that, a moment; for it will confirm our view, I think, of the essential attributes of a free nature. What is virtue, goodness, holiness? It is often spoken of, as if it could be created in the heart, or could be put into it, by an independent power. But can it be so? Virtue, love is the voluntary act of the soul. It is by *definition*, incapable of creation. It *cannot be put* into the heart. It is the heart's own voluntary putting forth. All that we can conceive of, as possible to be created, is the capacity to love. The act of loving is the sole act of the being created. It is as much so, as hatred is his own act. Both are alike free, voluntary, unforced; or they are not moral.

Whether we consider, therefore, the essential nature of good or of evil in the mind, we are brought to the conclusion, that the exposure to evil is one of the inevitable conditions of the problem involved in a moral, finite, and free nature. I have before expressed my surprise that Leibnitz, in his great work on theology, the Theodicèe, which is chiefly occupied with this very subject, nowhere distinctly points to the nature and ground of this inevitableness of evil. He does however *once* quote with *qualified* approbation the following sentence from Mr. Jacquelot: "Suppose," says Jacquelot, "that God could not prevent the bad use of free will, without annihilating it: it will be agreed that His wisdom and His glory having determined Him to make creatures free, the same powerful reason must preponderate over the unhappy consequences that would spring from this liberty."* This I regard as pointing to the true theory of the origin of evil. Only by being annihilated, could free will be secured from this liability to aberration and evil.

But I must now, to bring this theory fully before you, carry it a step farther; and I mean, farther back, to the origin of the human experiment. Every man begins his experiment in infancy. The race began in infancy. Every generation must begin so. *Could* it begin anywhere else? The point is material: for it is easy to see that if it were otherwise, if the man or the race could begin where their predecessor leaves off; if each generation had taken up all the wisdom of the past generation, and borne it onward; if the child had assumed all the virtues of his parent, and had proceeded on that vantage ground, then the burden of

* Theodicèe, p. 166.

human sin and misery would have been relieved to an incalculable extent. Again I ask, was that, in the nature of things, possible? Was it possible to put those results of past experience into any newly created heart? Was it not inevitable that every newly created race, every newly created soul should begin in infancy, and work its own way up to virtue and happiness? Such, we see, is the fact; but was any other thing possible? For myself, I do not see that any other thing was possible.

For experience, like virtue, by definition, *cannot be created.* Wisdom, by definition, *cannot be created.* It is what the moral being works out for himself. It is not God's act, but man's act. It implies choice, effort, resistance; and these are the works and acts of the human being. This being is created, not with certain virtues, but with certain faculties. Even if the body were brought into existence full-formed and in its adult state, as we may suppose the body of the first human being was, still there must be a time when this being puts forth his first act, and there must be an after time, when he puts forth the second and the third act. Can the first act have all the precision, certainty and strength of the second, the third, the hundreth? If not, then here is learning, here is progress. But present learning implies past ignorance; progress to-day, defect yesterday. In ignorance then, in weakness, by experimenting, the human being, the human race, must advance and grow and gain strength. In the nature of things, it cannot be otherwise.

Still and after all, I do not doubt the question will be asked—was there no alternative? Pressed by the hard strife of the problem, one may strangely say: "Well, but was freedom itself any necessary part of a moral and good nature? Could not God have made a being pure and good *without* freedom? Or, having given him freedom, could he not have held it back from all aberration? But do you not see that these suppositions violate the very conditions of the problem of moral agency?—that they are neither tenable, nor indeed conceivable? Nay, if the highest and noblest kind of existence, *i. e.*, a moral existence, *could* have been *made* and *kept* pure and happy, it is inconceivable that it should not have been.

The truth is, as I conceive, that the failure of this entire argument, if it fails with you, arises from my fault in stating it, or from yours, in not adhering to the premises. Let us change the terms of the question—let us put this, which is regarded as such a confounding and insoluble problem, into another shape—and ask, why *ignorance* is permitted in the creation. You find the most terrible and overwhelming calamities and miseries, springing from ignorance; from ignorance of the laws of health—of ventilation, food, drink, medicine; from ignorance of the laws of material nature, and of human nature. Indeed, almost all the evils in the world may be referred to this one source. And now you ask—quite confident that nobody can answer—disdainfully and solemnly shaking the head at any attempt to answer—struck blind by a perspicacity which sees that there is nothing to be seen—you ask, "What is the origin of ignorance?" What is the origin of ignorance? Why, it could not be helped. That is the origin of ignorance. It could not be helped. Do you wonder that man is not omniscient? Is *that* a confounding and insoluble problem to you? Why not go on, and wonder that man is not almighty, all-wise, and infinitely happy?

But now, I repeat, if any one goes into detail, and says—"Why this? Why that? Why such a race as the human? Why the Chinese or Africans? Why such degraded forms of being? Why creatures maimed and crippled by hereditary taint?"—I may well answer, that we do not know; that it is quite beyond us to know, in particular, why these special forms and conditions of being exist. Of the *degree* of imperfection, best for this world or for that world, it is, of course, quite beyond us to form any judgment. But surely it is something for us to consider, and something profoundly entering into the problem of our existence, that it was in the very nature of things impossible to remove from the system of a moral creation, all evil, all ignorance, all error, all suffering.*

Let me now detain you a few moments longer, while I attempt to carry this argument, necessarily abstract thus far, into some of its practical bearings upon life, and upon the state of mind, in our reasonings, which, as a matter of inference, it requires of us.

I say, then in the first place—let it be fixed in our minds, that the system of the moral world is a system of spontaneous development. It could not be other than spontaneous in consistency with its own nature. The agent is free. He must do, within the range of his permitted activity, what he will. You ask why things could not have been ordered or controlled so as to bring out a happier result; why such monsters in human shape as Tiberius, and Cæsar Borgia, or the petty tyrant in his own family or village, should not have been hindered from their excesses or their cruelties? The answer is, they could not, unless by being deprived of their natural freedom. If they had been animals they might have been guarded and governed by instinct. But they were allowed to be worse, by as much as their range was larger; and that range could not be contracted without giving up the essential, the *moral* character of the system. To all such hypothetical questions, the an-

* As I am anxious to relieve this conclusion from all unnecessary objection, I will add, that it is not altogether heterodox. Since I first delivered this course of lectures, I have read Archbishop King's work "On the Origin of Evil," translated and commented upon by Edmund Law, Bishop of Carlisle—some weight of testimony, certainly, from the Church of England—in which substantially the same view is taken. Substantially, but I may say, not precisely. The course of the archbishop's argument is mainly this: Take away anything that you call an evil, and I will show you that a greater evil would come in its place. But the ground taken in this lecture, is that it was in the nature of things impossible to exclude it; that it is an essential contradiction in ideas to put imperfection, choice, virtue on one side, and immunity from all evil, error, suffering on the other. There was a book published in Hartford, Conn., some years since, espousing, I think, mainly the same solution of our problem, and I was pleased to see a notice of it in the *New Englander*, in which this solution was commended as worthy at least of serious consideration.

swer is—*given* a nature moral and free: *given* a world for its sphere; and the consequences must follow. Let the enquirer seize this idea of spontaneous development and hold it fast. Interpositions, in certain circumstances and for certain purposes, we may and do believe in; but they are exceptions from the system, not the rule. As if, when the Creator had made the world and placed man upon it, He had then left, and, if I may say so, neglected it and cast it off, to run to its own free course—such is the general aspect and light in which we are to study its history. If in this study we meet, as we shall meet, with abundant evidence that this world is *not* cast off, that it is controlled and guided while it is left free, it will be our own wisdom and great happiness to see *that.* If we meet with the fact of Divine interposition, as we believe that we do, we shall receive it with most reverent joy and thanksgiving. But still we must clearly distinguish this from the general course of events. We must distinctly see that we are mainly to study, not a supernatural, but a natural development; and moreover, not an animal nor angelic, but a human development. We must firmly say—what man pleases to be, that he must be; what human reason, conscience, affection will, that they must do; and what human ignorance, barbarism, passion will, *that* they must do. It could not be helped, unless by unmaking this nature, deranging this plan, destroying this system of the world.

In the next place, that man's growth and action be free and rational, the system of treatment under which he lives must be one of general laws, and not of sudden and violent expedients; a system of gentleness and patience, of moral influence, and much of it, indirect influence. Our human shortsightedness and passion are ready often, to call down sudden and signal vengeance upon the evil-doer. "Is there not some chosen curse," we say, "some hidden thunder to blast the wretch who violates all laws, human and divine?" But suppose it were so. Suppose that the eternal retribution that dwells embosomed in the air around us, were to burst forth in thunder upon every atrocious crime. Suppose that the Infinite Intelligence were ever devising new penalties for guilty deeds. Or suppose that, by a genera. law, the lying lips were always smitten with an instant blow, or that there were a whip wielded by an invisible hand, for every villain in the world. It might be no more than justice; and you might say that the world would then be strictly governed. Yes, but the government would then be a police, and not a providence. Human nature would break down under such a system of treatment. Men would be like slaves under the lash; and their virtue, mere terror and cowardice. Therefore men are left slowly to learn the evil of their ways, and human wickedness is suffered to run far, that the experience of evil may be corrective, and contrition for it generous and sincere, and repentance deep and thorough.

Yet it is not to be overlooked, in the third place, that the system of this moral creation is one of restraint and correction. There is restraint here. There are limits to man's power and will and wickedness. He cannot overleap the barriers of the world; he cannot jump off from the globe which he inhabits. It rolls through the infinite void, a separate sphere and school; and the pupil cannot escape from it,—but by an act, rarely committed, and almost always to be referred to insanity. Material nature around us too, and so far as it enters into and forms a part of our own compound being, is full of restraint and retribution. Heat and cold and storm and night, and sleep and hunger and disease and pain, hold their place amidst all the strugglings of our will; and no man may deny or disregard their power.

There is a solemn control within us, also. I feel that there is an awful Providence over my mind. Amidst the thousand questionings of my spirit and the ten thousand moral emergencies of my experience, conscience rises up before me, ay, and *against* me if I do wrong, like a lifted finger. There is something within me, which is above my will, and despite my will, it proclaims a law. He who made our nature free, made it *not* free from that glorious, that tremendous bond. All written law, every covenant, promise, and oath in the world—all rest upon that inner bond. To obey that law within, is honor, peace, and fulness of joy. To disobey, is misery and ruin. Amidst all that is called ruin in the world, there is nothing like the ruin of guilt; and of all the miseries in the world, there is nothing like the agony of remorse. And though the sharpness of that agony be escaped through the dulness of conscience, though the solemn reality be veiled over by the haze of prosperity, yet I do not believe that any human being ever solved the problem of evil in himself, the problem of sensuality or avarice or malignant passion, without finding and feeling, ay, settling it in his deepest heart, that it was an unhappy course. Here, then, are restraint and retribution.

Such, in fine, and as a matter of incontrovertible fact, is the system of the world; material, and as such, a sphere of education; moral, and therefore free—and therefore liable in its very nature to aberration and evil, to sin and suffering; a system by its very nature, and inevitably, one of spontaneous development, a system necessarily, for its purposes, one of general laws; and clearly, by the intervention of a Power above humanity, a system of stupendous moral restraints.

Such, as I read it, is the problem of human life and history; and such, in the most general form, is its solution. We utter that phrase—human life and history—in a breath: but what infinitude of meaning is in it! What ages of tremendous experience does it describe! It is not a mere cold theme for philosophic disquisition; it is life, yours and mine, the world's life—intense, unutterable, steeped in joys and sorrows unutterable—wide as the spread of nations, comprehending the experience of unnumbered millions of creatures, swelling with the burden of long ages of existence. A solemn story, of things not one of which can be indifferent to him who is a man! History and biography have written it, and yet, they have not written a millionth part of it; fiction has illustrated it, and yet it is stranger than fiction; poetry has embalmed it in holy inspiration and sympathy, and yet the unwritten poetry is a thousandfold more than the written. Ay, everywhere has life—the now dead and vanished life of ages—been such. In crowded empires and among the scattered isles; in gay and gorgeous cities, and in solitary and lowly huts; in the fisherman's bark upon the Northern seas, and the shepherd's Arabian tent, and the hunter's Alpine path; by the hearth and the fireside, or in wandering and weariness; in the dark and dreary castles of the old Northmen, or upon the sunny slopes of Italy, of Persia, and of India, everywhere life, this same life, has had its lot—amidst wailings of grief and melodies of joyous hearts, amidst the desolations of war and famine and pestilence, and the green abodes of peace and plenty: age with its heavy sigh and infancy with its prattlings, have had part in this human lot; the joys and sorrows of parents and children, the secret, never-uttered ruminating, upon the mortal lot and immortal hereafter, of the private heart; passion and strife, and glory and shame; courage and aspiration, and defeat and despair—all that is life, and all that death is—all bound up in this tremendous bond of human existence!

Comparatively, nothing in the world is worth studying but that. God's wisdom in the stupendous problem of human existence, let me understand that; or let me understand what I can of it. All other sciences do in fact converge to that—the illustration of God's wisdom in the world. All arts—sculpture, painting, poetry, music, history, and every form of literature—are studies and illustrations of the great humanity. But the *philosophy* of it all—*that* do I seek above all things.

I believe that all is well. I believe that all is the best possible. Understand me, however. I hold to optimism in this sense; not that man's work is the best possible, but that God's work is the best possible—is the *utmost* that it was possible for Divine power and wisdom to do for man.

"What could I have done for my vineyard, that I have not done for it," saith the Lord. It is an essential part of the theory which I adopt, and one which I especially desire to illustrate, that the free will of man, *while* perfectly free, is yet surrounded by wise instructions and powerful restraints; that the world of nature and of humanity are full of them. I do not believe that the good Being would have *created* a moral system which in its freedom was certain to run down to utter destruction and misery. I believe he saw that it could, with his care and aid, travel upward, higher and higher through ages. But I do *not* believe that it was possible in the nature of things, to exclude pain and weariness, or stumbling and wandering from the path that shall conduct it to the heights, to the ever-rising heights of virtue and happiness.

But in this theory—to say one word more—there is no place for moral apathy. No man may fold his arms, and say, "Things must be so; and in erring, I yield but to nature." There is no fate in this world, like the fate that a man makes for himself. That is fate indeed—the inevitable necessity, that every man must freely work out his own weal or woe. If there be any practical value in this discussion, it is in having drawn your attention distinctly to this inevitable necessity—as the fact on which hinges the whole moral philosophy of human life and history. It *is* a fact, unalterable, fixed as adamant. Whether we build upon that rock, or break upon that rock—one thing is certain—it cannot be removed. But we may build upon it: and therefore to point it out, and, amidst the waves, the strifes and perils of human existence, to lift it up clearly to view, is to send out a challenge to all the spiritual heroism in the world, ay, and an alarm-call to all the sluggard indolence in the world; and to summon every man that lives, to do all that he can for himself, and to do all that he can for others, To arm the soul to look that dread fact of inalienable moral responsibility fairly in the face, and to arouse the soul to discharge itself of that stupendous trust with humility and resolution—these are the highest ends of all right study and of all true wisdom.

I say in fine, and I say plainly, that for sickly complainers, for poor voluptuaries, for weak worldlings—for ignoble creatures that had rather be innocent sheep and be happy, than wrestling angel-natures, taking blows and wounds in the lists of virtue—I have no doctrine to deliver. I say deliberately and firmly, that I had rather have com menced my existence as I have, than in some imaginary elysium of negative, stationary, choiceless, unprogressive innocence and enjoyment.

Give me freedom, give me knowledge, give me breadth of experience; I would have it all. No memory is so hallowed, no memory is so dear, as that of temptation nobly withstood, or of suffering nobly endured. What is it that we gather and garner up from the solemn story of the world, like its struggles, its sorrows, its martyrdoms? Come to the great battle, thou wrestling, glorious, marred nature! strong nature! weak nature!—come to the great battle, and, in this mortal strife, strike for immortal victory! The highest Son of God—the best beloved of Heaven that ever stood upon earth—was "made perfect through sufferings." And sweeter shall be the cup of immortal joy, for that it was once dashed with bitter drops of pain and sorrow; and brighter shall roll the everlasting ages, for the dark shadows that clouded this birthtime of our being.

LECTURE III.

THE MATERIAL WORLD AS THE FIELD OF THE GREAT DESIGN: ITS ADAPTATIONS TO THE END—HUMAN CULTURE.

I HAVE attempted to set forth in my first lecture, the apparent design proposed in the creation of the world—human culture; and in my second, the ground principles involved in that design—involved, that is to say, in those material and moral agencies, that belong to the present constitution of things. A scene there must be, a place, a sphere for human activity; a free will in man to act his pleasure; and from such a condition and nature I have contended that it was impossible—as far as we can conceive—that it was shown by the very terms of the statement to be impossible, to exclude all evil. This principle I believe to be incontrovertible. There are difficulties about its application; there are difficulties about the details, and to these it is my special business in these lectures to address myself; but there is no difficulty about the principle.

I shall now proceed, and especially in the present lecture, to consider this material world, as the sphere of human activity and culture.

The Rev. Thomas Burnet—an English divine of the 17th century—in a book of his, called "The Sacred Theory of the Earth," imagines the world originally to have been literally a perfect sphere. "In this smooth earth," he says, "were the first scenes of the world, and the first generations of mankind; it had the beauty of youth and blooming nature, fresh and fruitful; and not a wrinkle, scar, or fracture in all its body;"—(and what do you think he means by "no wrinkle nor scar"?)—why, "no rocks nor mountains," he says, "no hollow caves nor gaping channels, but even and uniform all over. And the smoothness of the earth made the heavens so too; the air was calm and serene; none of those tumultuary motions and conflicts of vapors, which the mountains and the winds cause in ours; it was suited to a golden age, and to the first innocency of nature." *

It is strange that, even to this eccentric writer, such a world should have seemed a desirable place, or even habitable. But suppose the reverse of this; suppose the earth to have been ridged all over with lofty mountains, without intervening plain, ocean or river, and it is still more obvious that it would have been completely uninhabitable; at least by any such race as now occupies it.

In a happy medium between the inaccessible mountain and the unbroken plain, lies the lap of earth to receive and nourish the children of men. They grow and multiply in the fruitful valleys; they nestle under the covert and shadow of mountain ranges, which send down refreshing breezes upon them; they line the river banks and the shores of the sea with their villages and cities, and launch forth from them their ships for distant voyages. And in the most obvious view, this arrangement is necessary to human growth, intercourse, and culture; and not only so, but to human subsistence. Without level grounds there could not be productive agriculture; without mountains there could not be gushing springs nor flowing streams; without oceans and the immense evaporation from their surface, there could not be cloud nor rain; and without refreshing rains and irrigating rivers, there could be no vegetable growth; and man and beast alike must perish from the face of the earth.

But this adjustment of the earth to human subsistence, comfort, and culture; let us consider it more nearly.

* P. 76, London ed., 1816.

The earth is a globe; and so small is the deviation from a perfect sphere caused by the highest mountains, that the Davalagiri in Asia, 28,000 feet high, stands above the level only as the twelfth of an inch would on an artificial globe of ten feet in diameter.* It does not belong to us to decide, scarcely to inquire, whether some other form for the world would have answered the purpose. It is evident that a square or any irregular figure, or simply a vast and level extension, would have been unfavorable to its revolutions on its axis, or its free movement in space. All the other heavenly bodies are spherical; this is the form chosen by the Infinite Builder and Maker. The earth then is a globe; and it follows that some portions of it must be less favorably situated for human comfort and culture than others. If it be asked why this inequality, this inconvenience, this evil is permitted; why the burning zone is assigned to some for residence, and the cold Arctic regions to others; the answer is, that in the system of things this was inevitable. Here, in fact, and especially in the northern cold, is the problem of evil again—the problem of evil for the Greenlander; and he can rationally solve it in no other way. But suppose that some other form *had* been chosen, by which these particular inconveniences would have been avoided; and while we are indulging our imagination, let us somewhat extend the field; let us conceive of certain other arrangements that might have been made for human comfort. Suppose, for instance, that the earth had been covered over, at convenient distances, with houses, built as a part of the world, of ever-during stone and rock; and that near these dwellings had grown trees, for shade and for fruit; and that around them had spread fields and farms. And suppose too, that roads, aye, and railroads, of nature's workmanship, had run all over the earth, just where they were needed; or that in the ocean, there had been vast currents, running opposite ways; one from America to Europe, to bear our ships, and another from Europe

* Guyot's Comparative Physical Geography, p. 34.

to America, to bring them back: suppose all this. Should we *like* this stereotyped *order?* Should we not wish to alter the houses, the grounds, the groves, the roads, to suit our taste or convenience? I scarcely ever knew a man to buy a house but he must needs alter it, to make it suit *him.* But the *same* houses, the *same estates*, the *same* arrangements, for *all generations*, rude and civilized—it would be intolerable. It would be a solid barrier against all improvement. No; better that the world, rough, wild, shaggy, be given to man as it *is*, to mould it as he will. And I do not doubt he *will* yet mould it into such a garden of plenty, such an abode of beauty and happiness, as we cannot now conceive of; far better than that exact plan—that world for drones, which some might prefer. No; man is better cared for, by not being cared for too much. The world is given to him, as the raw material, to work upon. That fact is the basis of his whole earthly culture.

But passing by this general form and structure of the earth, I wish to show how things are adjusted and adapted to human subsistence, development and improvement; and that, far more admirably and exquisitely, than they would be by any such arrangement of houses, farms, roads or ocean currents, as I have just supposed. For this purpose, I shall consider, first, some of the general arrangements of nature; secondly, some of the specific adaptations of the world to man, and of man to the world; and thirdly, certain ministrations of nature to still higher ends in the sphere of human culture.

Under the first head, I must mention certain arrangements—not, indeed, to convey any new *knowledge* to many of you; but I must *remind* you of them; they belong to the survey we are taking of the world as a place of human abode; and their very familiarity may lead us to overlook their importance.

The world is constructed to be the abode of human life, and to nurture the means and provisions of that life. For this purpose it must be supplied with food and drink; and it must be heated, ventilated, and refreshed with moisture.

The way in which these ends are accomplished is marked with such design, such adjustment, restraint and modification of nature's forces—nay, such actual departure from nature's ordinary methods, when it is necessary, that it is worthy of most reverent heed and consideration. It shows not only that there was care for a general material order, but care for *man*.

I. Thus, for *warming* the earth; is the *sun's* heat sufficient? I imagine that most persons never thought of any other as *necessary;* and yet it is certain that another *is* as necessary as the sun. The world-dwelling is warmed in part by a furnace; out of sight, and to most persons out of mind; and yet without which it would be uninhabitable. No doubt is now entertained, among geologists, that the centre of the earth, if not a molten and fiery mass, is far hotter than the surface; and that the surface derives part of its warmth from that source. But then, if the heat at the centre were far greater than it is, it might make a hotbed of the whole earth: it might produce enormous growths, like those of the pre-Adamite earth; when the fern and the brake grew eighty feet high—fit, indeed, to make coalbeds (which they *did* make), but not fit for human sustenance. If the central heat were greater still, it would destroy all vegetation. But if, on the contrary, there were *no* heat in the world itself, if it were a mass penetrated throughout with icy coldness, it may be easily seen that no heat from the sun falling upon its frozen bosom, could make it a fruitful, or desirable, or habitable abode for man.

But further, the regions of the equator, over which the sun passes and upon which he pours down his direct rays, are liable to be too hot; and the regions of the pole, upon which his rays fall slant and oblique, too cold. This, I have said, in the nature of things, was unavoidable. But what is there to modify and temper these extremes? On the line of the equator the earth bulges out, so that its diameter from east to west is twenty-six miles greater than from north to south. Now it is found, from boring into the earth, and from examining the temperature of mines at different depths, that the heat increases on descending, at the rate of about one degree for fifty feet; that is to say, that any swell on the earth, or any mountain mass, would be—the internal heat *alone* considered—one degree colder for every fifty feet of height—twenty degrees for every thousand feet. Doubtless other things are to be considered; and especially the warmth of the sun and air around the mountain sides; and we do not know the conditions of this central heat. Of course the calculation cannot be applied with any exactness; but taking into account simply the swell of the earth around the equator—inasmuch as the surface at the equator is about thirteen miles farther from the centre of the internal heat than the surface at the poles, it seems not unreasonable to infer that the warmth from this source is less within the tropics. That is to say, if there were no external source of heat, no sun shining directly upon it, the now burning zone would be the coldest part of the earth.

But above this swelling up of the earth in the equatorial regions, rise again the highest mountains in the world. From these heights the land regularly declines, all the way to the pole; each mountain range lower as you proceed, each plateau lower, from the lofty table land of Tubet in Asia, 14,000 feet above the level of the ocean, to the steppes of Tartary, and the great plains of Siberia in the extreme North; or to take it in the New World, from Chimborazo, 21,000 feet high, to the table land of Mexico, 7,500 feet high, and the plateau of Inner California, 6,000, and so onward to the plains of Oregon and Hudson's Bay. The equatorial mountains rise to the height of from twenty to nearly thirty thousand feet.

On ascending these mountains, at an elevation of about fifteen thousand feet from the base, we reach the point of perpetual congelation. Above this, rise the snowy heights —stupendous icehouses to cool the regions below—reservoirs of water too, to refresh them; and without which neither plant nor animal nor man could have lived there.* Now if a contrary disposition had been made; if low and level valleys had prevailed near the equator, and the highest mountains had risen within the arctic circle, it is evident that both would have been uninhabitable.

Let us now turn from the land to the water. Nearly three fourths of the earth's surface is covered with water. The Pacific Ocean alone, it is computed, occupies more space than all the dry land. It may seem a strange disproportion of waste and apparently useless water, to fruitful soil. But let us consider it. This soil can yield nothing without a certain amount of moisture. A certain amount—neither more nor less; too much would saturate and debilitate the vegetation, too little would dry it up. Now the sea is the source of moisture, the nurse of rains. Evaporation lifts up the watery particles into the air; whence they are borne upon the land, to fall in showers, to distil in dew, to bathe the mountain heights, whence they gush forth in springs, gather into streams, and form and feed the mighty rivers; and for all these purposes, the supply is, in the general, just what is wanted; neither too much, nor too little. But this evaporation from the sea; what does it give us? Pure water; an *extract* from the mass, as exactly separated as if it were distilled in an alembic. Suppose that the *saline* particles were lifted into the air, to fall in rain, and flow in the rivers; that it rained brine, and that brackish and bitter waters flowed in all our streams and fountains! What an element indeed—what a blessing is pure water!—the most exquisite refreshment of thirst, the only cleanser of impurity for the human skin and for all that pertains to human use, the only healthful solvent of vegetable food for the daily meal. And suppose that the pure springs or the *medicinal* waters were turned into bursting fountains of champagne wine; it would seem as if nature, in her secret caverns, had plotted for our destruction! And I confess that I am struck,

* I am indebted for these estimates to Guyot's Lectures.

not only with the blessing and beauty, but with the mystery of this element. We know nothing of the hidden connection between its particles, by which it is a flowing liquid, instead of a mere conglomeration of atoms. If it were poured into our cup and bowl, as disintegrated albeit golden sands, we could neither drink it, nor wash in it. More wonderful than any enchanted cup, is that which we daily put to our lips; choicer than all the cosmetics of Arabia, is that morning ablution; and well might it be, every morning, as an outpoured oblation of pure thanksgiving. And when it falls in refreshing rain—in the fine rain upon the mown grass—who can help sometimes thinking what it would have been if it had come down in sheets of water; how it would have deluged and crushed the tender herb beneath?

But why is the *sea salt?* Or what purpose is served by its saltness? Professor Maury, of the Washington Observatory, has given to this question an answer of singular interest. He has shown that the whole oceanic circulation depends mainly upon this quality of saltness. And upon this circulation depends again the tempering of all climates, both hot and cold. For if the ocean stood still, then increasing masses of ice in the north, and increasing heat at the equator, would make both zones uninhabitable. Of this oceanic circulation, the Gulf Stream is an example; but there are other currents no less remarkable. The arctic voyagers, wintering in Davis's Straits and Wellington Channel, found themselves drifted southward by a surface current—in one instance, a thousand miles in nine months—while, at the same time, icebergs, sunk deep in the water, and taking the effect of an undercurrent, were borne the very opposite way—borne northward, through crashing fields of ice, at the rate, in one instance, of four knots an hour.

But how is this effect produced? The immense equatorial evaporation—*i. e.* the taking up of immense quantities of water—lowers the sea level. A surface current from the north flows down to supply the deficiency. This indeed would take place if the sea were fresh. But in salt water, as the evaporation does not take up the salt, it leaves the surface water salter, *i. e.* heavier. Consequently it sinks; and thus, by its momentum, it prepares in the depths of the the equatorial seas an undercurrent, which flows northward. In an ocean of fresh water, this result would be superficial and partial.

But let us look at other ministries of the ocean.

At first sight it would seem as if this ocean barrier would separate nations—shut them up in solitariness and isolation. But what is made of this seeming obstacle? Why, in fact, nothing is made a medium of intercourse between distant nations like the ocean; and intercourse is the grand educator, civilizer. If Europe had been separated from us by 3,000 miles of land, we might hardly have reached her yet; or rather she might have hardly reached us—hardly have discovered this quarter of the world. Or if some wandering tribes had found their way over the intervening distance, there would nevertheless have been little or no intercourse. The vast plains of Asia were traversed only by here and there a trader or caravan, or else by invading armies. Invasion perhaps was better for the world's culture than sterile seclusion—than the sitting apart and alone, each people and nation alone, amidst hereditary and unbroken ideas and customs. But now the commerce of the seas is peacefully doing that which war did of old. It is bringing all nations acquainted with one another, interfusing their spirit and life blood, binding them together, and making brethren of hostile races; and, at the same time, opening the common fund of earth's bounties and blessings to every clime and country. The dread barrier of the sea has melted away into a liquid plain, best fitted to buoy up and bear on our vessels; better for intercourse than if it were spanned with bridges, or crossed in every direction by causeways of stone or railroads of ever-during iron. And if there be a few persons—and I confess myself to be one of them—who would prefer the causeways and the railroads—

prefer any conceivable locomotion to a sea voyage, yet nature's plàn is not to gratify the few, but to benefit the many. And I cannot help thinking that art will yet find means to relieve this horrible misery, this sickness of the sea.

It was indeed a dread barrier to those who first saw it; but what was its effect? It tempted their courage and enterprise: it called out their energy, hardihood and skill, and has thus contributed, along with intercourse and commerce, to make them the most prosperous and civilized people in the world; witness the Egyptians, the Phenicians, the Greeks, the Romans, and the modern European and American communities. Everywhere the highest civilizations have found their home upon the shores of the sea, and upon the rivers that flowed down into it. The ship is the most significant emblem in the scutcheon of freedom, polity, and progress. One has termed it "that swan of the sea;" but it is like anything but a swan, to the unpractised beholder. I remember the first time that I saw a ship part from the shore—the solid shore as one well feels it to be at such a moment: all was solid, firm, calm, quiet here; but there, all was alive, and seemed rushing upon some unknown fate; the roaring of the wind in the cordage, the swelling of the sails to the breeze, the straining of every yard and mast, and, as it seemed to me, of every mighty rib in the almost living mass, inspired me with a sort of terror. But the strong hearts that swayed it felt no terror; every motion was easy to *them*, every rope in the complicated network that bound it was familiar; and under their charge it swept over the deep, as free and fearless as if it were some huge seabird seeking its own natural element.

But before leaving this element, water, I must advert to another and still more remarkable arrangement. I have ventured to say, that nature, when it is necessary, departs apparently from her own laws. Thus it is laid down as a law in physics, that "heat expands all bodies," and so makes them lighter. Conversely, cold contracts all bodies, and makes them heavier. This is the law. Suppose, now, that the philosopher had never seen ice, or had never before thought of this remarkable fact, that cold, freezing *water* into ice, does not contract, but expands it, and thus makes it lighter than water. It certainly would seem to him like something miraculous; but how would his astonishment increase, when he saw the end to be accomplished by this deviation from law! Ice now floats upon the surface, and protects from freezing, the water beneath. But suppose that every drop of water frozen, became like lead, and sank to bottom. Then would our lakes, and probably our rivers too, become every winter solid masses of ice, which no spring gales nor summer suns could thaw—so as to make the earth habitable. "It struck me with awe, when I first knew this"—said one who mentioned this fact to me *—"nature violating one of her own laws for human benefit!"

But to return: I have spoken of evaporation from the sea. But evaporation would be useless, if its burden were not borne from the sea to the land. How is it borne? If there were vast curtain-like fans hung over the deep, and worked by some stupendous machinery above, to waft the ocean vapors to the shore, we should say, *there* is a provision! But equally a provision, though noiseless and unseen, is the power that sets in motion the boundless waves of air. *That* is heat. Heated air rises, and the colder air flows in to supply its place. Hence, as you know, the regular sea-breezes upon all islands and coasts. Hence the less regular alternations and changes of the wind daily, varied also by the intervention of trees, groves, hills, and mountains. But the same provision has a wider sweep, in the monsoons, and especially in the trade winds. The heated air upon and near the equator, constantly rising, creates a constant tendency in the lower strata of the atmosphere to that quarter; the motion of the earth on its axis gives it a turn to the west, like the water on a grindstone: on the ocean it has an unimpeded course, and is there a regular or trade wind; when it has spent its force in that direction, it turns back,

* Daniel Webster.

from reaction, from accumulation perhaps we might say, toward the north and east—thus giving us prevailing west winds; and thus it spreads its breezes, laden with refreshment, over all the continents. Thus by intermingled land and water, heat and cold, the earth is fanned with healthful airs; the extremes of every climate are tempered; the torrid zone parts with its heat to the north; the polar cold sweeps across continents and seas, to cool the burning line; and not one of those "sightless couriers of the air," goes without commission.

Kepler, the German astronomer, believed that the earth was a huge animal, that breathes in winds and tides, and bellows and belches out its fury in volcanoes, and shakes the world with throes, which are earthquakes. I once knew a man who held the same opinion. And as he took me over his plantation, it was curious, and if sometimes ludicrous, not altogether uninteresting, to see how he talked and felt about it. "There it wanted to be scratched"—where the plough was needed; and "there it needed a plaster"—where the spot was barren. It seemed a harmless thought, and better so to animalize nature, than to drive all life out of it. I had rather believe with Kepler or with Berkeley, than to see the world as a stolid substance—the petrified or fossil remains of an extinct energy. Everywhere, seen or unseen, is action, movement, life—free, flowing, endless. There are rivers in the *ocean*, like the Gulf Stream—aye, thousands of feet deep—that flow from continent to continent, bearing warmth in their bosom, and tempering the climates of whole countries. The earth, too, is bursting with vegetable life through all its pores; the flowing sap, the breathing leaves, the waving grass, all speak of *life*. Light, heat, electric fires, play over its surface; the air vibrates to perpetual sounds; the sea rolls with unceasing tides; the forest trees are filled with music; in summer and autumn days, it seems as if the hillsides and the thickets and the thick grass panted with singing, chirping, joyous, melodious life. The hum that comes up from all the earth is a living voice from its bosom. The summer breeze, that falls in frolic gusts and eddies upon the thicket and the shrubbery and the tall grass, makes them leap and dance and sway as to moods of laughter—like children turned out to play. The serene heaven that bends over us—meteor of beauty as it is—is not more beauteous, nor more filled with a celestial presence, than the fair world that lies beneath. Matter? It is time to give up the old Manichæan ideas; even science demands it, as well as religion. It is not obstruction, but manifestation of the Divinity. It is not the cast-off *exuviæ* of a dead and departed power, but the flexible and ever-flowing garment of the Infinite Life.

II. We have surveyed now, in their most general form, the great and palpable elements that go to make habitable and comfortable and agreeable this earthly home for man —land, water, and air. There is another view which I wish to present to you, and that is, not only of the general, but of the specific adjustment of things to human use, and of man himself to the sphere in which he lives.

It does not seem to me irreverent to look upon the Divine Power which is working in all things around us, as working with infinite skill; as adjusting things with wonderful adaptation to their purposes. I have said before that there are natural impossibilities; as for instance, a thing cannot be heavy and light, or opaque and transparent at the same time; as a thing's being best fitted for a general and permanent end, may *preclude* its being equally fitted for a limited and temporary emergency. But while that is not achieved which is not possible in the nature of things, the study of nature will delight us, by showing that all which *is* possible, *is achieved;* that all the good is accomplished that is possible, all the evil avoided that is possible.

Thus to take the physical adaptation of the human being himself to the scene: when a man falls into the water, we might for the moment wish he were light as cork, that he might not drown; his drowning is an evil, concerning which one may ask, why is it? or, why is it not avoided? And then again, if he were pushing against a beam that threatened to fall upon his child, one might wish, for the moment, that he were as heavy and solid as a rock. He is neither so heavy nor so light. In short, his weight is adjusted to more general purposes, to more permanent situations, to the entire sphere he moves in; and to the strength of the sinews which are to move the weight. Now this weight, you know, must depend on the size and density of the world in which he is placed; *i. e.*, upon the attraction of gravitation. In the sun, it would be twenty-eight times as great as it is here; in Jupiter, two-and-a-half times; in Mercury, only half as great; in the moon, only one-sixth. With the heavier weight, he could have done nothing; he could have neither worked nor walked. With the lighter, he would have lost the force, the momentum necessary to his daily taskwork, to his useful activity in every way. His weight, in short, is exactly adjusted to his sphere and strength.

Look again at the natural substances and products which he is cultivating or using in agriculture, in the mechanic arts in every form. If garden vines, instead of running on the ground, had risen up into the air, they could not have sustained the melon and cucumber. If wheat, on the contrary, had lain upon the ground, it would have lacked the sun and air to ripen the grain. The tree—the forest tree, that is—is to answer a different purpose; and what is that? To furnish timber for building. In its forest state the growth is thick; and the consequence is, that the lower branches die and fall off, and a long trunk is provided, which answers the purpose. If it had grown sparsely, it would have been, as we see it in the open field, unfit to be hewn into beams, or to be sawed into boards. And so if it had been much heavier or lighter, harder or softer, tougher or more brittle, than it is, it would have less well answered its purpose.

And what could we have done at all with it, if some metal had not been provided which could be sharpened into the axe, the saw, and planing tool. Iron—from which steel is made, and which is the only metal, I believe, capable of a similar hardening—is the most useful metallic substance in the world. I look upon its internal structure as one of the most wonderful proofs of design and skill. No other metal could supply its place; not gold nor silver, because they are too ductile and flexible; nor copper, because it is too brittle. Iron is malleable, and it can be melted, so that it can be moulded and beaten into all possible shapes; but its peculiarity, that which gives it its special value, is a certain toughness, a certain power of resistance, a texture making it fit for cutting, which is laid in its internal structure. We know nothing of that mysterious, interior constitution; but we see the result—that without which civilization would have been greatly impeded, if not forever held back even from its present degree of advancement.

And, accordingly, iron is more abundant in the world than any other metal, or all others put together. Gold is comparatively rare, and depends upon this consideration, as well as its freedom from liability to rust and tarnish, for its extraordinary value. Both fit it for that most important agency of being a circulating medium, or a current representative of all sorts of value. Nor is it likely that the mines of California and Australia, will yield much more than a needful supply, for the growing wants of commerce and civilization. This is not the first time that the world has been dazzled with visions of boundless accumulation. The mines of Mexico and Peru, awakened very much the same feeling in the sixteenth century. And among the Phenicians of old, as Heeren tells us,* there was a very similar excitement about the mines in Spain. The ships of Tarshish, mentioned in Scripture, were Phenician vessels sailing out of Tartessus (Tarshish), in Spain; and it was said in that time, that not only were the ships laden with gold, but that their anchors were made of gold.

We might pass now, in this brief survey, from the

* Works, vol. i. p. 328–329.

mineral to the animal kingdom. That certain quadrupeds, birds, and fishes were destined to be food for man, is a point not questioned, I believe, in any sound physiology. I confess for myself to a feeling of dislike to this system of destruction. I do not like to hunt or fish for the same reason; but I believe that the feeling is more scrupulous than wise. It is no greater hardship for animals to die by the hand of man than by the claw or fang of their fellows—not so great; and sudden destruction is better than to die untended, of lingering decay. Indeed, if they died of disease or decay, the very carrion of their remains would fill the world with pestilence. Nor is the amount of animal happiness lessened; immediate transformation into new life takes place; and the world is always as full of animal life as it can bear.

But there is another use of the animal kingdom to man, which indicates a no less striking adaptation. Certain animals were evidently made to be domesticated—to be the companions and helpers of man. For this there is a fitness in their nature, structure, size, strength, habitudes, and very instincts. Not the lion, the tiger, the hippopotamus and the hyena are so fitted, but the horse, the ox, the cow, the camel, the ass and the faithful dog. And it has been well observed that the want of most of these animals among our own aboriginal races, was of itself enough to prevent any great advance in civilization.

Nor are the wild tribes of creatures useless to man. They make the scene of the world gay and beautiful. They make nature vocal. They supply man with food; they clothe him with furs. They preserve the world from putrefaction and pestilence. Offensive smells would make our summer walks hateful, but for them. The hyena, the vulture, the very worm is a scavenger. The cleanliness of the animal and insect tribes themselves, is most worthy of notice. The feathers of birds, the hair of quadrupeds, the sharded wings of insects, take no soil. The most delicately kept child is not neater, than the bug in the dunghill. And thus, by structure, by instincts, by the pursuit of food, life is caused to spring from decay and corruption; and the house of nature is kept clean and pure, without service or drudgery or toil.

III. But I must leave these details, in order to find space for two or three observations on the general and yet urgent adaptation of material nature, not merely to human support and comfort, but to the higher spiritual culture. We shall not exhaust the theme here; for we cannot consider the human constitution, as we propose to do in a future lecture, without referring to the circumstances in which it is placed, to the outward agencies by which it is developed. But there are two or three views of nature's influence, which press themselves upon our attention now, because they help to complete the general survey of it as a material organization. For it is not enough to say that nature has provided a home for man through the combined agencies of the earth and ocean and atmosphere, or that she has adjusted the objects of the vegetable, mineral, and animal creation to his use; for she has still more distinct and significant appeals to his intelligence and moral culture.

There are certain arrangements in nature, then, which are evidently fitted to answer a double purpose to man—a lower and a higher; to give sustenance and pleasure and practical direction, and at the same time to impart higher knowledge and guidance. The arrangements I shall instance are the fertility, the order, and the beauty of nature.

In the first place, with regard to the fertility of the soil: the primary object is manifest. But has it never occurred to any one who cultivates the soil, to ask why it was not made twice or ten times as fertile as it is now; or why, when exhausted by a crop, it could not have been entirely, as it is in part, restored and replenished by the air. By these means labor would have been relieved to an immense extent. We are apt unthinkingly to take the existing system as if it could not have been otherwise. But a slight change in fertility—*i. e.*, a soil twice as fertile, or a human organization demanding only half as much food, would have relieved many a heavy burden. Ay, there is a hard strain upon human energy. It is the straining of the very sinews to the task. Nay, *all* work is hard, because field-work is hard. For if this had been relieved, human energies might easily have achieved the rest—the building, the manufacturing, the artisan's work in every kind.

Look, then, at this fact of moderated fertility, and see what it means.

I say *moderated* fertility; for it might as easily have been less as more. You sometimes, as you travel, pass through a district, or by a farm, of which you rather disdainfully say, "it must be a hard scramble for life here; you would not try it, for your part." But suppose the whole world had been as barren and intractable, or worse. What then? Why, then had we been a race of miserable drudges. Then too had there been no place for society; no place for the cultivation of the sciences and elegant arts; no seventh day of perfect rest, no altar nor priesthood; but all the refinements of life, all its mental culture, its graceful arts, its religious ordinances, and all the splendor of its cities, palaces, and temples, would have been buried under the crushing oppression of cheerless toil. You, my friends, would not have been here, listening to a lecture upon this subject, or any other subject; but you would all have been abroad upon the sterile earth, cutting away the intractable forest, levelling the rugged hills, digging, delving, drudging for a bare subsistence.

But turn now to the more attractive side of the picture; and suppose a soil so prolific that the labor of an hour would suffice for the wants of a week; and what *then* would follow? Why, then would man have been turned out to idle vagrancy, or sunk into voluptuous sloth: and the moral fortunes of the world would have been as certainly wrecked and ruined by indulgence as, on the former supposition, they would have been by hardship.

But this leads me to notice a still more exact and careful

adjustment of the law. The zones of the earth are as much marked by difference of strength and of wants in the inhabitants, as by difference of heat in the climate. The men of the torrid zone have not the physical vigor of the Northmen. The labor, therefore, that is light and easy in the North, to the more delicate frame and languid temperament of the inhabitants of the torrid zone, would be an overwhelming task, crushing both to body and mind. Accordingly their wants are fewer. They require less food, less clothing, less fuel, less expensive buildings. In the northern regions, where man is more vigorous, more protection is needed, and stronger diet—more of animal food. The Hindoo's dish of rice, would not suffice for the hunter and miner on the steppes of Siberia. To the Esquimaux and Greenlanders, a bountiful dish of whale oil is said to be a delicacy. The northern voyagers, Parry and Franklin, found that their crews were obliged to live almost entirely on animal food; they lost vigor and cheerfulness without it—a fact worthy of some account with our extreme dietetic systems.

And then, observe, in fine, by what means, by what agents this general adjustment of fertility is effected—the air, the wind, the rain, the mouldering forest leaves and disintegrated particles from the surface of mountain rocks, the fire in the woods, the volcano in the abyss. Wild elements, undefined instruments seemingly they are; and yet they all conspire to produce a certain degree of fertility. Any considerable swaying either way, and that balance would have been disturbed in which the moral destinies of the world are weighed. Truly, "the winds are His angels, and the flaming fires His ministers." Truly, "He weigheth the mountains in scales and the hills in a balance."

Again, in the *order of nature*, we see a double purpose—the one referring to practical convenience, to the guidance of daily action and industry; the other, to the cultivation of the mind—lying, indeed, at the foundation of all science. Without the first we could do nothing; without the last we could learn nothing.

The first purpose is answered by many obvious arrangements. If the sun did not daily rise and set; if day and night did not duly succeed each other; if the year did not bring about its circuit, and the seasons did not revolve in fixed cycles; if summer and winter, seedtime and harvest, did not know their place; if all the elements did not obey certain laws; if the fire did not burn, nor water fall, nor food nourish, nor the seed produce the plant, nor the plant yield seed, with invariable sequence, we could do nothing upon any regular plan; the whole action and industry of life would be brought to a stand. Throw all this into confusion, and man would stand aghast, and would soon sink and perish, the victim of that boundless disorder. He cannot take a step but by lines, which nature has drawn all around him for his guidance.

But now let it be observed that the order of nature is not limited to the purpose of furnishing this palpable guidance. Because the order of nature embraces a thousand things which the common eye cannot see; with which common prudence has nothing to do. The law, for instance, of definite proportions in chemistry—that is, that so many parts of hydrogen mix with so many parts of oxygen to form water, and so in all the chemical compounds, and that they will mix in no *other* than certain definite proportions—this has nothing to do with the common uses of water or iron, of lead or tin, in their common forms. So the laws of crystallization in minerals, by which gold takes one form and quartz another; the wonderful system of genera and species in plants and animals—the resemblances and differences so marked; and the geometric laws that reign over the heavenly bodies—these have no palpable, practical uses. Then again to go into the animal creation—though the horse, the ass, and the ox had *not* stood before us as distinct species; though their forms and qualities had been blended and mixed in such utter confusion that it had been impossible to classify them, still they could have drawn loads and borne burdens. Whereto then serves this order in nature;

which partitions it out into realms and ranks; which penetrates the most secret cells of animal or vegetable life or mineral structure, and stretches its sceptre over the boundless spheres of heaven, and binds the universe in sublime harmony? The answer is—to *teach* man. I need not deny that it was chosen for its own sake; but I say it has this further advantage and purpose—to *teach* man. Only through this order is science made possible. If it were not for this order, and the scientific classification founded upon it, the human mind would sink helpless amidst boundless diversity and detail. Only through this classification is any available *language* possible. The words animal, mineral, vegetable—beast, bird, fish—stand now for distinct classes of objects, bound together by definite affinities. Break that bond; make every object to differ essentially from every other; and then every object, to be pointed out, must have a different name; and the human mind would sink as helpless beneath the burden of words as beneath the burden of thoughts. There are objects enough on your farm or in your warehouse to occupy a life in learning to designate them; the catalogue of your farm or warehouse would be as large as a dictionary; and every other would require the same; and the metes and bounds of knowledge would be as narrow as the metes and bounds of your estate. *Now* nature spreads itself before us as a volume, with its books and chapters and sections: but let its order be broken up, and it would be as a volume in which the words were printed hap-hazard, without connection or consequence, without statement or conclusion; and we should learn comparatively nothing.

This is that sublime order, so attractive and beautiful that philosophers, both ancient and modern, have endeavored to resolve it into some one primordial principle—Pythagoras and Plato into number or form; the Germans, Schelling and Hegel into some subjective, metaphysic law. Auguste Comte imagined at least, that it may be reduced to some principle in nature like gravitation. Some such all-comprehending unity is the dream of many minds still. But fanciful or wise as the search may be, certain it is that, without this sublime order, the universe would not be a temple of knowledge and worship, but a Babel of utter confusion and frustration to all study and inquiry.

Finally, *beauty* in nature has a double function, though somewhat less distinctly marked.

The colors, green and blue, and the neutral tints, scarcely less common, are naturally agreeable to the eye; and if red and yellow were the pervading hues, the organ of sight would be dazzled and blinded by them. Then again variety, both in color and form, is naturally grateful; and if all the objects in nature were of one shape and of one hue, no *prison* could be so dreadful. To our constitution, therefore, nature's garniture is almost as necessary as her substantial supplies of food.

But the beauty of her works ministers to purposes far beyond convenience, far beyond utility. It is connected with higher laws in us; it touches a finer sense than of good, than of advantage. Beauty, to all who truly know it, is a thing divine. Its treasures are poured with lavish abundance through the world, its banners are spread upon the boundless air and sky, to entrance the eye and soul with visions of more than earthly loveliness.

The whole influence of nature's beauty, and of all that is akin to its beauty—how manifestly is it divine! It holds no compact with anything base or low. Man may mar and desecrate its fairest scenes; but he can never say to the majesty or loveliness of nature, "*Thou* hast tempted me!" Wicked and hateful passions may break out—jarring upon her sublime symphonies, disturbing her holy quiet; but *nature* has no part with them. Did ever the grandeur of the midnight heaven, or the thunder in the sky, or the answering thunder of the ocean beach, make any man proud? Did the murmurings of the everlasting sea, or the solemn dirge of the winter's wind, or the voice of birds in spring, or the flashing light of summer streams, or the mountain's awful brow, or the vales

"Stretching in pensive quietness between,"

did ever these make any man rude or ungentle? Did ever the fulness and loveliness of the creation, weighing upon the human sense and soul almost with an oppression of joy, make any man selfish and grasping? No; the true lovers of nature are never ignoble nor mean. She would unnerve the oppressor's hand, or melt the miser's ice, or cool the voluptuary's fever, this hour, if he would open his heart to her transforming companionship.

Nor are the treasures of her beauty yet half explored. A finer culture of the senses and soul will unfold new wonders. "What powers," says Herder, "are there in each one of our senses, which only necessity, sickness, accident, or the failure of the other senses, brings to light! The blind man's acuteness of hearing and touch seems at times almost miraculous. May it not be a hint of what is possible to all the senses—of powers yet undeveloped in us? Bishop Berkeley observes," he continues, "that light is the language of God, of which the most perfect of our senses can yet spell but a few elements."* Looking at that grand kaleidoscope made on the back of the pianoforte, and which doubtless many of you have seen, I was led to think of these undeveloped powers of sense, and what visions of supernal glory may yet be opened to the eye. What unfolding wonders *shall* yet burst upon us; what pictures shall be unrolled to the vision of purer natures; what seals shall be taken from the great deeps of beauty—it may not be for us to know in this world. Our sense is dim, our power feeble; the present revelation, I suppose, is all that we can bear. But the time may come, when there shall visit us melodies, such as were never drank in by the ravished ear, sights, such as never entranced mortal eye; when perpetual raptures may be felt without exhaustion; when lofty states

* The Philosophy of Humanity.

of mind, such as noble genius and heroism inspire, may become the habit of the soul, and ecstasy may crowd on ecstasy forever.

Full of moral influence, full of prophecy, full of religion, is the true sense of beauty. When I sit down in a summer's day, with the shade of trees around me, and the wind rustling in their leaves; when I look upon a fair landscape —upon meadows and streams, stealing away through and behind the clustering groves; when the sun goes down behind the dark mountains or beyond the glorious sea, and fills and flushes the deeps of the western sky with purple and gold; when, through the gates of parting day, other worlds, other heavens come to view—spheres so distant that it takes the light thousands of years to reach us: then only one word is great enough to embrace all the wonder—God! Beautifully says a great poet, and no less justly:

"He looked—
Ocean and earth, the solid frame of earth,
And ocean's liquid mass, beneath him lay,
In gladness and deep joy. The clouds were touch'd,
And in their silent faces did he read
Unutterable love. Sound needed none,
Nor any voice of joy: his spirit drank
The spectacle; sensation, soul, and form,
All melted into him; they swallowed up
His animal being; in them did he live,
And by them did he live; they were his life.
In such access of mind, in such high hour
Of visitation from the living God,
Thought was not; in enjoyment it expired.
No thanks he breathed, he proffered no request;
Rapt into still communion, that transcends
The imperfect offices of prayer and praise,
His mind was a thanksgiving to the Power
That made him."

LECTURE IV.

THE BODY AND THE SOUL, OR MAN'S PHYSICAL CONSTITUTION: THE MINISTRY OF THE SENSES AND APPETITES.

The body and the soul—the relation of the body to the soul—the ministry of the body to the soul—this is the subject of the lecture before us: and I say at once, that it is my wish and purpose to vindicate man's physical organization from the charge that it is naturally low and debasing, or was ever meant to be so; that it is my wish and purpose, in approaching this heaven-built sanctuary of the soul, to offer, not scorn and desecration, but reverence and worship.

There are two kinds of houses that a man lives in. There is the house that the carpenter built. And there is *this house*, that God hath built for the spirit's dwelling. The former is built for an end: for the use, for the accommodation, and, justly considered, for the moral cultivation of its inhabitant. Can we suppose less of the latter? The body is an organic structure, with a thousandfold more contrivance in it than a house, or a whole city of houses. But organization is a means to an end. Now this relation is what I understand by the term philosophy: and I might have *said*, that my lecture this evening is on the philosophy of the human organization, senses, and appetites.

Let me pause upon this point a moment: for I must try to keep distinctly before your minds the object of these lectures, and to make it constantly appear how legitimate, practical, and important that object is; nay, of what interest it is to all thoughtful persons.

Organization, I say, is a means to an end; and the perception of this *relation*, is philosophy. The philosophy of a thing is the knowledge of the end to be answered by that thing, and of the means embraced in it to accomplish that end.

I confess that I am somewhat tired of hearing this word, philosophy. It was formerly a mystery; then, afterward, it was a terror to religion and faith; and now, perhaps, it has become a weariness. We have philosophies of everything. Nevertheless, this constant repetition of the word, this fixed direction of thought, I hold to be a very remarkable sign, ay, and a very good sign of the time.

That which is indicated by it, is immeasurably the highest kind of knowledge. Observe that the two elements must go together. The knowledge of the means by itself, or of the end by itself, is not philosophy, but a very inferior thing. Thus, for example, a man may understand the end or use of a machine, engine, or implement, without understanding the organization or adjustment of its parts; and then he is not a philosopher, but a mere handicraftsman. Or he may consider the parts alone; he may pore over the details of an instrument, the mere isolated facts—and so of the great system of nature and life—and go no further, think nothing of an ultimate aim, nothing of order, plan, or purpose; and then he is not a philosopher, but a mere matter-of-fact man. He who comprehends both the means and the end—sees the parts with their relations, and the result—is in that regard a philosopher. He may never have thought of calling himself such; he is perhaps a humble laborer in the field of life; but he is, in relation to one thing, and may be to many more, a philosopher. Suppose—to illustrate still further the superiority of this kind of knowledge—that a small section from the great field of nature were offered for inspection, and that it were a quarry of granite. The examiner enters it, and ascertains what may be called the *facts* presented; that is to say, he discovers and distinguishes the three elements—quartz, feldspar, and mica. But if he knows nothing further, if all his knowledge and thought are shut up in the heart of this quarry, of what interest can it be to him? He might as well know anything else, or know nothing. But now suppose that he goes out into the world of adaptations and uses; that he sees the bedded rock as a material for building; and further, that he marks upon its upper surface how its particles are crumbling away into a soil; and then traces that soil through vegetable, through animal, through human life, to all the majestic purposes for which man and nature are made; what then does he say? "Philosophy!"—might he not exclaim—"well art thou called divine; for thou dost unbar the gates of wisdom, and pour light and beauty through the world."

So regarded, the action of life would become thought, and its experience, wisdom. Some tendency of this kind, I believe, is to be observed, at this day. The world is entering upon that state of early manhood whose natural impulse it is to ask the reasons of things; and I cannot but think that this word, *philosophy*, so often repeated, so often printed, heading and lettering so many books, is like a blazoned banner, going before and leading on a nobler progress than the world has yet seen.

To proceed now with the subject of this lecture: I have already explained to you, that my theme is not Natural Theology, not a discussion or illustration of the Divine Perfections, as manifested in nature and life. We do indeed teach all this indirectly; it is the grandest interest of this subject, as it is of every subject of high philosophy; but our specific object is to show how things in nature and life, and so in the human organization, senses, and appetites, are framed to answer a certain purpose—to minister to the highest of all purposes, the culture of the human soul.

Now the human frame has much in common with the animal organism. All this, though it abundantly manifests the wisdom and goodness of the Creator, and would demand attention in a system of Natural Theology, I shall leave out of the account; save and in so far as it serves especially to elicit and train the human faculties. With the benefit of this exception we may fairly say, that the eye and the ear, though common to man and animal, have for man a peculiar, that is to say, a mental and moral instrumentality. In considering the ministry of the body to the soul, I shall keep in mind this distinction between the human and animal organization, because it touches the very point in hand. The animal organism ministers to instinct merely; the human, to intellect and moral culture. Take, for instance, the sense of touch; which animals possess indeed, but in a degree so inferior that, comparatively, they may be said not to possess it at all. If, instead of this sensitive vesture of feeling, man had been clothed with hide and hair and hoof, the human soul had been imprisoned in obstruction and stupor. It is the mother's caress that first wakes the infant soul to life. The fond embrace is the earliest nurture of affection and seal of friendship. In all the animal world there is no kiss. The grasp of the hand—all over the world the sign of comity and kindness—is a significant token of the human destiny; it is the sign manual upon the great charter of human brotherhood. Shaking hands—it may be a very wearisome thing to a popular favorite in a long summer's day; it may seem to many a very unmeaning ceremony; but it links and binds the race in the bonds of moral fraternity. But the whole frame, too, is thus sensitive. The air that falls upon it, in softer than veils of down, breathes exquisite pleasure through every pore. The sense of touch, the eldest born and earliest teacher of all the rest, imparts in fact a character to all the other senses, and to the whole nature; so that I am tempted to say that the delicacy or torpor of this organization is, for any child, one of the clearest prognostics of his future development; and I doubt whether a man, who can let a fly walk all over his face without knowing it, though deep powers and passions may dwell within, is ever a man of fine, quick, and sympathic sensibility.

Next, the faculty of speech is peculiar to man. This is

given for expression; but mark that it is given for the expression and culture of higher things than are found in animal natures. Much may be revealed, it is true, in dumb show, in pantomime, or by inarticulate cries; and animals do this: and man's most ordinary wants could be so expressed; and those who maintain that speech was an immediate, Divine gift to man from his Creator, because it was an immediate necessity, seem to me to overlook this fact; besides that a miracle is not to be supposed where a miracle is unnecessary; and I have *known* two children playing by themselves for a single summer, to form a language of their own. Neither dumb show, however, nor childish prattle, suffices for the higher wants of humanity. For the finer discriminations of thought and feeling, for the opening and culture of the human understanding, *cultivated speech* is necessary; and such, we cannot doubt, is its special office.

I cannot altogether pass over the wonder of this thing in our humanity, though I must not dwell upon it. Language, the breath of all human thought, the living tissue of all human communication, the telegraphic line that stretches through thousands of years, the texture into which are woven the character and history of nations and ages—all other devices, all other arts sink in comparison with this grand instrument, at once of Divine intelligence and human ingenuity—the common speech of men. To describe the *organs* of speech, their structure, relations, and action; and then the corresponding organ that receives it, the ear; and then the medium of speech, the subtile and elastic air, would require ample treatises. And yet the act of an instant calls all these agencies into play. A man utters a word, but one word; and a volume could not describe all that has been concentrated in that utterance. Nor to one ear alone does the utterance pass, but to many. A man utters a word; and instantly it breaks, as it were, into a thousand particles, which pass like sunbeams through the air, and, in one moment of time, print an intelligible thought upon the minds of thousands. And the *might of speech*, the power given to a word, the living strength that girds a man when his whole nature speaks out—there is no force in the world that is felt like that. Justly therefore is the power of God represented by a word. "By the word of the Lord were the heavens made, and all the host of them by the breath of His mouth."

There is another peculiarity in man, of a totally opposite, and yet perhaps of a no less significant character; and that is laughter. Some men question much about recreation; whether they will have it or have it not; whether they will admit it into their plan. But Heaven has sent it into their plan; and they must have it, whether they will or not. Nay, they laugh about *nothing*, too—which makes it yet more significant in this view. But laughter has a still further and higher significance. It is the expression of the mind's freest enjoyment. It is like the clapping of hands in an assembly—the riotous outbreak in us of pleasure, delight, sympathy. It is healthful too, I might say, by the by. It helps more to digest a dinner than old wine, or anything else fancied to help it. But its highest office is in the delicacy of apprehension which it indicates. There are twenty kinds of laughter, with as many meanings. Laughter is the relish of wit, the mockery of folly, the utterance of joy, the murmur of approbation, the shout of welcome. It expresses what words cannot. It is the flower that bursts from the hard, logical stem of talk. Sad were the life in which there was no laughter; sad and bad, I should fear. Men do not laugh when they are meditating wicked deeds; the guilty face is serious enough—stern or livid with its seriousness. Sad were the life to which nothing ludicrous ever presented itself; it were scarcely human. In fact, laughter is perhaps the most distinctive visible mark of our humanity. If an anomalous or masked being were presented before us, concerning which we doubted whether it was a man—that which would most immediately decide the point in his favor, would be a burst of laughter. There are sighs and screams, and there is singing in the animal world, but not laughter.

There are other peculiarities in the human organization to be noticed.

One is the countenance. You can conceive, though perhaps with difficulty, that on striking an ox or a dog with a cruel blow, the animal might turn around upon you, with a distinctly human expression of indignation or reproach; as much as to say, "I have my thoughts, and this is cruel." If no other feature could express that, the eye might. It does not; that power is not *given* to the animal face; if it were, it would be such a metamorphosis as would fill us with terror, and would penetrate with horror every reckless or savage abuser of the uncomplaining, dumb creatures that God has given for his service. But man is made to stand erect, and the crowning glory of his person is a countenance, every lineament of which is clothed with moral expression. The lowering brow of defiance, the cheek blanched with indignation, the eye challenging truth, or killing with accusation, or veiled and shaded with softening pity, the winning sweetness of smiles, the whole manifold mirror of radiant goodness and honor—all is moral ministration. And indeed, speaking of smiles, I think I never *saw* a smile that was not beautiful. Hardly less remarkable, perhaps, is the circumstance of every man's face being his own, clearly distinguishable from all others. We see the inconvenience, and sometimes fatal inconvenience, of not being able to distinguish one man from another, in the very few and rare cases of remarkable resemblance. If this were common, it would hardly be too much to say that the intercourse, the business, the very civilization of the world must stop. Not to know certainly whom we talked with, whom we traded with, who had told us or promised us this or that, whom we had married or who our children were; the world would be thrown into utter confusion; and all good relations would become impossible. To prevent this, there is achieved in the human countenance, what seems to me scarcely short of a miracle. Here it is—a little patch of white ground, nine inches long and six wide, with the parts the same, the configuration the same, and the hues generally the same; and yet, if all the hundreds of millions of the human race were brought together, every man could pick out from them all, his friend, with a certainty equal to that of his own identity.

Finally, the human hand is to be mentioned. It serves indeed one of the purposes of the animal claw or forefoot—*i. e.*, to obtain food. Taking into account the forearm, the arm, and shoulder, it is worthy of note, that a similar formation prevails throughout the entire animal economy, as if nothing more perfect could be devised. That is to say, there are the scapulæ or shoulder blades, the clavicles or collar bones to keep them from pressing upon the chest, the arm, the forearm, and the hand, claw, or hoof, as the case may be. The same general construction is found in the fins of the fish, the wings of the bird, and the foreleg of the quadruped. But in man, this organ, I do not say, comes to its perfection—for all is perfection, every animal has that which is best for itself—but this organ comes in man to answer purposes peculiar to himself; and most of these are mental and moral. "The indefeasible cunning" that lies in the right hand, has more to do than to procure food. For instance, it has to fashion clothing, without which there could not be comfort in all climates, nor civilization in any. No animal could cut cloth, or sew it, or thread the needle. Then again, all the practical arts depend upon the hand—building, the use of tools, all skill in making fabrics, which is *called manu*facturing. Then, all the fine arts require the hand—painting, sculpture, music. Then, once more, all writing is handwriting. All human communication, beyond that which is oral, all literature, all books, all works of genius, all the grandest agencies in the world depend upon the hand. Yes, in the human hand lies the whole moral fortune, the whole civilization, the whole progress of humanity. The right arm is a lever that moves the world.

I have thus spoken of certain parts of the human organism as superior to the animal, and as evidently intended to answer a higher purpose—touch, speech, laughter, the human face and hand. Let us now consider, in the next place, the general ministry of the senses, appetites, and passions.

Some of you, I have no doubt, will feel, when you hear these words, appetites and passions, as if I named things that are not friends, but enemies to human culture. You have associated with them perhaps *only* ideas of temptation. But in the good order of Providence, I am persuaded it will always be found that temptation and ministration go together, and that ministration is the end, and temptation only the incident. Temptation is but another word for strong attraction to a thing; that attraction is necessary, and was never meant to be injurious, but useful. I do not say, therefore, with some, that powerful passions and appetites were placed in man on purpose to try his virtue, but that they were placed there for other ends; that they are, in fact, a necessary part of the human economy; and that the trial is purely incidental, and in fact unavoidable. Just as fire was not meant to burn the house, nor, as the main intent, to make the keepers vigilant, but simply to warm it, though it could not warm, without being liable to burn it.

I shall solicit attention particularly to this part of the human economy, to these fires of appetite and passion in the house of life; because here arises the only moral question about our sensitive constitution; and I am persuaded the question can be met. But I ask the inquirer to see, in general, what his simple senses teach him. I ask him to consider his own physical frame, fearfully and wonderfully made, as the very shrine of wise and good teaching, and to listen to the oracle that comes from within. Ay, to the oracle; but remember, it is when nature's flame burns upon the altar, and not the strange fire of idolatrous passion. I appeal to nature against sensualism; and am willing to risk the cause of virtue on that issue. I will show you—I think, at least, I can show, that simple, natural appetite it is *not*, that leads to vicious and ruinous excess, but something else. I concede the liberty in our physical constitution—provided it be truly understood—to follow nature.

"Fatal concession!" I hear it said. "Fatal concession!" exclaim both ancient philosophy and modern religion. "What can the body teach, but evil, error, excess, vice?"

Let us see. You find yourself possessed with a nature other than your spiritual nature; different from it, inferior to it; and you hastily conclude that because its qualities are lower, its uses must be lower, and its tendencies all downward. You say, or think, perhaps, that if your being were a purely spiritual essence, you would be free from all swayings to evil. But how do you know that? Nay, keener than the temptations of sense itself, are the spiritual passions—ambition, envy, revenge, and malignant hate. You imagine that if your present frame were exchanged for some ethereal body, you would have passed out of the sphere of evil and peril. That again, you do not know. Come then to the simple fact, and let it stand unprejudiced by any theory, or any fancy, or any comparison. God has given to us, in the present stage of our being, this body—this wonderful frame. Sinews and ligaments bind it together, such as no human skill could ever have devised. Telegraphic nerves run all over and through this microcosm, this little world, and bear mysterious messages, vital as thought and swift as sunbeams. Now I say that these are all moral bonds, good ministries, channels meant to inform and replenish the soul, and not to clog or corrupt it.

I hardly need say this, in the first place, of the five distinct senses—touch, taste, smell, sight, hearing. They are the mind's instruments to communicate with the outward world; instruments so varied as to convey every kind of information; servants that need not to be *sent* to and fro on errands, but that *stand* as *perpetual* ministrants—before the gates of morning, and amidst the melody of groves, and by the bowers of fragrance, and at the feast of nature, and wherever the pressure of breathing life and beauty comes to ask admission to the soul. The body is a grand harmonicon, a panharmonicon, strung with chords for all the music of nature. Serving all needful purposes also—to walk, to run, to move from place to place; to work, to achieve more than all animal organisms together can do; it is, at the same time, an *organon scientiarum*, an organ of all knowledge. It is more than a walking library, it is a walking perception—of things that no library can teach; it is a walking vision—of things that no language can describe: like the wheels that appeared to the rapt Ezekiel, full of eyes within and without.

All this, then, it will not be denied, is good and useful ministration to the mind. One might as well inveigh against a telescope or an ear trumpet as against the eye or ear.

But now to this system belong certain distinct susceptibilities; which are not classed under the head of senses: these are called appetites. Such, for instance, is hunger; or, in other words, the general relish for food and drink, which, when denied for a certain time, becomes hunger or thirst. I have before alluded to the *uses* of this particular appetite, but I wish to say a word further and more distinctly of it in this connection.

You can easily conceive that a being might have been made without this appetite—made to move, to act, to live; but not to eat. Or you can conceive that he might have had the relish for agreeable food and drink, without the intolerable pain he feels when they are long denied. Why, then, this pain? I look upon it as a distinct provision, designedly, and, if I may say so, gratuitously put into the system, to arouse man from indolence, to arouse him to activity. I look upon it just as if nature had provided a whip; just as if there were an organ attached to the human body as the arm is, and fashioned like a scourge, and, when the man is sinking to ruinous indolence, lifting itself up and striking him with a blow, to stir him to action. It *is* a *sting*, and answers that purpose. And moreover, it is a stimulus exactly adjusted to the strength of the agent, and also to the means of gratification. If hunger returned every hour, instead of two or three times a day, human sinews could not bear it, nor provide for it, nor the world-supply of food suffice it.

And is it a point too low for philosophy to observe, furthermore, that hunger, with the peculiar needs of that appetite in man, promotes social intercourse? I say, with the peculiar needs of that appetite in man; for *his* food must be cooked. He cannot pursue his prey or pull up his root, like the wild animal, and eat it on the spot, alone. He must bring it home, he must have arrangements for cookery; and the convenience of this process makes it almost necessary that families should assemble at certain times of the day and eat together. I am persuaded that we little suspect the immense social and civilizing effect of these daily gatherings around the social board.

But admitting that the appetites have their uses—which is the first position I take—it is said, nevertheless, that they have bad tendencies, tendencies to excess, to vice, to ruin. On this point, there is, in the second place, a most important distinction to be made; and that is, between appetite in its simple, natural state, and appetite in its artificial and unnatural state; a state brought on by voluntary habit and corrupting imagination and mental destitution; for which man's *will* is responsible, and not his constitution. Look then at simple, unsophisticated, unperverted appetite. Is the draught of intemperance, or the surfeit of gluttony, naturally agreeable? Far otherwise. Moreover, all those stimulant and narcotic substances and those rich condiments, of which excess makes its principal use, are naturally distasteful and disgusting in the highest degree. I do not say that even *they* were created in vain, or must necessarily be injurious; for everything is good in its place and degree—even poison is so; but I say that there is no natural demand for these strong stimulants. On the contrary, fever in the veins, poison in the blood, sickness, nausea, are remonstrances of simple appetite, remonstrances of nature against them. And show me what diseased and vicious passion you will, and I will show you that it is the mind's guilt, and not the body's defect; that it is not the passion let alone, still less duly controlled by the higher nature. It is not nature, but bad example or companionship, that leads to evil. It is imagination that nurses passion into criminal desire. There is a natural *modesty* which unhallowed license always has to overcome. Let no man lay that flattering unction to his soul, that God has made him to love evil—made vice and baseness to be naturally agreeable to him; for it is not true!

But these appetites, besides their general uses, and besides their natural innocence, seem to me, in the third place, to bear a specific relation to the mind. They are urgent teachers.

They teach, first, *moderation*. They teach the necessity of self-restraint, of self-denial. I have no doubt that a being not clothed with flesh, a pure spiritual essence, would feel the necessity of self-restraint. But if any physical organization, belonging to an intellectual nature, could be made to enforce this law, it appears to me it would be that of our human senses and appetites. Because it is manifest that their unrestrained indulgence works the direst ruin to the whole nature. What! does this our sensitive frame teach lessons of evil, lessons of vice? God and nature forbid! Open, patent, everlasting fact teaches the very contrary. The woes of intemperance, gluttony, licentiousness, excess, are the very horrors and calamities of the world in every age. They are so horrible that we dare not describe them. Here, then, is "elder Scripture writ by God's own hand" written before ever voice was heard on Sinai or by the shores of Galilee, written all over the human frame, and within every folded leaf of that wonderful system. Yes, upon the ghastly form it is written, and upon the burning cheek, and deep in the branching arteries, and along the secret and invisible nerves is it written. And sometimes you may read the writing by the literal, alcoholic fires, kindled in the veins; which, with visible flame, burn up the man; and sometimes by such haggard lines of deformity as nothing but the *worst* license of vice ever drew upon the human frame. I once saw in Paris a collection of wax figures taken from life, and designed to present such an illustration. I do not wish to speak of it, nor of the vice illustrated, nor of the nightmare horror felt by the beholder for hours after it is seen. But it seemed to me that no preaching on earth, was ever like that silent gallery.

You must have patience with me, my friends, for I *must* overthrow entirely, and utterly demolish this plea of the senses for vice. My argument for the ministry of the senses and appetites, cannot stand at all, unless I do that. The truth is, the senses, fittest for virtue, happiest in innocence, are only *capable of vice*—that is all, but no conceivable organization could be surrounded with more tremendous remonstrances against evil. So the *mind* is *capable* of evil, and so is the mind, too, guarded. And it might as well be said that the *mind* seduces to ill, as that the body does—nay, I think, *better*—with far more reason. But because sensual aberration is more apparent, and the effects are more visible, therefore the world, with little insight as yet into the truth of things, has agreed to charge this fact of temptation especially upon the body. It would be coming nearer to the truth to say, that the mind is the real culprit.

What *are* the comparatively poor, puny, and innocent senses, but servants of the mind—compelled to do its bidding? I know it is a doctrine of old time, that the body does all the mischief; that the body is the enemy of the mind, a clog, an encumbrance, a corrupter. The philosopher, Plotinus, affected to have forgotten his birthplace and parentage, because, says Porphyry, "he was ashamed that his soul was in a body." He imagined that the mind had good cause to complain of the body. But I believe it would not be difficult, and scarcely fanciful, to set forth a counter plea. "I have wandered"—might the substance of the body say to the mind—"I have wandered through all the regions of existence, and never was abused, till I came in contact with you. I have made a part of animal natures, that were innocent; I have lived in the beautiful forms of vegetable life; I have flowed in the streams and sported in the air, all purity and freshness and freedom; and never till I was subjected to your influence, was I breathed upon by any bad spirit; never till then, was I tainted by the diseases of vice, or made a loathsome mass of sin-wrought corruption; never till then, was my nature perverted from its uses, and made the instrument of evil."

But to speak most seriously: What a wonderful, moral structure is our physical frame! If a command to be pure were written, imprinted in visible letters, upon every limb and muscle, it could not be a clearer mandate, and by no means so powerful. It was said to the mad and rebellious Saul, "It is hard for thee to kick against the thorns." Such a message comes indeed from no open vision, but from his inmost frame, to every raging voluptuary. Thorns and tortures does it shoot out against him from every part. If, every time he indulged in any excess, he were covered with nettles and stings, the intimation would not be a whit more monitory than it is now.

How different is it with the animal! You may feed him to repletion; you may fatten him into a monster; and there is no disease, no suffering; there is only enjoyment; and so far as he is destined for food, he is the more fitted for his purpose. But if you do this to man, disease and pain enter in at every pore.

The ancient philosophers, in their theories, desecrated matter; the moderns, and especially the sensual school in France, have deified it. They boldly proclaimed—I speak of the French infidel philosophers of the latter part of the eighteenth century—they boldly proclaimed matter to be the true divinity; the human frame, its altar; and the appetites, its priesthood. Selfishness with them was the only motive; sensation, the only good; and life a bowing down in worship to the appropriate divinity. But whoever tries that theory, will find that matter *is* indeed a god, too powerful for him; the fleshly altar will be burned up and destroyed by the strange fire that is laid upon it; and the priests, the appetites, will perish in that profane ministration.

The Government builds prisons for culprits, and protects the honest house. All men pronounce that to be a moral administration. But what if, when wrong was perpetrated in the honest house, and it had become the habitation of the base and vile, it should, by some wonder-working intervention of the Government, grow dark and desolate, and should gradually turn into a prison—the windows narrowing year by year, and grated bars growing over them; the rooms, the ceilings, slowly darkening; the aspects of cheerful and comfortable abode gradually disappearing, and gloom and filth coming instead, and silence, broken only by the sobs and moans of prisoners, or the sadder sound of cursing or revelling? Such, mark it well! becomes the body, the more immediate house of life, to every abandoned transgressor! Not alone the mount that burned with fire, utters the commandment of God; not alone the tabernacle of Moses, covered with cloud and shaken with thunder; but this cloud-tabernacle of life, which God has erected for the spirit's dwelling, and the electric nerves that dart sensation like lightning through it—all its wonders, all its mysteries, all its veiled secrets, all its familiar recesses, are full of urgent and momentous teaching.

But there is something further to be observed concerning this teaching; there is one respect in which it is yet more urgent. For it demands not only moderation and self-denial, but activity: it forbids not only excess, but indolence. It demands of those who do not labor, daily, out-of-door exercise—not a lounge in a carriage only, but a walk, or some bracing exercise in the open air—demands *that*, or says, "pay for your neglect." Some inuring, some hardness—hardship, if they please to call it—nature exacts even of the gentlest of its children. The world was not built to be a hothouse, but a gymnasium rather. Voluptuous repose, luxurious protection, enervating food and modes of life, are not the good condition, not the permitted resort, for our physical nature. Half of the physician's task with many, is to fight off the effects of such abuses. The laws of the human constitution are moral laws; they address the conscience, the moral nature; they exact penalties for neglect. And doubtless the penalties are severe. That is not nature's fault, but nature's excellence. Doubtless the penalties are severe. I am persuaded, indeed, that if they could be enumerated; if all the languid and heavy pulses could be numbered; if all the miseries of nervous and diseased sensation could be defined; if all *that* could be described which surrounds us with wasted forms, or sequesters them in silent chambers, an aggregate of ills could be found which would match the statistics of pauperism, or of intemperance itself. I believe there is less suffering among the idler and more luxurious classes, from violent disorders, than from those chronic and nervous ailments, which do not always inflict acute pain, which do not alarm us for the patient—well if they did!—but which enfeeble the energies, destroy the elasticity of the frame, undermine the very constitution of the body; which depress the spirits too, wear out the patience, sour the temper, cloud the vision of nature, disrobe society of its beauty and despoil it of its gladness, and send their victim to the grave at last, from a life which has been one long sigh. And all might have been prevented by one brisk daily walk in the open air.

This subject—and I mean now this whole subject of the right training and care of the body—is one, I conceive, of unappreciated importance. Our physical nature is more than the theatre, more than the stage, it is the very costume, the very drapery in which the mind acts its part; and if it hangs loosely or awkwardly upon the actor, if it weighs him down as a burden, or entangles his step at every turn, the action, the great action of life must be lame and deficient. What that burden, that entanglement is *now;* and what is the genuine vigor and health of a man; what is the true, spiritual ministry of the body to the soul, I am persuaded, we do not yet know.

I confess that I sometimes think that this subject—what old Lewis Cornaro denominated in his book "the advantage—not the duty only—but the *advantage* of a temperate life," is one that goes behind all the preaching. The physical system, though not the temple, is the very scaffolding without which the temple cannot be built. We call from the pulpit for lofty resolution, cheering courage, spiritual aspiration, divine serenity. Alas! how shall a body clogged with excess, or searched through every pore with nervous debility; how shall a body, at once irritable, pained, and paralyzed, yield these virtues in their full strength and perfection? We ask that the soul be guarded, nurtured, trained to vigor and beauty, in its mortal tenement; that the flame in that shrine, the body, be kept bright and steady. Alas! the shrine is shattered; and rains and windflaws beat in at every rent; and all that the guardian—conscience—can do oftentimes, is to hold up a temporary screen, first on one side, and then on another; and often the flickering light of virtue goes out, and all in that shrine is dark and cold and solitary; it has become a tomb!

I am endeavoring, in this part of my lecture, to defend man's physical constitution in general from the charge that it naturally develops evil, vice, intemperance, excess every way. I before showed that the specific organs and attributes of the physical structure—the sense of touch, speech, laughter, the human face and hand—are fine ministries to the intellectual nature. I came then to what is thought the more questionable tendency of the senses and appetites; and I have shown, first, that they are useful—as hunger, for instance, impelling to industry; secondly, that they are naturally innocent, *i. e.* that they do not like, but naturally *dislike* excess; and thirdly, that they powerfully teach and enforce wholesome moderation and healthful activity.

I deny, therefore, that the bodily constitution naturally ministers to evil, to vice. A similar organization shows no such tendency in *animals.* It is the mind, then, that is in fault. But now I wish further to show, before I leave the subject, that vicious excess is a complete inversion of the natural relations of the mind and body; that instead of being according to nature, it turns everything upside down in our nature.

Certainly, in the natural order of our powers, the mind was made to be master; the body was made to be servant. Naturally the body does not say to the mind, "Go hither and thither; do this and that;" but the mind says this to the body. The mind too has boundless wants that range through earth and heaven, through infinitude, through eternity; and it must have boundless resources. Can it find them in the body?—in that for which "two paces of the vilest earth" will soon be "room enough." Our physical frame is only the medium; as it were, an apparatus of tubes, reflectors, Æolian harpstrings, to convey the mysterious life and beauty of the universe to the soul. So far as it loses this ministerial character, and becomes in itself an *end* on which the mind fastens, on whose enjoyments the mind gloats, all is wrong, and is fast running to mischief, misery, and ruin.

For suppose this dreadful inversion to be effected; suppose that the all-grasping mind resorts to the body alone for satisfaction—forsakes the wide ranges of knowledge, of science, of religious contemplation, the realm of earth and stars, and resorts to the body alone, and has, alas! for it, no other resource. What will the mind do *then?* It will—I had almost said, it *must,* with its boundless craving, push every appetite to excess. It must levy unlawful contributions upon the whole physical nature. It must distrain every physical power to the utmost. Ah! it has so small a space from which to draw its supplies, its pleasures, its joys. It must exact of every sense, not what it may innocently and easily give, but all that it *can* give. What ere long will be the result of this devotion to the body and to bodily pleasures? *There comes a fearful revolution in the man!* The sensual passions obtain unlawful ascendency—become masters—become tyrants; and no tyranny in the world was ever so horrible. None had ever such agents as those nerves and senses—*seductive* senses, call you them!—say rather those ministers of retribution, those mutes in the awful court of nature, that stand ready, silent and remorseless, to do their work. The soul which has used, abused, and desecrated the sensitive powers, now finds in them its keepers. Imprisoned, chained down, famishing in its own abode, it knocks at the door of every sense; no longer, alas! for pleasure, but for relief. It sends out its impatient thoughts, those quick and eager messengers, in every direction for supply. It makes a pander of the imagination, a purveyor for indiscriminate sensuality of the ingenious fancy, a prey of its very affections; for it will sacrifice everything to be satisfied.

Could it succeed—could it, like the martyr, win the victory through these fiery agonies—but no; God in our nature forbids. Sin never wins. Ruin falls upon soul and body together. For now, at length, the worn-out and abused senses begin to give way: they can no longer *do* the work that is exacted of them. The eye grows dim; the touch is palsied; the limbs tremble; the pillars of that once fair dwelling are shattered, and shaken to their foundation; the whole head is sick, and the whole heart faint; the elements *without* become enemies to that poor, sick frame; the fires of passion are burning within; and the mind, like the lord of a beleaguered castle, sinks amidst the ruins of its mortal tenement, in silent and sullen despair, or with muttered oaths and curses and blasphemies.

Oh, let the mind but have had its own great satisfactions, its high thoughts and blessed affections, and then it could say to these poor proffers of sense, "I want you not; I am happy already; I want you not; I want no tumult nor revel; I want no cup of excess; I want no secret nor stolen indulgence; and as for pleasure—I would as soon sell my body to the fire for pleasure, as I would sell my soul to *you* for *pleasure*."

Such is the true and natural relation of the mind and body; such is the law of their common culture. Under this law the body would be fashioned into a palace of delights, hardly yet dreamed of. We want a higher *ideal* of what the body was made and meant to be to the *soul*. Sensualism has taught to the world its terrible lessons. Is not a higher æsthetic law coming, to teach in a better manner? Sensualism is but the lowest and poorest form of sensitive enjoyment. One said to me, many years ago, "I have been obliged, from delicacy of health, to abstain from the grosser pleasures of sense; neither feast nor wine have been for me: perhaps I have learned the more to enjoy the beauty of nature—the pleasures of vision and the melodies of sound." The distinction here taken, shows that the very senses might teach us better than they do. For I say, was that witness a loser, or a gainer? Vision and melody; shall grosser *touch* and *taste* carry off the palm from *them?* Vision, that makes me possessor of the earth and stars!—the eye, in whose mysterious depths is pictured the beauty of the whole creation!—and what comprehensive *wonders* in that bright orb of vision! Think of grosser touch and taste; and think, for one moment, what sight and hearing are. It is proved by experiments, that, naturally and by mere visual impression, the *eye* sees all things as equidistant and near—close to us—a pictured wall. By comparisons of apparent size and hue, we have learned to refer all objects to their real distance. Sky and clouds, mountain-sides and peaks and rocks, river, plain and grove, every tree and swell of ground, all are fixed in their place in an instant of time. Hundreds of comparisons—hundreds of acts of mind, are flung into that regal glance of the eye! But more than the telescopic eye, is the telegraphic ear. More, to my thought, lies in the hidden chambers of viewless sound; in that more spiritual organ, which indeed expresses nothing, but receives the largest and finest import of things without; in that mysterious, echoing gallery, through which pass the instructive, majestic, and winning tones of human speech; through which floats the glorious tide of song, to fill the soul with light and melody. Instruments of godlike skill, types and teachers of things divine, harbingers of greater revelations to come, are these. Not for temptation, not for debasement, was this wondrous frame built up, let ancient philosophers or modern voluptuaries say what they will; but to be a vehicle of all nobleness, a seer of all beauty, a shrine of worship, a temple of the all-pervading and in-dwelling Life.

LECTURE V.

OF MAN'S SPIRITUAL CONSTITUTION—MINISTRY OF THE MENTAL AND MORAL FACULTIES.

From the statement of the problem of human destiny, to the ground principles of it, as laid in the finite and free nature of man; from the general structure of the material world as the place of human abode and culture, to man's physical organization, and the ministry of his senses and appetites—this has been the order of discourse in our previous lectures. Let us now proceed to the mind itself; to that presiding power which dwells within the bodily organization, and yet is as distinct from it in its nature and essence, as if it were ensphered in heavenly splendor; to that life within, that cannot be wanting to the purpose which all life around it subserves.

On any theory of human nature, this field of inquiry is fairly open to us. For though the theory about the soul be this—that it is by nature spiritually dead, and can wake to life only by a regenerating power; though the soul were regarded as a dry and dead mechanism, helpless and incapable of moving itself, yet when the stream of influence *is poured* upon it, that stream, it will not be denied, finds and sets in motion a machinery fitted to answer high purposes. It is into this grand mechanism that we are now to look.

In its nature, I say, it stands completely apart from the physical mechanism. Thought, feeling, conscience, is one thing; bone, sinew, brain, is another thing. Because they are intimately associated, because thought, feeling, con-

science operate *through* bone, sinew, and brain, therefore to say, as the materialist does, that they are of the same nature, is as if he should say, that because light, to be perceived, passes through the eye, therefore light and the eye are of the same nature; or because *life* dwells in the plant, therefore the material structure of the plant, is the same thing as the mysterious life that animates it. Or if he says that thought is the *result* of a bodily organization, he says that which *can* be no matter of perception or knowledge to him—which *is* nothing, in fact, but the merest imagination. He may imagine, if he pleases, and he might as well, that thought is an exhalation from the earth, that it comes up through the soles of the feet, that it passes, like raw material, through the mechanism of the human system, till it issues from the brain the finished product. To all such dreaming, we may say—if mind is not one thing, and matter is not another thing; if mechanic organization is not one thing, and the conscious and living will is not another; if these substances or modes of being do not, in fact, lie at the opposite poles of thought; then there is no such thing as difference in the universe.

And let me say also, that the mind, the inner being, is not, as an object of thought, enveloped in that peculiar obscurity commonly ascribed to it. Metaphysics may be abstruse, and far away from the ordinary paths of thought, but the mind is not. It is imagined to be far more mysterious and inaccessible than matter. But, strictly speaking, in the nature of things, the very contrary is the truth. Things without me, are matters of observation; things within, of consciousness. The things within are nearer and more certain to me. I know myself, as I know nothing else. I know my thought better than I know any object without me. When I compare thought with thought, and draw a conclusion, that process is far more intelligible to me, than when I put heat to fuel, and produce combustion. The outward world is phenomenal and shadowy, compared with the inward. Some philosophers have doubted whether it exists at all; but none have doubted their own existence. I can easily believe, that if we could get back to our original experience, we should find that, at first, the bodily organs themselves seemed as external and foreign to us, as the material world—the foot no more a part of ourself than the ground it trod upon; but no such mistake could be made with regard to our thought, our feeling, our consciousness: *that is ourself.*

Into this innermost home of our humanity, then, let us enter; and see what is created there, to minister to the great end of our being.

In the mind then, considered as distinct from bodily sensation, there are three great faculties, or classes of faculties.

First, there are the intellectual powers. And what is their ministry? Plainly to discover truth. This is the one object, the destined result of their entire action. There is the intuition of truth, which embraces mathematical axioms and the original moral conceptions; which embraces ideas of truth as superior to error, of right as higher than wrong, of cause and effect, of time and space, both finite and infinite; ideas native to the mind, created, embedded in it; ideas which are the foundation of all reasoning. Then there is perception of facts around us, and consciousness of facts within us; and judgment, which compares these facts and draws conclusions; and imagination, which ranges through the creation, and gathers new and analogous facts and principles; and memory, the storehouse of knowledge—without which there could be no comparison, no process of thought. All these faculties obviously have one design, the discovery of truth.

Secondly, there are the æsthetic faculties, whose office is the perception of beauty. Certain forms, proportions, colors, and sounds are naturally agreeable to us; others are disagreeable. I am not aiming at any full or detailed analysis of the mind. I only wish, in the general, to direct your attention to its cardinal principles. And certainly there is such a part of our mental constitution as I now indicate; which has no direct regard either to truth or right, though it is in many ways connected with both. There is nothing strictly intellectual nor moral in the agreeableness of certain forms and colors, in the sense of proportion and harmony and melody. These belong to the æsthetic part of our nature.

Thirdly, there is the moral faculty—that is, conscience—and its nature and office cannot be mistaken. *What it is*, there can be no doubt; though the questions, how it arises in the mind, and how it acts, have admitted of various explanations. They are very familiar—those of Hartley, Adam Smith, Paley, and of the later and better philosophers, German, French, and English, who hold that conscience is a distinct and original faculty. But it is unnecessary to consider them in detail; because they all admit that there is such a thing as conscience; that it is a discrimination of the right from the wrong; that it is an approval of the right, and a condemnation of the wrong. Neither does a misguided conscience, of which the world has seen enough, and of which flippant sceptics have made so much, any more prove that there is no such thing as conscience, than a misguided reason proves that there is no such thing as reason. Beneath the rubbish of all human errors lies the indestructible basis. Nay more; within, wrapped up within every moral *mistake* that ever was committed, lies the *nucleus*-conviction that *something* is right. Conscience, however imperfect, unenlightened, erring, has ever held that there was something right in the very wrong which it sanctioned. It has sanctioned cruelty, oppression, war. Why? Because it *believed* them to be *right*. The very persecutor, like Paul, thought he was doing *God* service. That inborn element was never worked out of the moral judgments of men. That great and solemn word, *right*, was never erased from the tablet of humanity, howsoever worn and defaced, and never will be.

Let us now consider how this spiritual constitution of

our humanity, intellectual, æsthetic, and moral, conduces to the end for which we say that it was made; how, indeed, it is a kingdom built up within us, with laws and ordinances and powers all conspiring to that end. In doing this, we must take care to distinguish, in human nature, the permanent from the casual, the necessary from the contingent, the fundamental from the superincumbent, God's work in the mind from man's overlaying. In works of human art, if the critic or student should neglect to make this distinction, if he should confound fragments and defacements and ruins with the original structure and design of statue or temple, he would stumble at the first step. And the original, the Divine work in the *soul*, is to be distinguished from all that mars it, or there will be no proper ground for any study of it. Ground there *is*, however; and this consideration of the matter—the distinction, that is, which I here make—is most pertinent and practical to the present state of men's minds. For the aberrations of our humanity, by many, *are* mistaken for its laws and principles. Because men have fallen into deep and sad erring, they seem to suppose that nothing better than erring is to be expected of them. Depravity as a doctrine, is made an apology for depravity as a life. And man, "made but a little lower than the angels," made for angelic aspiration, suffers himself to be low and vile almost without shame, certainly without any keen and converting self-reproach.

The error is as old as the most ancient philosophy, and as new as almost the latest. The Persian sages, the Greek philosophers, Plato himself, the Gnostics generally, and even some of the Christian fathers, held that the world and its inhabitants were so ill made that they would not ascribe the work to the Supreme God, but charged it upon some inferior being—Demiurge or Satan. Even the learned Cudworth, so late as two centuries ago, maintained, and his opinion is countenanced by the acute and liberal-minded Le Clerc, that all things here below are arranged and ordered by a certain power, which he calls "Plastic Nature," a power, he says, "incorporeal, but low and imperfect."

Assuredly we have learned better things than these, and can vindicate a better philosophy. Humanity ill made? Indeed the best argument for that theory would be the blindness that could see no better. Ill made? It is made, first of all, to recognize the sovereignty of truth. Errors and deviations and controversies there have been, and enough of them, in the world; but the one challenge of all dispute, from the first hour that ever a man debated anything with his neighbor, has been this—"I have the truth; and you have it not." All intellectual erring, at least in the regions of abstract inquiry, has been involuntary, and has evermore been a seeking for the truth. If it had *found* nothing, *then*, indeed, would a case be made out against us, of stupendous abortion. But what do the words —science, philosophy, literature, art, poetry, common sense —mean, if the search has been in vain? And if there stood upon the earth, now and here before us, one who had *discovered* all the truths, the secret and mysterious truths of nature and life and humanity, that being would draw from the whole world a homage such as was never paid at the throne of monarch or pontiff. So is man made; so to bow down before the truth, before the simple, naked, invisible truth, as he bows before no outward shrine. The eternal reason speaks in him; and its word is an oracle. Above all earthly power and grandeur, sits sage wisdom. The monarchs of the world are such as Plato, Homer, Milton, Shakspeare.

Homage to such is natural. Truth leads not downward, but upward. There is something ennobling in the bare pursuit of it, in the most abstract forms. One cannot *listen* to a clear and lofty discoursing, without feeling his very frame to expand with swelling thoughts. There are books, and even those of the abstrusest philosophy, like Dugald Stewart's, which I cannot hear read without feeling as if I wanted to rise up and stride through the room, and were a head taller. I am reminded, in this connection, of the beautiful eulogium which Sir James Mackintosh passes on Dugald Stewart. "How many," he says, "are still alive, in different countries, and in every rank to which education reaches, who, if they accurately examined their own minds and lives, would not ascribe much of whatever goodness and happiness they possess, to the early impressions of his gentle and persuasive eloquence!" *

Turn now to the department of Science. It does not fall within my present design to speak at length of its vastness—of the grand fabric of scientific knowledge which man has built up in the world; to show how he has stretched the compass of his investigation from the earth to the skies; how he has analyzed every known substance, and studied the laws of invisible agencies, and penetrated into the beds and layers of the old creation, and deciphered its history; how he has descried millions of living creatures sporting in a globule of water, and then risen to follow the millioned globes of heaven in their courses; how he has traced out astonishing analogies of structure between the flower of the field and the system of heavenly spheres—between the arrangement and development of the solar system, and the branchings of our forest trees—showing them all to be of one type, one order, one creative idea. But whither can all this stupendous knowledge lead, but to God? Where can man bow down his awe-struck reason but before the throne of the invisible Might? Science is the natural ally and minister of religion. And this, notwithstanding the assumptions of some philosophers, whom not science, but irreverence, has made Atheists, has now come to be regarded as the established truth.

"Still"—I hear it said—"the mass of mankind is buried in ignorance." It is curious to observe how constantly we use the word ignorance, as if there were no knowledge but that of books and theories. The active classes, I think,

* View of the Progress of Ethical Philosophy in the Seventeenth and Eighteenth Centuries, p. 213.

have some right to complain of this book-learned assumption. What are we to say of that vast accumulation of knowledge, called common sense; the light of daily life; the light of guidance that shines upon all the paths of human pursuit? All the philosophy in the world, could not supply the place of that; all the philosophy in the world, in utility, is perhaps inferior to it. It has been reserved for some of the French philosophers, Jouffroy, and others, to raise this truth to its proper place. M. Jouffroy has raised it, perhaps, something *above* its place; for this is his view of the matter. "*Seeing* and *observing*," he says, "are different things. Seeing is universal; observing is the philosopher's province. Observing is the seizing and examining of particular aspects of things; and although keener than the common and general seeing, and having its own immense importance, it is apt to be narrow and one-sided. Hence the varying and conflicting systems of philosophy. But seeing is broader, though less clear; sight is the mirror that holds all things. The common man sees all things, in nature and humanity, as truly as the philosopher, and having no bias, no theory to support, is likely to see them more justly, though far less deeply." Common sense therefore corrects the aberrations of philosophy. Thus he says, "The history of philosophy presents a singular spectacle; a certain number of problems are reproduced at every epoch; each of these problems suggests a certain number of solutions, always the same; philosophers are divided; discussion is set on foot; every opinion is attacked and defended with equal appearance of truth. Humanity listens in silence, adopts the opinion of neither, but preserves its own; which is what is called common sense." *

But it is more especially to my purpose to say that common sense has come to distinctly moral conclusions. These are embodied in a mass of maxims, proverbs, apothegms, the hived-up wisdom of all ages, which, if I had space to repeat them, you would see to possess only less truth and

* See the Essay translated in Ripley's Specimens, Vol. I.

authority than Holy Writ itself. Such are the maxims that "honesty is the best policy; all is not gold that glitters; handsome is, that handsome does; time and tide wait for no man; forewarned, forearmed; right wrongs no man; every door may be shut but death's door; man's extremity is God's opportunity; man proposes, God disposes; no cross, no crown; better the child weep than the father;" and a multitude of others. Common sense, though leaning much to prudence and worldly wisdom, is nevertheless a moral censor, and sometimes a profound teacher of the highest things. It is always the corrective of fanaticism, the satirist of folly, the condemner of vice, the reprover of injustice, the patron of truth, integrity and well-doing.

In the next place, the æsthetic part of our nature, the sense of beauty and melody, though not in philosophical strictness of speech either intellectual or moral, is most immediately associated with our noblest faculties, and ministers to their growth and perfection.

I have before spoken of the beauty of nature, and of the power of music. I have spoken of the eye and ear. Let us now penetrate beyond them—beyond the sphere of sights and sounds, beyond those organs of seeing and hearing, to the *sense*, the *feeling* of beauty and melody, in our æsthetic and spiritualized nature. The animal has eye and ear, and outward world, but, properly speaking, no feeling of beauty or of music. Who ever saw one gazing upon a landscape, or upon the silver orb of night unless it were to "*bay* the moon?" Who ever saw one testify delight in music, save as it was *associated* with his master's presence, or with his going forth to hunt or to fight? These higher things are reserved for higher natures.

Again, this sense of beauty is innate; as much so as reason or conscience. Outward sights and sounds do but wake it up—do but nurture and cultivate the inward power—do but answer to it. A fair landscape does not create the sense of beauty. That already existed within; made *ready* by the hand of its Creator, to receive the outward impression. The soul *demands* beauty and harmony, just as it demands truth and right, to satisfy it. It can no more admire deformity and discord, than it can admire falsehood and injustice. It is not education that creates these finer instincts. If a human being were brought up amidst ugly forms and jarring dissonances, the moment that lovely sights and sweet melodies broke upon his eye and ear, he would turn to them delighted.

Nay more, this inner sense is never satisfied. All that fills the eye and ear, does but awaken the desire of things more beautiful, of sounds more melodious. The realm of cultivated taste and imagination is forever widening, and forever leading the soul onward and upward.

I say distinctly, *upward;* from things seen to things unseen ; from things earthly to things heavenly. It is possible indeed, but it is *not* natural, to behold all the glory and goodliness of the creation, without being led to the Infinite Glory. It is not natural. It is as if one should look upon a lovely countenance, and never think of the loveliness which it enshrines.

No, the grandeur and loveliness of nature—sunsets and stars, and the almost literally uplifting deeps of the blue sky, as we gaze upon them—and earth with its beauty, soft, wild, entrancing—with its glorious verdure, its autumn splendor, its sprinkled wilderness of charming hues and forms ; and ocean, bathing its summer shores, and bearing like many-colored gems upon its bosom the green and flowery islands—these things are not only beautiful, but they are images and revelations of a glory and a goodliness, unseen and ineffable. They steep the soul in reveries and dreams of enchantment, unearthly and immortal. How has the radiant vision kindled the poet's eye and lighted the torch of genius, and come down as fire from heaven upon the altars of piety, in all ages ! A bed or a bouquet of flowers —who can read anything upon their soft and shining petals and delicate hues, but sweetness, purity, and goodness ; and how many silent thanksgivings from those who bend over them, have ascended to Heaven, on the breath of their fragrant incense! And music—what chord in all its wondrous harmonies ever touched any evil passion? I have heard of *voluptuous* music; but I never heard it, and cannot conceive of it. Words may be voluptuous, or wrathful, or revengeful; but not melodies. Hotbeds of musical culture there may be, that corrupt the heart; but it is not music that does it. I should as soon think of a sunbeam's soiling the atmosphere it passes through. No, there is no possible concord of sweet sounds, there is no combination of tones within the range of harmony, but it weaves garments of light and purity for the soul. All melody naturally bears the thoughts into realms of holy imagining, sentiment, and worship. I would cultivate music in a family, with the same intent as I would build an altar. Away with the unworthy notion of it, as a mere fashionable accomplishment! It is a high ministration. And the highest musical culture, so far from being time and means thrown away, is really as a priesthood in the household.

In the third place to be considered, with reference to our argument, is the moral part of our nature—conscience. And there are three elements in conscience, to which I wish to draw your attention; its directive, its authoritative, and its executive power.

We are saying in this lecture, that the whole interior constitution of man was made to guide him to truth, to virtue, to the supreme good and Goodness. The most powerful aid to this end is, doubtless, the conscience.

It is directive. Do you say that you know men with very queer consciences; and that nations and ages differ about what is right; and so infer that there is no direction? A moment's reflection must convince you that these differences do not touch the principle of conscience, but only the applications of the principle. To plead these differences in denial of the principle, would be as if one said that because there are errors, there is no such thing as truth; because there is a great deal of darkness, there is no such thing as light; or because there are variations of the needle, there are no magnetic poles. Nay, but how knew you of variations, if there were no direction? How knew you of darkness, if there be no light? And what *is* error, but distorted truth? And so the very aberrations of conscience, prove that there is a conscience.

Nay, but it *is directive.* It approves of justice, truth, integrity—gratitude, generosity, disinterestedness—gentleness, pity, kindliness. It says, "This is the way;" nobody can doubt it. And now suppose that across the field of life there fell from heaven, before every man's eye, a bright track of light, such as you have seen the moon cast athwart the troubled waters; or suppose that on your hand were a compass and a needle, pointing ever to the right way; what guidance, you would say, is here!

But more than sunbeam or needle points the way. An awful sceptre is stretched over us. Conscience is more than guidance; it is authority. When a man says, "I OUGHT"—may I beg of you to pause a moment upon that expression, and to consider what it means? When a man says, "I OUGHT," he has an indescribable sense of *allegiance*—to *something.* He knows not *what*—it may be; no visible power commands him: he does not think what it is; but that word, "*ought*," binds him—to an unseen Lawgiver. I know, gentlemen, that the lecture room is not the place for preaching or for rhetoric; but I do feel that here is a fact of awful significance—too little considered. This silent reign of *right* in our humanity—this magnet in the soul, ever drawn by an invisible influence, to the *right*—what *is* it? What does it mean? What does it proclaim? I answer—there must be a God!—for God only could have impressed that mysterious law upon our humanity. Ah! poor, human trembler beneath that awful mandate!—great witness, shall I not rather say, to that sublime authority!—does he think to escape from it? Go to the deepest and darkest cavern of the earth; go where thou art alone and no eye sees thee—where no power of the Church shall coerce, on enactment of law bind, no hand of government compel—where there shall be nothing save thine unutterable consciousness with thee; but when thou sayest, "I ought"—altar and throne sink to the dust; they are but symbols of that eternal authority that speaks within you—an authority that *binds* altar and throne, and empire, and the world together.

Does any man think to evade it? Nay, by Heaven and the eternal law! that shall he not. Conscience is executive too. No infirm aid does it offer to the right; no inefficient hindrance to the wrong. It announces no idle requisition. It has rewards for the good, sweet as the most precious happiness; and penalties for the bad, dire as the most dreadful misery. No human government was ever so urgent and imperative as this power of conscience. It goes down to the depths of the heart; it touches the secretest nerve; it penetrates where no human tribunal can go. The human law may be evaded; but let a man carry down into his heart the thought that he has done wrong; and that thought is misery—is misery amidst all the blandishments of pleasure and the splendors of fortune. And let a man bear, in a bosom lacerated with every wound, the blessed consciousness that he has done right—*has done right;* and no floods of disaster nor fires of martyrdom can deprive him of the sweetness of that conviction.

No man, I repeat, shall evade this law. Retribution is more than a doctrine, it is a fact. No violation of conscience is so hidden or so slight, but it pays the penalty. There is one great error on this subject, old as the world, and new as the delusion of to-day, but it is an error still—and that is, that concealment is escape, that punishment comes only with disclosure or catastrophe. But suppose the concealment to be effected—the theft, the fraud, the lie, the bad base deed to escape detection—does the *man* escape? The *man!* Why, *he* knows it. If all the *world* knew it, and *he* knew it *not*, then, in a sense, might he be said to escape; he *would* escape from his own reproach. But even then he would not escape the worst—the very and essential curse of evil in *himself*. "Maxima peccati pœna, est *peccasse*," says Seneca; "the greatest penalty of sin, is to have sinned!" Are men punished only by and by, or when they grow old? Nay, says Plutarch, "they are not punished when they grow old, but they are grown old in punishments. Can we say," he continues, "that a man is not punished when he is in prison, or hath his fetters upon him, till his execution comes? We may as well say that a fish, which hath swallowed the hook, is not taken, because it is not fried or cut in pieces? So it is with every wicked man; he hath swallowed the hook, when he committed the evil action." * Lysimachus, Alexander's general, is said to have given away a kingdom to the Getæ, for a draught to quench his extreme thirst: when he had taken his draught, he exclaimed, "What a wretch was I, to lose a kingdom for so short a pleasure!" This may be fable; but how many a man, to quench the thirst of some raging passion, gives away the kingdom of all inward tranquillity and fortune. It has been well said that our English salutation—"How *are* you?"—touches the heart of all welfare. Ay, how *are* you?—that is the question.

Again, the taint that is in a man, however concealed and however slight, is breathed out into the very air around him, steals through the very pores of his life, infects his conversation. His family, his children, society around him, those dearest to him, all suffer for it. If it be selfishness, avarice, vanity, though he himself be but half conscious of it, it lowers the whole tone of his character, conversation, and influence. If it be an act of gross fraud or vice, he cannot heartily speak at all for the right, for virtue, for what is noblest in the world. What a retribution is *that?*—to be dumb where good men talk—to flee from the converse of virtue! Concealment only increases the evil. If it were known, the whole power of society might be united to crush and stamp it out of existence; but now, like a poison or a gangrene, it spreads its secret blight through all the rela-

* Origines Sacræ, B. III. c. iii. p. 116.

tions of family, friendship, and society. All this too *reacts* upon the offender in many ways. And in palpable cases it is often a saving reaction. How many have forborne the inebriating cup, lest it should ruin their children! And if the parent forbears not, and they are ruined, what can inflict a deeper pang! And if he is brutalized to that extent that he cares not, that, I repeat, is the deepest retribution of all.

The adjustment of this law of retribution to our humanity, the mingled severity, forbearance, and discrimination, with which it is exercised, are worthy of further attention.

It makes, for instance, a significant distinction between palpable vice and that more indefinite erring, of which the world is full. Palpable vice brings a swifter judgment, because it is a more manifest wrong. I do not deny that *some* forbearance is shown even here. Providence waits a little with the youthful voluptuary, that he may see the evil and reform. It does not take many experiments with vice however—with the inebriating cup, for instance—to show him the evil; and it very soon appears that nothing will do but blasting disease and smiting shame. But with ordinary and decent selfishness, with the world's covetousness, pride, and vanity, the case is different; it takes more time to solve the problem; and more is given. But by and by, with every thoughtful man, the problem is solved—solved, if not sooner, amidst the shadows of declining years. Then life begins to spread itself around the selfish man, cold and barren and cheerless; over one green spot and another, the waste stretches; there are none truly to love him, who never truly loved anybody but himself; there are none to care for him, unless it be with a care purchased, or paid to the sense of duty; the man may be rich, but wealth does not make him happy; feasting, wine, faring sumptuously every day, do not make him happy; splendor, equipage, a crowd of attendants do not make him happy; and the poor, starved nature within, which the wealth and garniture of a thousand worlds could not suffice, sighs for some better thing.

Or turn to a different scene; where evil goes to that extent, that it seems to be *only* misery and exasperation; where amidst want and woe, amidst oaths and blows, life goes on like a wild and wrathful battle with calamity. If there is anything that fills me with horror and despair, beyond all things else, it is some vile and abandoned city quarter, where wild uproar and mad revellings go on amidst filth and raggedness and wretchedness unspeakable; with fiery draughts poured out at all corners; with pale and haggard brows leaning against the posts and gates of the streets; and in the chambers, horrible diseases, untended, shrieking in agony. Is this Stygian pool, this midnight of the world, this blackness of darkness—is it Hell? No, misery is merciful, even here; nature is not devilish; sighings and tears mingle with these horrors—ay, and prayers for deliverance; and it may be God will hear; and man may help. Poor, forsaken wretches!—outcasts from the world—exiles from the light of many homes—could they see that God hath stricken them in mercy, that a paternal Providence knocks at all their gates—could human entreaties mingle with their mad blasphemies—they might return and find a Father in heaven—though there be none below—perhaps they have killed him!—none on earth to receive them.

Sad and heart-sinking spectacle!—but is there no counterpart to that picture? Can retribution find its way only through broken gateways and "looped and windowed raggedness?" Nay, through castle walls and plating gold, as well. On pillows of down and beneath planks of cedar, there are agonies as bitter as those which men are wont to pity so deeply. Vice desolates all where it comes—makes the full house empty, and the great house mean. There is a certain destitution in evil, even when there is no remorse. As cold is but the absence of heat, so a vice, like avarice, may be but the absence of virtue; but it is very cold and deathlike. And even where, in other forms, it kindles a fire in the veins, it leaves the *heart* cold and dead. To the *soul*, it is all poor and paltry. Search the records of its most prosperous career, and there is nothing but dust and desola tion in the path. Thus the gayest and the most fortunate in the evil way, have always become the greatest complainers. The poor man's complaints and scorns and rages against the world, are nothing to those of the broken and worn-out man of pleasure. So it has been with them all, from the Imperial Tiberius to the Aspasia of modern French gayety, Ninon de l'Enclos, who said, that if she could have foreseen what her life was to be, she would rather have died upon the threshold, than to have lived that gay and guilty life.

Or turn to the Emperor Tiberius. What bad man could be happy, if he could not? He had an empire, when that empire was the world, to use for his ambition—to farm for his pleasures. But what was his life? Read a letter of his to the Roman Senate. "What I shall write to you, conscript fathers, he says—or what I shall not write, or why I shall write at all—may the gods plague me, more than I daily feel that they are doing, if I can tell!" "Than I *daily* feel that they are doing." This spreads the confession over a portion of his life. It was a miserable life; and every bad man's life is a miserable one.

Such, then, as it presents itself to me, is the picture of our inward nature. Its original faculties are all instruments constructed, pointed, sharpened for the work of aiding virtue and resisting vice. And thus, in fine, do I state the case, and in the form of a comparison. If you were to examine a machinery which you knew was designed to produce a certain result; if you saw, in the first place, a general preparation and tendency of all its parts to that end; if you saw, in the next place, certain sharp instruments exactly formed and fashioned to cut and shape out the very thing to be made, your mind would rest with satisfaction upon it, as a well-adjusted piece of work. But what would be your astonishment, if, when you saw things going wrong in that mechanism, you observed a secret spring suddenly lift itself up, to resist and correct the wrong tendency. Such admiration and wonder, I believe, justly belong to the constitution of our humanity.

But now, on the whole, it may be asked, "What has this humanity done? You say, it was made for culture. Where is it? You say it was made to produce certain results? Where *are* those results? Bring your theory to the test of facts. This fine nature, intellectual, æsthetic, moral—what has it done? *Culture*, do you say, is the end of Providence! Is it not *production* rather? Multiplication of the species, seems to be the end; with little care for its development and growth. Transplantation to another clime may be the ultimate object; and would seem to be—so thick and stunted is the growth of men here."

There is one singular and emphatic refutation of all such reasoning, in the fact that the children of a single pair are not fifty, but commonly five or six. This fact shows that care is to be taken of them; that culture is the object, and not mere multiplication.

But let us look at this objection, for a few moments, in two views.

In the first place, with regard to the mass of men, the least cultivated—Hindoos, Hottentots, what you will—I say that the objection overlooks the actual amount and value of their cultivation. If all human beings died in the earliest infancy, the objection might seem to be valid; but even then I should doubt it: we know not what valuable impressions even infancy may, in a single year, acquire. But follow this being through twenty, thirty, fifty, seventy years, and how much has he learned; ay, without school or institute; without book or Bible—on the Ganges or the Niger! He has looked upon nature, seen and classified thousands of objects, and understood the uses of many. He has learned to labor—to provide for a family; and by skill in tillage, or hunting, or the care of flocks, he has become lord of the surrounding scene. He has learned to distinguish between right and wrong; and though he has abused, he has cultivated the moral sense. And within his range have come still higher things. Tradition has poured into his ears its mystic love. He has lifted his eyes to the heavens, and his thoughts above the heavens to the Infinite Being. Is this passage from blank infancy to the crowded page of human experience; from the conception of nothing to the conception of Infinitude—is this, I say, no progress, no culture? Measure these few mortal years, and mark the steps passed over; then measure the years of eternity; and whither shall they not bear a being who has begun thus?

But in the next place, I say, it is unfair to the argument, to take the lowest examples of human culture. If there were a hundred similar machines submitted to your examination, and one of them in its working far surpassed all the rest—the rest halting or breaking down through the bungling of artisans—you would take that *one*, as the proper illustration of the design and wisdom of the original inventor. Not the ignorant, the low and base, then, but the sages, philanthropists, heroes, the noblest men in the world—these proclaim the end for which human nature was made, and for which its original powers are fitted.

I will not dwell upon this human nobleness; I have not space left, nor power to do it justice; but I will for myself simply profess what I think of it; let the cynic or the satirist, or the desponding skeptic or complainer say what he will. I look around upon the universe, and I see many bright points; a dome of brightness above; and stars that are set in the brow of night; and mountain tops that kindle their altar fires with the beams of morning. But in all this universe, there is nothing, save the majesty of God most High, that draws forth my reverence, my enthusiasm, my delight, like a noble and good man. Of all things known to me, this is the brightest spot. There may be angels; there may be seraphim—supernal natures above the reach of my sympathy. I know them not; I never saw such an one; I never saw book of his writing, nor action of his performing, nor life that he lived, nor death that he died; but I have seen *men*, through struggle and weariness, and pain and death, soaring to knowledge, to virtue, to heaven; through lonely studies, through the trampled fires of passion, through mortal infirmity, through baits and snares of evil, thick strown upon all their path and trodden under foot, mounting to the heights of the world. They are seated on the thrones of the world, compared with which the Cæsars held the dominion of a day. They are indeed "the representative men" of the earth; the representative men of our humanity.

LECTURE VI.

THE COMPLEX NATURE OF MAN, PERIODS OF LIFE, SOCIETY, HOME, BALANCE OF THE PHYSICAL AND MENTAL POWERS.

I HAVE spoken in my last two lectures of the physical and spiritual constitution of man. There is a union of both, a complex nature of man, which requires to be considered with reference to its end.

Under this head are to be mentioned, in the first place, the different periods of life. These steps of life all have their place, and give their aid in the process of human development. The physical adaptation in these periods of life, images and helps a moral adaptation. Look at the supple and flexible limbs of a child, at the strengthening bone of manhood, and at the relaxing fibre of age. How necessary are these; the one to the safe training of life, the next to its stable vigor, and the last to that loosening of the hold upon life's labors and cares, which is necessary to the quietude, the meditativeness, the ripened wisdom that befit the closing period of our earthly existence. This remark is familiar in physiology, but it is equally applicable to the moral economy of the human constitution.

Childhood is the world's great experimenter. It is the season, not of the deepest, but of the most rapid learning. It wants, therefore, a peculiar susceptibility to feel, a freedom to choose, and a flexibility to change. It must try this and try that, and not fix too strong a grasp upon anything. It must be full of hope and buoyancy and facility. Lay the weight of prejudice or custom, or matured vice, upon childhood, and it would be crushed entirely. We are alarmed when we see in a child a disposition to prevaricate; but we should be shocked beyond measure if that practice were clothing itself with the strength of fixed habit. We are vexed when we see a boy taking on airs of superiority to his mates, on account of the homage paid to his parent's wealth or fame; but, thank Heaven! the great enslaving law of opinion yet bears lightly on his ignorance and innocence. But what should we think, if we saw the full-grown vices of sensuality or worldly ambition developing themselves in the body or mind of a child? We should give him up in despair.

You will be more sensible of this guardianship thrown around the earliest period of life, if you observe the barrier that separates childhood from manhood. In youth, and in its passage to maturity, there is a very singular crisis; the form, the face, the voice, the temperament, the sentiments, the passions, pass through a remarkable change. The previous time of life seems to have been a dispensation by itself; marked by a certain indifference, by a certain mingled levity and apathy with regard to the wider interests of life. The child has a safeguard in his profound *ignorance* of much that is around him. He lives in the midst of the world; but a friendly veil is thrown around him, that tempers its bright and deceitful glare. He lives in an enclosure protected from temptations that would be as wild beasts to his gentle innocence. His ambition does not wander beyond the school and the play ground. The impulses of sense and passion yet slumber in his bosom. His loves are school-day friendships and family regards. His life is comparative joyance and repose. But now at length, the time comes when the great veil that hides the world begins to rise; when the first battle with the stronger powers that sleep in the human breast, is to be fought; and the previously secure and calm house of life becomes, as it were, a forge, an arsenal, a citadel. There are flashings out of new and unwonted fires;

there is solemn and even sad brooding over the enterprises and destinies of existence; there are trumpet calls in the courtyard of the guarded house; there is the disturbance and disorder, the dust and confusion, the thronging thoughts and energies, that betoken the entrance upon a new and momentous scene. Forces like these would have split and shattered in pieces the frail and delicate tenement of childhood; but now, to virtuous resolution and youth's first struggling prayer to Heaven, strength is given to meet them.

The next stage is manhood. *Now* something is to be decided on, and something is to be done. *Before*, there was activity; *now* there is to be work. There is to be plan, pursuit, profession—some end to be chosen; and there is to be a concentration of energies to gain it. The field is wider. Before, the word was,—"Learn these lessons and continue to learn them, and you shall be at the head." Now, many things are to be learned and many things done, to get to the head, or to get along at all. The head is, not a certificate, a diploma, a valedictory oration, but the leading-staff of empire, of authorship, of art, of business, of social or professional distinction. The world is full of varied interests, full of exigencies, full of competitors. The business of life is complicated, urgent, exhausting. Think of a child, a boy of fifteen, charged with all this care, this responsibility. It would confound and crush his faculties. Especially would it crush down all joyance and free growth. But all this, to right-hearted manhood, is a noble culture. Manhood has powers for the task. It has strength of muscle to work, strength of mind to act, strength of heart to endure. And the innocence of childhood is well exchanged for manhood's strength, for its courage, its manliness, its high integrity; for that grand equipoise of the faculties in which it holds itself erect and firm, and stands before the world with foot and hand, and heart and mind ready for its work; ready to do business, to cope with difficulties, to subdue obstacles, to speak and act in the affairs of men and nations.

But the toil and strife at length are over; the bustle

and turmoil of life have passed away; age lays its chasten ing hand upon the vigorous frame and the fevered passions; sager and more sacred thoughts take possession of the mind; the race is run, the battle is fought, the world is changed; and when that winter day of life is come, and the blossoms of hope and the fruits of ripened friendship are all scattered in the dust, the man says: "Let me depart, it is good for me to die."

And age too, like every other period of life, is not without its own special fitness and personal vocation. How else—says the poet—

"How else couldst thou retire apart,
With the hoarded memories of thy heart,
And gather all, to the very least,
Of the fragments of life's earlier feast—
Let fall, through eagerness to find
The coming dainties yet behind?
How ponder on the entire past,
Laid together thus at last;
When the twilight helps to fuse
The first fresh, with the faded hues;
And the outline of the whole
Grandly fronts, for once, thy soul."

And now I say, that all this is naturally a progress in virtue. In one respect the visible is not an emblem of the spiritual life. Age, that declines in vigor, naturally grows in virtue. Its affections, I think, are usually as vigorous as those of youth; its wisdom is, of course, far greater. I do not forget that it is, in some respects, peculiarly tried. It is hard to give up some things to which it has been accustomed—the activity, the control of affairs, the indulgence perhaps of appetite. This last point I have sometimes seen to be one of especial difficulty. These however, are but flaws upon the deep and quiet stream.

Still, age is naturally the maturity of virtue, of piety, of all that is noblest in the mind. Not till approaching the grand climacteric, perhaps, does the character usually arrive at its highest perfection. Great intellectual power, no doubt, is attained earlier; the culminating point of talent, authorship, statesmanship, military skill, is reached sooner; but not till a later day does humanity, even when thus distinguished, arrive at its highest wisdom, self-control, and sanctity; not till then, perhaps, are the great problems of the inmost life solved; the conflicting tendencies of the nature brought into harmony; and the utmost aims of human existence achieved. To me the grandest form of humanity is the aged form. I had almost said the most attractive beauty, taking into account the manners, bearing, and *expressions* of countenance. Youth, I know, carries off the palm, with most persons—the fair complexion, the glossy hair, the smooth brow and painted cheek. It is a sort of barbaric taste, I am tempted to say; but it is so prevalent, that I am quite sure a good-natured indulgence will be extended to an opposite opinion; it has so very little chance of prevailing. "Ay,"—it will be said—"criticize as much as you please, the claims of youth to all beauty and outward charms; they can bear it." But, in truth, the form that stands erect after the storms of seventy or eighty years have beat upon it; the face that bears on it the marks of all human triumph, of the last triumph, that over itself; the calm dignity and gentle courtesy and forbearance, in man or woman, that come from long reflection and patient culture; the holy serenity and assured trust, caught from the heaven that is near, and shining through the parting shadows of life; why, nature, I say, is not false to herself; *there is* the nobleness of humanity, and there are some of its noblest expressions. That aged form—how often, in fact, does it draw a thoughtful man in a gay company, from the charms of youth, and all the importunity of their attractions, to the side of its venerableness, wisdom, and beauty! The contrary tendency in this country or any other country, the tendency in society to separate the aged and the young, is one that is to be looked upon with the greatest reprehension. This pushing forward of the young to take all the places in society, to *be* the whole of society, ought to be repressed by their elders, with dignity and authority. Depend upon it, that all such breaking away from the great bonds of nature, from the venerable sanctities of life, is essentially degrading even to the taste of a people; and you may be sure that it is a vulgar tendency of society that leads the young to wish, in their chosen happy hours, to separate themselves from their aged friends. I am not wandering from my proper theme. The point which I have ventured thus plainly to touch, concerns not only good manners, but good culture. It was meant, I believe, that youth and age should exert upon each other a mutual influence; that the aged should not want the cheering presence and attention of the young, nor the young, the wise and tranquillizing influence of the aged; that aged life should not lack entertainment, just when perhaps most needing it, and that young life should not rush into it, without the restraints of filial tenderness and respect.

Montaigne says, quoting, perhaps unconsciously, almost the very words of Cicero, "I had rather be old not so long, than to be old before the time." But we, in this country, think ourselves old before we are so, and actually grow old before we need. Society forces it upon us. "I have done with the world," says one; "I am getting to be an old man." And so he sits in his solitary room, perhaps; afraid that he shall be a burden upon the young company in an adjoining apartment. And suppose he is an old man—and not fifty, which is old for our pushing society—suppose he *is indeed* an old man; does it follow that he has done with the world? Nay, if wisdom and experience and perfected character mean anything, he has now to exert a finer, nobler, and more beautiful influence upon the world, than ever.

From the progress of life, let us now turn to the general structure of society, as another sphere in which the double nature of man plays its part.

The world, it is said, is a corrupter. *Nature* has wholesome influences, but the world none. A comparatively safe abode man has, amidst the hills and waters and the free air; but the moment he comes into the presence of moral natures all is peril and evil. Hence convents, hermitages, the anchorite's cell. Hence, the non-intercourse with what is called worldly society and its worldly ways, enjoined by many churches upon their members.

But can that be altogether *so?* A sacred watch indeed for all young minds, nay, for all minds, over the influence that others exert upon them—this is well. But can it be that society, the bosom of universal nurture, bears upon it nothing but peril, but pollution? Can it be that the human generations are brought forward in succession, only to be trained by selfishness, treachery, injustice, pride, and sensuality? Is this the school of humanity?

No, no; we do not, and cannot think so. Let us see what we do think, and ought to think.

Society then, like man, is liable to err; so and no otherwise. Society is but collective humanity, the aggregate of individual character; and whatever there is in the physical and moral constitution of man, to urge him to the right and to restrain him from the wrong, must be found in that same world which we dread and condemn. Found there; but mark one difference—found sometimes, in greater, in collective strength. For after all, the world sometimes is even a stronger reprover than the individual conscience; and a man is all the more in danger for being alone—for not feeling the pressure of social opinion. Some dark iniquity is perpetrated in secret, and the light within fails to shine upon it and show what it is; and its hideousness is not seen, till it is revealed—till it is *reflected*, in the mirror of all-surrounding conscience. But let us look at the great social ministry, and see whether it is for good or for evil; for there are serious questions about it. Selfish interests—inequalities—competitions—solidarity—and the general social influence; these are the points to be studied.

We say the world is selfish. Let it be ever so true—I shall soon have occasion to qualify the admission—but let it be ever so true; yet can you pass over the remarkable fact that the very selfishness of *society* is engaged on the side of honesty, self-restraint, visible virtue? *Individual* selfishness may *not* be; it may choose to steal, defraud, indulge itself in evil ways, in any way, it cares not what, nor how much to the hurt of others; but the common selfishness resists all that. What does every man want of his fellow, in conversation or in business; what is it the interest of all to demand, but truth, honesty, honor, virtue? A man may not choose to practise them himself; but he wants them to be practised toward him. Mark it well, then; in all ages, among all nations, amidst all other fluctuations and convulsions of opinion, stand fraud, intemperance, licentiousness, branded and blackened with universal opprobrium. Selfish interest, mere selfish interest writes on the table of the world, the laws of virtue. Why? Because God has ordained them to be the laws of the common welfare. There they stand! There they stand, deep and high. The mountains on their everlasting bases, stand not so firm as these foundation laws of right, in the common, the great Humanity.

But, it may be said, selfishness, though it protects the right, is a bad thing still. Yes, it is a bad thing; but is all selfish that we call so? Let us not mistake here. Let us not champion general virtue, to the hurt of our own—like a man crying "famine!" and starving to death to prove it. *My* pursuing my own interest, cultivating my own farm, conducting my own business, is not selfishness. I may till my field, and be heartily and none the less glad that my neighbor's is yielding him a good crop; and that surely is not selfishness. I *must* attend to my own affairs; I have no business to meddle with his. This may be called the isolated principle, or the selfish principle, or by whatever hard names men please; but busybodies in other men's affairs—men that were often going to their neighbor's fence, and saying how glad they felt at his prosperity, and offering excellent advice perchance, would be very troublesome people, at any rate. There is doubtless enough selfishness in the world, and it is odious enough; the basely ambitious, the miserly, the inebriate, and the debauched live in the world; but there is a great deal of generosity in it also there is a great deal of sympathy and feeling for one another and the common indignation that darkens the very air in horror, around vice and crime, has a far deeper source than selfish and politic resistance to a common foe.

Let us pass to another point. One of the most annoying forms of selfishness is competition for the goods or honors of the world. This, it may be said, is not simply a pursuing of one's own interest, but an infringement upon others' interests, or a wish at least to surpass them—to get what they are seeking.

Now I am not obliged to defend anything beyond the degree in which it actually exists; and I am not obliged to defend anything which Providence has not appointed; and finally, I am not obliged to defend anything which, from the very nature of the case, could not be prevented. I say then, in the first place, that in the general industry of life, there is little or no *actual* competition. The bounties of nature are not so stinted, that I must starve, or my neighbor. There is enough for us all. And men, generally, cultivate land, build houses, make ploughs and scythes, with little thought that their neighbor's successfully doing the same things, is any disadvantage to them. Competition is usually seen in trade, in the professions; and then only or chiefly in the crowded centres of society. But I say, in the next place, that there is very commonly committed an egregious blunder here; for which Providence is not responsible. And that is the blunder of supposing that there *is* a competition of *interests* to the extent commonly imagined; that another's success is proportionably an injury to us. Individual success adds to the general wealth and prosperity; it builds houses, employs laborers, rears ships, makes beautiful gardens and grounds; and is a common benefit. Successful manufacture increases demand. The fame of a lawyer, physician, or clergyman adds to the dignity and honor of his profession. But suppose, in the third place, that we do unavoidably come to the sharp edge of competition; two of us want, and cannot help wanting, the same thing—the same office, honor, emolument. Then, I say, as one of the *inevitable* trials of virtue, must we meet it. Then must that sharp edge carve out a nobleness for us, above all that the ordinary contacts of life can do. In no relation, perhaps, can men be so noble to each other, as in that of rivals; and though prejudice, jealousy, and envy too often make the contest odious and the *men* odious, yet candor, kindliness, and generosity might, and sometimes do, clothe them with brighter honors than any they seek for.

The third feature in the social condition, presenting difficulty to most men's thoughts, is inequality of lot. There is nothing, perhaps, about which so many minds are sore and vexed, as this. Reformers have considered much how they could remove it. Radicals have demanded that it be swept away entirely. "That all men are born equal" is taken literally by some, and held to be a good ground for keeping them so. Nothing in the world is inveighed against with such bitterness as wealth and rank.

Now hereditary rank, supported by entailed estates, I admit to be a great social injustice. But passing by these human arrangements, and coming down to the general fact, to the providential order, I should like to have some one tell me, how it is possible to prevent inequality, ay, and great inequality of lot, without breaking down entirely the free will, the free energy by which the world *is* a world, and not a mere system of machinery. Make all men equal to-day; give them equal property, equal means, equal comforts. Difference, ay, the hated distinction, begins to-morrow, as surely as they are left to act freely.

Let us accept, then, this fact of inequality as inevitable, and see whether it is at war with social justice or improvement. Is it at war with social justice? Certainly the very opposite is the truth. Perfect and perpetual equality of lot would be the most manifest *in*justice. It would not be rewarding men according to their deeds, but the very contrary. Sluggards and knaves might like it, but nobody else could.

And then with regard to improvement—if all men stood upon an exact level, how much of the necessary and palpable stimulus to exertion would be taken away! If I saw no man above me in any respect, I should be apt to be content with what I am; I should fail perhaps to be reminded that there is anything higher for me to attain. The child, for instance, stands to his parent in the relation of inequality; but suppose he did not; suppose he saw, or thought, his parent to be no wiser nor stronger than he; he would be in a deplorable condition for his improvement. Indeed this whole strife for visible preëminence overrates the prize altogether—undervalues the inward strength and nobleness, of which it is properly nothing but the symbol; and ought to drive men upon that inward sufficiency as the only relief from envy, jealousy and base ambition.

But it may be said, there is something more trying in the problem of society, than competition, and that is, this terrible solidarity—the suffering caused us by others—suffering of the innocent for the guilty; suffering, proceeding from individuals, but spreading far and wide; running through all the fibres of social existence. The answer is—could there be society without this exposure? Manifestly not. Without sympathy, there could be no society; with it, there must be pain for others' afflictions; ay, and suffering, loss, trouble, from others' errings.

And this necessity, like every other in the system, is turned into a beneficent law. The care for one another—that most anxious and watchful care, that others, our children, our relatives, our friends, should do well; the feeling on the part of the tempted man, that a thousand eyes are turned toward him—eyes that will kindle with joy at his well-doing, and that would weep bitterly over his fall; all this is a conservative force, to preserve the virtue of men, and to prevent aberration—a force lent by the union of all the bonds of human interest, and all the ties of human sympathy; and without which, it is manifest, society could not stand. As in the system of nature, it is said that every particle of matter, though it be upon a dunghill, contributes to the universal order; so in the system of society, the poorest creature in the world, one that lies upon that dunghill, has relations to the welfare of all; all power and wealth and well-being are worse off for him. It is true; it is inevitable; it is well; and well were it, if we more thoughtfully laid it to heart.

Having thus attempted to meet the leading questions that arise with regard to the great social discipline of Humanity, let us now turn to its direct and unquestionable instrumentality.

Society is the great educator. More than universities, more than schools, more than books, society educates. Nature is the schoolhouse, and many lessons are written upon its walls; but man is the effective teacher. Parents, relatives, friends, associates; social manners, maxims, morals, worships, the daily example, the fireside conversation, the casual interview, the spirit that breathes through the whole atmosphere of life—these are the powers and influences that train the mass of mankind. Even books, which are daily assuming a larger place in human training, are but the influence of man on man.

It is evident that one of the leading and ordained means by which men are raised in the scale of knowledge and virtue, is the conversation, example, influence of men superior to themselves. It seems, if one may say so, to be the purpose, the intent, the *effort* of nature—of Providence, to bring men together, and to bring them together, for the most part, in relations of discipleship and teaching. The social nature, first, draws them to intercourse. Perpetual solitariness is intolerable. But then, much of their intercourse is on terms of inequality. Equals in *age*, people in *society*, seldom meet, but one is able to teach or tell something, and the other is desirous to learn it. The lower are strongly drawn to the higher. Children are not content to be always by themselves; curiosity, reverence, filial affection draw them to their superiors. In the whole business of life—tillage, mechanism, manufacture, merchandise — a younger generation is connected with an elder, to be taught by it. Barbarous tribes go on forever in their barbarism, till they are brought into the presence of superior culture. The Chinese exclusion has kept that people stationary, though civilization has been knocking at their gates for more than three centuries.* And it is better—I speak of mere results, not principles—that the way for light should be opened into that country by English cannon balls, or the rending asunder of the empire, than never to be opened. But such a fixed barrier to civilization is a solitary phenomenon in history. Nations, the barbarous and civilized, by some means or other, in the everlasting ferment of human interests and passions, are thrown into communication and interfusion —if by no better means, by war, by subjugation, by capture; for Providence, if one may say so, *will* have them come together. Human injustice and cruelty are not to be abetted in this matter. There are better ways, which Christian civilization ought to learn—travel, trade, missions of light and mercy; but, some way, the nations must mingle together, or the ignorant will never be enlightened, the savage never civilized.

Where are the ruder peasantry of Europe now resorting, for work and for subsistence? To the heart of England and America. Many an enlightened man, building a railroad, or improving his estate, many a refined woman in her household, is made their teacher—little suspecting the office, perhaps. It were fortunate, I think, for both parties, if they did; it might make the relation more kindly and holy; but any way, the work will be done.

How fine and delicate and penetrating is this power of man to influence his kind! A word, a tone, a look—nothing goes to the depths of the soul like that. The dexterous hands, and the embracing arms, the commanding eye and the persuasive lips and the stately presence are fitted for nothing

* Williams's "Middle Kingdom," chap. xxi.

more remarkably than to teach. Travelling on a railroad, one day, I saw a little child in the company of some half a dozen affectionate relatives. From hand to hand it passed—to be amused, to be soothed, to be taught something from moment to moment—to receive many lessons, and more caresses, all the day long. "Here," I thought with myself, "is a company of unpaid, loving, willing, unwearied teachers. Such governesses could scarce be hired on any terms." Well, it was not a nobleman's child; it was not a rich man's child, that I know; every man's child has such training. The same thing, substantially, is passing in every house where childhood lives, every day.

How sharp, too, and jealous, is the guardianship of society over the virtue of its members! How preventive and corrective are its sorrow and indignation at their failures! A parent's grief is such a warning and retribution as prisons and dungeons could not bring upon his erring child. And then it is to be observed that the grosser and more ruinous vices are such as soon betray themselves, and cannot be long concealed. The police of society is very likely to find them out. And selfishness, covetousness, vanity, do not escape. The repulsive atmosphere of common feeling about the selfish man, the cold shadow in which the miser walks, the stinging criticisms upon the vain man, proclaim that society is not an idle censor. What does public opinion brand, what does literature satirize, all over the world, but the faults and foibles of men? Society has thrones for the good and noble, and purple and gold are but rags and dust in the comparison. Society has prisons and penitentiaries for the base and bad, and stone walls and silent cells are not so cold and death-like.

Let us now proceed to a third subject presented by the complex nature of man, and that is, the relation of sex, and the consequent order of the family.

This great bond of many interwoven relations—home—is deserving, at the present day, of some special attention and study. The facility and extent of modern intercourse tend to create a kind of cosmospolite feeling in the world. Colonization, too, weakens the family ties. Increasing luxury, the expensiveness of living—one of the worst effects of our artificial civilization—is unfriendly to marriage. Engrossing business, especially in cities, is drawing away the attention of many from home and home culture. Withal, some of the social reforms are directly proposing to substitute joint-stock corporations for separate and independent households. Amidst these tendencies, let us see if we can find what is the order of nature, and why it is established.

What, then, makes the family? What is it that carries man beyond community, neighborhood, society, friendship, to this inner circle of life? What makes the family? It is an institution so established and universal that few, perhaps, have ever asked themselves the question; and yet it involves, as I conceive, some of the profoundest views of the wisdom of Providence.

In the human relation of sex, then, is laid the foundation for home. In this, that is to say, is laid the foundation for a peculiar and permanent *attachment*, which leads the subjects of it to wish to dwell together, and apart from others. Thus the great Master says, that God *made* them male and female, that they two should become one; that they should be united in an interest that separates them from others. On this purpose and intent of Heaven, He founded the sanctity of marriage. Suppose the distinction of sex not to exist, and that there were no such attachment as is now founded upon it, and no such relation of two persons to certain other persons who are their children, as is now established; and then it is evident that although there might be social ties and temporary unions of friendship, and even a common residence, there could be no family. Men might be gregarious, but they could not be domestic. They might live together, but they could not be *one*, in that almost mysterious tie of affinity and kindred.

Next, to strengthen the family bond, another provision is made. Why does not the infant child, like the young of animals, arrive in a few days or weeks at its maturity, and the ability to take care of itself? I know of no ultimate reason for this, but the purpose of Heaven to "set the solitary in families." Children might have been formed as well to come to maturity—certainly to physical maturity—in twenty weeks, as in twenty years. A twenty *years'* care of their offspring is assigned to parents, in order to establish a school of natural and moral influence. The school-houses of a nation, indicate its purpose to give its children a certain technical education. The domestic abodes of the world manifest a purpose of the overruling Providence, no less clear and explicit. Youthful love and parental affection, which are of God's creating and not ours, lay every corner-stone in them, and raise every protecting wall. In idle unconsciousness may that love between the sexes grow up; the theme of jesting comment may it be, to those around; but such is its great mission; such is the solemn bond which it lays upon the world. The problem of *parental* love and filial subjection, may be wrought out with weariness and sorrow, or with thoughtless, or with reflecting and holy gladness; but such is the momentous solution of that problem.

We have said that society is the great educator. The family is the primary school of that education. The pupils are children—delicate in frame, docile in spirit, susceptible of influence. Nor is it easy, if indeed it is possible, to conceive how the object could have been effected without that relation. I have said in a former lecture, that the only conceivable beginning of existence for a rational being, is infancy—a state, that is to say, of ignorance and destitution; in which impressions, knowledge, virtue, holiness are to be *acquired;* since those things are by definition matters of experience and volition, and incapable of creation. Had man been full formed at once then—*i. e.*, not in knowledge and virtue, but in mere *strength* of body and mind, which *is* conceivable—had there been thus far a state of physical and mental equality, the rigid fibre would have found its fellow in the obstinate will, and *neither* would, nor could perhaps, have yielded to the voice of instruction, nor to the sway of discipline. But a child's docility, a child's meekness—could we understand it—is something heaven-sent, something, I had almost said, fearful to contemplate. The mingled veneration and love, with which it looks up to a good parent; the mingled wonder and fear, with which it looks up to a bad parent, who has lost in vice or rage the government of himself; what contrast on earth could be more touching! Alas! in how many dwellings stands that poor stricken child, gazing with awe and terror upon the frenzy of inebriety or the fury of anger, and parting not with its meekness and submissiveness, amidst all its agonies and wrongs. It is God's child, not man's; and might well be the minister of God to the evil man—nay, and *is* so.

Scarcely less remarkable is the influence of the family state upon its elder members. Marriage recalls man from what would be otherwise his wild roving through the world, and assigns to him a home. That home becomes the natural centre of his affections, cares and labors. But for this bond, life would be nomadic, and its ties transient as the traveller's footstep. This gives a sphere, a locality to human pursuit, makes of it a regular, concentrated industry, makes frugality, foresight, care, self-restraint necessary, calls sympathy to the bedside of sickness and suffering, and turns man's dwelling into a sanctuary of sorrow, a memorial of death, and threshold of eternity. But I need not dwell longer upon so familiar a theme as the good influence of home.

I only wish you distinctly to see what is the origin of this institution. It is divine; and because it is divine, it is universal. Amidst the wide wandering of men upon earth, diversified by all the varieties of condition and culture, there is one tie, drawing evermore to one spot—one heart-drawing evermore to one magnetic centre; and if I were to put the question to the whole human race—what is that?—the answer would be, it is *home*. Before government, before society, city, community existed, there was a home. It is no human, no civil, no factitious institution. God made it. It was rooted in the foundations of the world. From the brooding darkness of primeval time, the first objects that emerge to sight are homes—not nations, but families. It was a home that floated upon the waters of the great Deluge. The first altar built on Ararat was the home-altar. It was the home-altar that lighted the steps of men and generations in their wide dispersion over the earth. It was "the pillar of cloud and fire;" and if that light had gone out, the human race would have become extinct.

The first brand of misery upon the human brow, and the darkest to-day, is excision from home. God pity such an outcast! But how few such are there! Outcast from every other tie a man may be;—but find the veriest wretch that roams the earth or the sea; and one spot there is to which he clings with a saving confidence, if there be any saving for him: he knows—he *knows* that there is one place on earth where the memory and care of him linger, and live, and can never die.

I have spoken now of the one grand object of the distinction of the sexes. I say nothing of the direct, personal relation considered by itself. It is difficult to speak of it—a difficulty lying in the very delicacy and depth of the relation. There is, perhaps, a mystery in this marriage of hearts, which we cannot understand. It is a union beyond worldly interest, beyond selfish attachment, beyond friendship; it is the union of natures, counterpart to one another, of which the two make *one*, in a sense pertaining to no other human relation. Certainly if the world were occupied by men or by women alone, it would be but half a world. The grace and charm of life would be gone; and each would roam through the earth, in comparatively sad and solitary isolation. And whoever would blend the sexes, blot out the distinction, make their pursuits and callings the same, their very dress the same, would be guilty of treason, not to man or woman only, but to the majesty of Providence itself.

Finally, there is, in the complex nature of man, a bond

and a balance of its powers and tendencies, most worthy to be observed.

The union of the mind and body commonly called a mystery, is more than that; it is a wonder. The rushing tide that pours through the heart, swollen and discharged sixty or seventy times a minute, for eighty years, without wearing away its channel—this is a commonly cited instance. But more miraculous still, perhaps, is the human head. That the mind should be linked with a substance so frail and fragile as the brain, seated in a mesh like gossamer, not on a marble throne; that its fiery thoughts should not tear it in pieces; that its swelling emotions should not burst the delicate integument; that it should keep sane and strong when one thread diseased deranges all; that it should so long keep touch and time, when thrilling nerves and throbbing ganglions are its ministers—this is the wondrous bond and balance of soul and body.

Look at this balance of the faculties, mental, moral, and physical, in a larger view. See how all those tendencies and impulses, which left to themselves would go to destruction, are restrained by one another, and by the union of all. By the constitution of our nature, the raging appetites, the wayward passions themselves are bonds. Anger is exhausted by its own violence, and sinks to pity at the wound it inflicts. Natural affection in its rudest state, is yet to tie to something. Passion, I say, is itself restraint. Bonds are woven out of the free and wild affections. Man must love. Then something must he love—wife, children, home, friend. He must sustain relations—to cherished childhood, or to beseeching weakness and tenderness. All his passions, then, his loves, hates, hopes, fears, unite to put and press and drive him into some controlling and protecting order. The leading, visible form of that order is Government. That great bond that holds a nation together, is spun and woven out of the texture and strife of all human passions and interests. Government is not a thing of chance or of will, but of necessity, of God.

Nor only so; not only is there a bond, but there is, as I was saying, a balance among the human powers that tends to control and keep them right—to keep them, at any rate, from the uttermost wrong. Man is a kingdom; and no political balance of powers was ever so exquisite and admirable as the equilibrium of forces in him. There are the citizen affections; there is the populace of the passions: and their interests are opposite, their control mutual. There is the mob of reckless and raging desires; but sobriety, thoughtfulness, order come to meet it. Or ambition arises, and would sweep to its end, over a kingdom in ruins, but private regards come to check it; those human hearts that it would tread and crush beneath its feet, put forth tendrils and snares that entangle and fetter its reckless strides. And everywhere, sobering fact, sobering labor, tame down the impulses of imagination and appetite—of wild dreaming or wild craving of fortunes, honors, splendors, gratifications. Everywhere the rushing tides of passion are met by cross currents, and are met too by the rugged shores of circumstance and necessity. Ay, necessity, like an iron fate, stands in the way; weakness, sickness, pain, death, stand in the way; and heat and cold and storm, and ocean waves, and rocky heights, and the cold bare mountains of limitation and difficulty, stand as barriers against the wide-flowing desolations of passion and vice and violence.

Thus it is in all nature and life; for humanity, in this balance of its powers, is both influenced and imaged by the universe around it. Any one of the agencies within us or around us, left to operate alone, would destroy alike the order of nature and humanity. This atmosphere, you know, in which we move so easily and lightly, sustains us, as it were, with millions of elastic and invisible cords; so that if a vacuum were suddenly produced beneath us or by our side, we should be instantly crushed to the earth, as by the weight of a mountain. So it is with the balance of our intellectual powers; let one faculty be struck away, and everything falls into ruins.

Thus man stands, amidst universal nature and life, in the very equilibrium of contending forces; where attraction balances attraction, and power checks power; where heat and cold, winds and waters, swell up to the point that is necessary to sustain him; and his sport and his play is amidst waves of infinite motion and heavings of boundless might—on the very verge of precipices from which he never falls, and amidst the vibrations of vast elements which hold and rock him as a child in their protecting arms. Thus the powers of nature, both material and moral, like reined coursers, are held beneath some mighty hand; and man is borne onward in the car of life, amidst all but bursting thunder and whelming earthquake; borne gently and smoothly; his repose the product of infinite conflict; and the very music of his joys the harmony of that which, unrestrained, would be boundless discordance and destruction.

LECTURE VII.

ON THE SPECIAL INFLUENCE UPON HUMAN CULTURE OF THE DISCIPLINE OF NATURE, OF THE OCCUPATIONS OF LIFE, AND OF THE ARTS OF EXPRESSION; OR, THE MENTAL AND MORAL ACTIVITY ELICITED BY MAN'S CONNECTION WITH NATURE AND LIFE.

THUS far in these lectures, we have done, or attempted to do, two things. First, we have laid down the foundation principles, the basis in theory, of the problem of human destiny: and that we found, in the necessary character of a *creation*, whether material or moral; and especially in the natural impossibility of conferring unmixed and unconditioned good upon rational beings. Next, we have shown the actual basis of the problem; the basis of it, so to speak, as a working problem; and this we found in the frame of the world; in the arrangements of material and animal nature, in the physical organization of man, in his mental and moral constitution, and in his complex nature.

Now, out of this basis spring certain forms of human activity. These are to be considered in this lecture; and the conditions of that activity, the helps and the hindrances, in the next.

I am about to lead you, my friends, into actual life, into the bosom of human experience. But because it is the actual, common, daily scene that will be before our eyes, I must pray you not to overlook the stupendous moral, the sublime end, to which it points. I do not propose to teach you a transcendental philosophy, but a philosophy that mixes itself up with the very life that we live, and the very being that we are.

We are then to consider, at present, certain forms of human activity that are developed from nature and life. With this view we shall consider man in two points of light —first, as *nature* takes him in hand; and next, as *Providence apprentices* him to certain life-tasks. I say he is apprenticed to them; and that, by an indenture of older than feudal or Roman date. In all that is circumstantial, man is less free than he is apt to think. Thus, he does not sow nor reap, does not fabricate things, nor trade in them—does not write deeds nor prescriptions, nor sermons nor poems—does not paint nor sing, nor make statues nor buildings nor books, simply because he fancied to do so, but because there was an irresistible necessity or impulse to do these things. The activity, art, occupation of life, could not have taken other forms, at man's pleasure; he was obliged to adopt these. He walks in the leading strings of a Wisdom higher than his own; and one of the objects of this lecture, is to show how they are fitted to influence him, and to affect the general order of the world.

But, in the first place, we are to consider how it is that nature takes him in hand—to move, to influence, to instruct him.

I have already spoken of nature's influence. I have spoken of its fertility, order, and beauty, as ministering both to human convenience and human culture. But I wish to press the consideration to another point—to that development and specific direction of the human faculties, to which it drives and compels us. It is necessary to return to this subject of nature's influence again and again, in order to meet the objections that arise from this quarter. Objections, I say; for it is a problem that I am dealing with; and it is natural that my discourse should often be colored by this aspect of the matter in hand.

There has always been a theory in the world, that matter is essentially antagonistic, hostile to mind. And a very strange theory it is certainly; that the very sphere for man, the very house of life, should be regarded, not as built for his convenience, comfort and growth, but as thrown down in his path, to be an obstruction and hindrance to him. But such has been a very prevalent way of thinking. There is much ancient philosophy and much modern poetry, to this purpose, whose effect needs to be examined. One of the old Manichæan writers—and they professed to be Christians too, some of them—speaks of the "bad principle" in the world, as self-existent; and hostile not only to man, but to God. Sometimes he calls this bad principle nature; sometimes matter; sometimes Satan, and devil.* Plato, wisest of the heathen, makes Socrates say, in the Phædo: "There is another pure earth, above the pure heavens, where the stars are, which is commonly called ether. The earth *we* inhabit is properly nothing else than the sediment of the other: upon which we are scattered, like so many ants dwelling in holes, or like frogs that live in some marsh near the sea. We are immersed in these cells, he says—mewed up within some hole of the earth;" and he maintains that it is the great business of a wise man to prepare to *die*, and to escape from a world full of fetters, clogs, and obstructions.

Let us see if with better lights we cannot better understand this constitution of things—*i. e.*, of nature and of humanity as placed in the midst of it. Nature, it is true, does not spread for man a soft couch to lull him to repose; nor does she set around that couch abundant supplies, which it requires only the stretching out of his hand to obtain. For the animal races she *does* so provide. She *prepares* food and clothing for *them*, with little care of theirs. She spreads their table, for which no cookery is needed; she weaves and fits their garments without loom or needle; and her trees and caves and rocks are their habitations. Yet man is said to be her favorite, and so he is; but thus does she deal with her favorite: she turns him out, naked, cold and shivering upon the earth; with needs that admit of no

* Lardner's Works, vol. ii. p. 189.

compromise; with a delicate frame that cannot lie upon the bare ground an hour, but must must have immediate protection; with a hunger that cannot procrastinate the needed supply, but must be fed to-day and every day; and now, why is all this? I suppose, if man could have made of the earth a bed; and if an apple or a chestnut a day could have sufficed him for food; he would have *got* his barrel of apples or his bushel of chestnuts, and lain down upon the earth and done nothing—till the stock was gone. But nature will not permit this. I say, will not *permit* it. For hers is no voluntary system. She has taken a bond of man for the fulfilment of one of her primary objects—his activity; because, if he were left to indolence, all were lost. That bond is as strong as her own ribbed rocks, and close pressing upon man, as the very flesh in which it is folded and sealed. So is this solid and insensible world filled with meaning to him; the blind and voiceless elements seem to look upon him and speak to him; and the dark clothing of flesh and sense which is wrapped around him, becomes a network of moral tissues; and everything says, "Arouse thyself! up and be doing! for nature—the system of things, will not have thee here, on any other terms."

But what, again, does nature demand of this activity. The answer is, *discretion.* Immediately and inevitably a principle of intelligence is infused into this activity. Immediately the agent becomes a pupil. Nature all around, says even to infancy—what all human speech says to it—"take care!" It is, all over the world, the first phrase of the parent's teaching, the first of the child's learning—"take care!" And this phrase but interprets what nature says to all her children. Not as an all-indulgent mother does she receives them to her lap, but with a certain matronly sobriety, ay, and "the graver countenance of love"—saying, "take care—smooth paths are not around thee, but stones and stubs, thorns and briers; soft elements alone do not embosom thee, but drenching rains will visit thee, and chilling dews, and winter's blast, and summer's heat;

harmless things are not these around thee, but, see! here is fire that may burn, and water that may drown; here are unseen damps and secret poisons, the rough bark of trees and sharp points of contact. Thou must learn, or thou must suffer."

Ay, suffer! What human school has a discipline like nature's? In these schools, we are apt to think, that punishments are cruel and degrading. But *nature* has *whips* and *stripes* for the negligent. Her discipline strikes deep; it stamps itself upon the human frame — and upon what a frame! All softness, all delicacy; not clothed with the mail of leviathan, nor endowed with interior organs like those of the ostrich or the whale, and yet a frame strong with care, while weakest of all things without it. What a wonderful organ, in this view, is the human stomach! the main source of energy to the system, strong enough to digest iron and steel, working like some powerful machine, and yet, do you let it be overworked or otherwise injured, and it is the most delicate and susceptible of all things—trembling like an aspen leaf at every agitation, and sinking and fainting under a feather's weight of food or drink. What a system, in this view, is that of the nerves! insensible as leathern thongs in their health—trembling cords of agony in their disease!

I would not dwell upon these matters as abstract facts. I would have my discourse teach, as nature teaches. Do you not see the wonder which nature and humanity thus present to us? Do you not see man as a frail and delicate child, cast into the bosom of universal teaching? Ay, that teaching comes out to him in tongues of flame, and it penetrates his hand in the little, seemingly useless, thorn, and it assails his foot with stones of stumbling; and it flashes into his eyes with the light of day; and it broods over his path with the darkness of night; and it sweeps around his head with the wings of the tempest; and it startles him to awe and fear with the crash of thunder. The universe is not more filled with light and air and solid matter, than it is filled and crowded with wisdom and instruction.

But more, far more than this does nature teach; not activity or self-care alone, but a larger wisdom. To show this fully, we should be obliged to enter the vast domain of modern science. What can we possibly say, in the few words for which we have space here, upon a theme so immense and magnificent?

But in what I shall say, let me still speak of man as nature's pupil. It is common, I know, in this connection, to celebrate the achievements of man; to say "how much has he discovered and learned." But the true philosopher is disposed rather to say, how much does nature teach, and how much have I yet to learn! The dying words of the great La Place, when he withdrew his eyes from those depths of heaven which he had so profoundly studied—his last words were: "That which I know is limited; that which I do not know is infinite." What noble devotees indeed have been found at the shrine of nature! Anaxagoras and Aristotle, and Copernicus and Kepler, and Galileo, and Newton, and the Herschels, and Boyle, and Davy, and Cuvier, and Ehrenberg, and Blumenbach, and Berzelius, and many who bear up the honors of those great names at the present day, besides a multitude of a kindred spirit, though of less fame, who morning and evening, at noonday and at midnight, are watching by all the avenues and at all the gates of this sublime temple. Secrets unimaginable are yet to be detected, wonders upon wonders are yet to be unfolded; and *that* the wise well know.

But let us glance a moment at some of its actual revelations.

Light passes at the rate of twelve millions of miles in a minute.* Sir William Herschel was of opinion that by the aid of his 40-feet reflector his eye descried nebulæ (now mostly resolved into stars,) from which it would take the

* It is not material to the statement whether light is regarded as a substance, or whether, according to the later theory, the effect of light is produced by the vibrations of some substance—some infinitely diffused ether. In this case the *vibrations* pass with equal rapidity—a fact, more wonderful still.

light nearly two millions of years to reach us.* Professor Nichol says that Lord Rosse's telescope certainly penetrates a depth from which the light would require 60,000 years to come to us. Struck with these statements, and feeling as if there must be some extravagance or vagueness about them, I turned to Sir John Herschel's Elementary Treatise on Astronomy, and there I find it stated that the period cannot be less than a thousand years; how much more is unknown. Subsequent calculations have proved, I believe, that it cannot be less than ten thousand.

Let it be observed that I am now speaking of our own system; not, indeed, the *solar* system, but that vast bed of stars called the Galaxy, which, in the line of its extension, gathers so many stars to the sight as to present that whitish appearance which we call the Milky Way. And yet this is now discovered to be but one of many universes. Rosse's telescope has dissolved into systems of countless stars, the nebulæ that had been descried in the far-lying regions of space. And of these systems—these universes--vast perhaps as our own, more than 2,000 have been seen and numbered.

Well may *ours* be called a *universe*—whether we consider its vastness or its order. We have said that from some of its bodies a ray of light takes 10,000, and it may be 50,000, years to reach us. It scarcely matters, to any conception we can form, *which* estimate we adopt. But think of it! Before the time of Sesostris, before the earliest date of recorded time, it may be, that ray of light left its home, and through distances awful and inconceivable it has come, traversing twelve millions of miles in a minute, and reporting of unnumbered millions of resplendent suns, scattered like star-dust through that illimitable infinitude of space.

But again, all these millions of spheres which compose our universe are revolving around one central point—the star Alcyone, in the constellation Pleiades—at the rate of about

* Philosophical Transactions for 1802, p. 498. See note in Humboldt's Cosmos, vol. 1, p. 154, Am. Ed.

400,000 miles each day. And all these universes, it may be, are revolving around another centre—the throne of the Infinite Might.

And yet, when we turn to the opposite extreme, scarce less a wonder meets us. Millions of creatures, organized, active, sportive, live in a drop of water. The galionella, an extinct species of animalcule, was an organized being, and had a kind of integument like a shell. And Ehrenberg tells us that in a single cubic inch of the polishing slate of Bilin are forty thousand millions of the silicious frames of the galionella.*

In this awful universe, we need not say, is stupendous power. It is in the roll and sweep of infinite systems; but it is also, and long was unsuspected, in the very bosom of the air around us. Take four cubic feet of the vapor that softly steals from the river's bosom; and it is seemingly nothing; you wave your hand in it as if it were nothing; and yet in the expansion and contraction of those four cubic feet of vapor, is power enough to move long trains of heavy-laden cars through our fields, as swiftly almost as the bird flies. For myself, I must confess that I can never cease to look with wonder at this marvel that is daily before my eyes. And for the swiftness of nature's messengers—what are these that are darting on telegraphic lines over our heads, and bearing living thoughts, hundreds of miles in an instant! The time may soon come, when a man shall send his fireside talk in a moment, from the tropic to the pole, and tell of marriage or birth, of sickness or death, even while it is passing, to his friend, half across the globe. The time may come when the earth shall be a vast whispering-gallery, and thoughts shall circulate around it, as freely as sunbeams.

Why do we not tremble with fear, amidst the swiftness and power of these tremendous agents in nature? It is, because we believe in an infinite Order—an infinite Goodness. It is a marvellous confidence. It is a solemn thing to live

* See Humboldt's Cosmos, vol. 1, p. 150, Am. ed.

as we do—to live thus as children of faith. We recline upon the bosom of this tremendous Nature, where there is power enough within the wave of our hand, to tear us ten thousand times in pieces, as confidingly as in the lap of a parent. Our knowledge of things around us is small; but our faith boundless. To the little child, nature is a stranger, and has some rough points about her; but how soon does he come to look upon her as a mother! See him basking in the sunshine, bathing in the water, running in the fields, with his bright locks floating in the wind: everywhere he feels as if kind arms were around him. He confides in the uniform beneficence of nature. If he had studied her millions of years, he could not be more sure. How knoweth he this so surely? It is because not you nor I, but God, hath taught that weak and innocent child. "And thus," says Chalmers, with equal justness and beauty, "a truth, the uniformity of nature, which would seem to require Omniscience for its grasp, as co-extensive with all nature and all history, is deposited by the hand of God, in the little cell of a nurseling's cogitations." *

From this survey of nature, not merely as the theatre of human training, whose general structure is fitted for that end—which was the subject of a former lecture—but of nature as effectually enforcing and impressively teaching certain things—activity, self-care and a wider and diviner intelligence, let us now turn to the specific tasks that are set for man in the field of life. These are the occupations of life; embracing in their range, all its laborious pursuits, its practical arts, and learned professions. And I wish to make it appear, as I have already said, that these are all a part of the *system of things*, in which we are placed. Some of these occupations are looked upon as degrading; some as hard and almost cruel. In some—and this is sometimes particularly felt in the learned professions—many persons so little distinguish themselves, that there is nothing to gratify their ambition, and they become discouraged and dis-

* Chalmer's Bridgewater Treatise, p. 203, Am. Ed.

heartened in their callings. Now in all these pursuits and professions, it ought to be felt that there is a *duty* imposed by the Great Taskmaster; which it is well and right and honorable to discharge. I have been struck with observing how much, in the popular literature of England, in the ballads and songs for instance, this sense of *duty* is urged, and especially upon one particular class. I mean military men. In the songs of Dibdin for instance, this is very striking. The common sailor is taught to feel that he is to stand in his lot, however humble, because it is his duty. And equally true is it that this is to be every man's strength and stay in his daily tasks—*duty*. We cannot get along without it.

Let us, in the first place, cast a glance at these tasks, to see how they spring from the necessity of things, and are the ordained vocations of men.

The feudal system, and its predecessor, the slave system, never wrought a greater or more pernicious falsehood into the history of human life, than this—that labor is degrading, a thing to be deprecated and shunned; and that idleness—doing nothing—is the honored and happy condition. The great visible fact of the world, is *work*, and first of all, work upon the world itself; that is to say, tilling the soil. The entire human race draws subsistence from the earth upon this condition—*work*, as truly as all plants and trees derive their life through the roots that connect them with the ground. Instead of roots, human hands are stretched out to draw supplies from the earth and from the sea. Not that every man is a farmer or a fisherman; but every man —artisan, merchant, or professional man—does something that connects him with that supply. Next, manufacture— the cooking of food, the weaving of wool and cotton into clothing, the fashioning of stone and wood and the metals into houses and furniture, and a thousand conveniences—it is an ordinance. Then again, trade—the merchant's vocation—the exchange of the productions of different countries and climates; it is an ordinance. How idle to say, by way of objection, that it produces nothing! Exchange is as necessary to human comfort and civilization, as production. Are the learned professions any less ordinances—functions ordained in the very nature and necessity of things? All men cannot study the laws of the human constitution, the symptoms of disease and the methods of cure; therefore there must be physicians. Men generally cannot devote themselves to the education of their children; therefore there must be teachers of reading, writing, numbers—of sciences, languages, music, painting, etc. Numerous relations necessarily spring up between persons, estates, lands, chattels. The rights of men to property and personal security; the ascertaining and defining of those rights by able treatises and carefully-drawn statutes; the necessity, to prevent infinite confusion and injustice, of general principles, and of instruments, covenants, testaments drawn in accordance with them—all this is the subject of a complicated and profound science. There must be men to understand it; there must be lawyers. Worship is a duty, religious instruction a need of humanity; therefore there must be pastors, preachers, divines. Some persons do not see the need of *this* profession, and propose to abolish it; but the world has judged otherwise. There must be somebody, at least, to preside over the rites of public worship. Finally, statesmanship, the guidance of the affairs of nations, is an indispensable vocation in the order of all civilized society. And all these vocations, I still say, are natural ordinances of life, necessary results of the human nature and condition, bound up with the constitution of the world; without which the world cannot exist, civilized society cannot exist.

Let us now look at these pursuits and employments of men, in the next place, as the means of development and culture.

The world, we say, is a school; the object is culture. Let us *look* at it in this light. Do we imagine that something better than the present plan might have been devised to answer the end? Let us see. Suppose that to *learn* and to *teach* had been the sole and immediate business of human life. Suppose that the generations of men, housed, fed, clothed, provided for without any care of their own, had been placed, as it were, on school forms, rank behind rank; and that a few, the aged and the wise, had stood before them to give instruction. Would that seem to us better than this incessant, varied, voluntary activity? That is to say, instead of finding his education *in* this activity, would he have found a more abstract system better?

I would not make any unfair representation, or draw a picture that does injustice to the supposition in question. Suppose that in any way—in families, or under the most attractive circumstances—direct teaching and learning were the sole business of life. And I say again, does it seem to us that this would be better? Assuming that development, culture is the end of life, does it seem to us that having nothing to do but to study the works of God would have been the better plan? Does it seem to us a great *waste* of time, to dig and delve, to plough and sow and reap, to manufacture and buy and sell; or to cook and wash and keep the house? Should we account it a blessed fortune, if we had nothing to do but to read and study and meditate?

Abstractly, perhaps, it may appear to be so, and in some other state of being this may be the method of culture. But we have now to look at *this* state; and we have a large range of considerations to take into the account. There may be *individuals* far advanced on the path of improvement, to whom a life of study may be better suited than to others; and yet the scholastic life, compared with the active, is questionable. But we have to consider the race, and the race as beginning in infancy, and as travelling up slowly on the path of progress, and little qualified even now, in the mass, for a life of study. Men in general would find it very dull to spend their time in the contemplation of facts or theories. They must obtain their development in some other way. Nature can hardly be a laboratory to them yet; still less a library: it must be a workshop. The life of every child before us is a picture of the general life. We do not begin with giving it books or lessons. For four or five years it is left very much to its own activity—a period during which, nevertheless, it has been said by a celebrated statesman,* that we probably acquire more ideas—not mere knowledge, which comes partly from reasoning on ideas—but more *ideas*, more of the elements of reasoning than we acquire during our whole life after.

But let us look next at the whole course of life and of generations, at the discipline for all men. Would study, as the sole business, be better than action?

It must be a very strong being that can afford to think all the time, and do nothing but think. Colleges would become madhouses, were it not for vacations. Schools of abstract speculation have often proved themselves to be wild enough, even when composed of the most learned men. The extravagances of the old school-men is proof enough of this.

Perpetual thinking, at any rate, is more than anybody can bear. We should be cast, and flung helpless down in the toils of thought, if the line were never broken; and it is well that event, action, circumstance, comes to break it. The question, indeed, is not between thought and action, but whether it is best that they should be blended; and of this I have no doubt.

For it is further to be considered that this mingling of action with thought introduces into life an element of individual experience, of untaught, self-taught knowledge, of personal experimenting, which is of immense importance to the character. It brings truth to the test of fact, and makes it more vital. It makes every attainment more thorough, and fixes it more deeply in the mind. Other things being equal, he will best understand the law who practises it; or the physical constitution of man, who studies it with a view to healing; or theology, who puts in order his thoughts to state them to others; i. e., to preach them.

* Lord Brougham.

And finally, I do not see how he can be said to understand *virtue at all* who does not put it in practice. All the moral, i. e., the highest ends of life, seem absolutely to require action in order to their accomplishment. The mere contemplation of virtue or of truth, however divine, is apt to degenerate into sickly sentiment. It is liable to become dreamy, inefficient and superficial. And there are too many examples to prove that in the upper surface of the character many noble, ay, and religious thoughts may have their place, while in the layers and depths beneath all may be bad and wrong. It requires action to develop the true moral energy. It requires that the very deeps of character and life be stirred up. It requires contact and conflict with toil, trial, difficulty, with sickness, sorrow and pain, with all that makes the moral discipline of life.

On the whole, then, I am persuaded that this discipline, which is found in the ordained occupations of life, is a good training—is the best conceivable. I do not accept as at all reasonable the common complaint that these occupations are mere drudgery to the spirit, mere waste time to the soul, mere toiling and moiling, mere buying and selling, mere writing deeds or prescriptions—with no end but to get bread. They do a great deal for man beyond this, in his own despite; and they would do a great deal *more* if he saw what they were *meant* to do—if he but had the reflection and wisdom distinctly to say with himself, "There was no need in the nature of things that I should be a worker; God could have provided for me without *that*, as he has for the birds of the air; but I am made a worker for the development of energies, for the culture of virtues. I am made a worker that I may be something higher, stronger, nobler, than a mere enjoyer, or a mere idler, or a mere learner."

But observe now the actual process. See a man who cultivates his farm. He must work. But that is not all he has to do. He has to think, and to think a good deal, in order to do the work well. There are various soils on his farm, suited to various uses; there are different products to be reared; there are successive seasons, demanding attention and foresight; there must be a general plan, and the details must be wrought out with care and judgment. So much is indispensable, and much more might be easily added—a knowledge of agricultural chemistry, a scientific cultivation of the land. And with this connects itself the whole circle of family duties and affections; the *home* stands in the midst; the visible guardian and presiding genius of the scene; the holy altar, the sacred hearthstone that shed light and warmth like the sun upon all around. Such the centre and such the circumference of rural life—the best bond to virtue, and sphere of healthiest activity; the great page of nature spread around and within, some thoughtful inquiry and some reading to understand it—what better school, what holier sanctuary could there be for man than this!

Go now to the manufactory and the workshop. Here the materials which nature provides are to be wrought into a thousand forms, for human convenience and comfort. Intellect, invention, skill, dexterity, are here brought into the most adroit and brilliant activity; revolving wheels, the swift-flying shuttle, the sharpened instrument, best image the mechanic intellect of a people. No man can pass through our workshops and factories without being astonished at what is there achieved. This is not a dull school. When Heaven ordained that man should be an artisan, a manufacturer, it did not appoint the task to benumb his faculties, but to quicken and sharpen them to the keenest exercise.

And again, I ask with regard to the merchant's calling—does Heaven frown upon *that?*—as some of the satirists and reformers do? Beneficent exchanger of the products of all climes and countries, bringer of comforts to all firesides throughout the world, promoter of peaceful intercourse, civilizer of the nations; whose sails whiten every sea; in the bright track of whose empires, are Phœnicia and Carthage, and old Spain and Greece, and Holland, and England, and America—is this to be rated as a barren and unproductive calling? Is it the misfortune of the world that it must have this instrumentality? "But it corrupts the *individual*"—will some one say? Only as everything corrupts him who will. Some of the noblest virtues—some of the noblest *men* in the world, are reared in this field.

Turn, in fine, to the learned professions. These too take their place in the order of Providence. Let us see *what* place: and what *functions* they may be for those who discharge them.

In this distrustful, this all-doubting age, it has fallen to the lot of the medical profession, I think, to be brought into question more than any other. The reason is, that the field of its investigation lies in the dark; so that the processes of cure, and the principles of evidence, are more obscure; and the generality of men are more incompetent to judge here, than anywhere else. Dr. Abercrombie, in his "Intellectual Philosophy," mentions the case of a physician, who retired in disgust from his profession, saying, that "The practice of medicine was like a man striking with a club in the dark; if he hit the disease he killed the disease; if he hit the patient, he killed the patient." Now I think that this man was himself striking in the dark, when he said that; and not only so, but leaving all the rest of the world in the dark. The darker the matter is, the more need to seek for light. The science of healing, however imperfect, the study of *constant* cause and effect for thousands of years, must have some value; it is a good study; and for the *practice* of what is thus learned, I know not what can call out finer sympathies than this ministration of relief to sickness and pain, nor any that wins for itself a more enviable place in the confidence and affection of society.

The legal profession, again, has no small amount of prejudice to contend with. It cannot be denied that it is necessary; somebody must understand and administer the laws; and to do this requires a life devoted to it. But still —this enlistment in the cause of bad passions, this espousal and defence of the wrong side, is thought by many to be unprincipled. I have long wondered that some member of this profession, does not take up and thoroughly discuss the moral questions which thus press upon it. It really very much concerns, not only the honor of the profession, but the healthiness of the public conscience, that this should be done. In brief, the principles are these: In every legal question, there are two parties; in the minds of judge and jury, there are two sides, which have a claim to be considered and weighed; counsel represent these parties, espouse these sides. The *original* party has a right to state his case; then surely another, better qualified, may do it for him. And in all ordinary cases the lawyer does not and cannot *know* which side is wrong, till the evidence is all given in and the case fully argued. This is the theoretic ground for legal practice; and certainly there is nothing in it that is at war with the great ends of Providence—nothing that forbids a high moral culture; everything on the contrary that requires it. It is, rightly viewed, a high and noble vocation. It is the sphere of justice, the forum of eloquence, the school of statesmanship.

Of the clerical profession, in the present connection, I need say nothing but this: it is the ultimate and culminating ministration to the highest life of the world; and of the teachers of youth—that fourth profession—that they must learn before they teach; that the very condition of their function is intelligence, and its end, instruction; that they, more than any other distinct class of men, lay the very foundations of all human culture.

Let us now come to consider, in fine, as forms of human activity, *the arts of expression.* Nature teaches and enforces many things for human development and instruction; the ordinary occupations of life assist the same design; but this is not all. Men are possessed of great and divine ideas and sentiments; and to paint them, sculpture them, build them in architecture, sing them in music, utter them in eloquent speech, write them in books, in essays, sermons, poems, dramas, fictions, philosophies, histories—this is an irresistible propensity of human nature.

Art, inspiration, power, in these forms, naturally places itself at the head of the human influences by which the world is cultivated and carried forward. The greatest thing in the world doubtless is a sacred life; the greatest power, a pure example; but this is the *end* of all, and we do not here contemplate it as a means. As means, art is greatest. A beautiful thought, a great idea, made to quicken the intellect, to touch the heart, to penetrate the life—this is the grandest office that can be committed to human hands. Every faithful artist of every grade, belongs to this magnificent Institute for the instruction of the world.

Criticism in literature, within the last forty years, has passed through a very remarkable change. Any one may trace it in the leading journals, of that standing; as for instance, in the *Edinburgh Review*. Formerly literary criticism was very much occupied with form and details in art, and had very little reference to the true design. Now it has come to be received as an unquestioned canon of criticism, that there *can* be no high art without moral elements; that irreverence and atheism would kill all high artistic excellence, as surely as they would kill all high moral excellence; that the most sublime and beautiful things, whether in nature or humanity, are imprints and signatures of the Divine hand; and that to express these things, the soul of art must commune with what is divine—must be breathed upon by the sanctity of religion. It is not as it was in the days of Voltaire and Helvetius and D'Holback, and Hume and Gibbon; *now* it is understood that no man can be a *great writer*, a great poet, novelist, or philosopher, who does not recognize and feel what is greatest in man—the spirit of humanity and the sense of what is above it. I hardly know of any more significant mark upon the world, indicative of the world's progress, than this.

There is one grand mistake often made in the appreciation of art, arising from the honor and fame that attend it. I suspect that it is quite a common notion that men study, write, speak, paint, build, for *fame*. Totally and infinitely otherwise is the fact with all true men. They live for an idea—live to develop, embody, express it; and all extraneous considerations only hinder and hurt their work. But this is often misunderstood. I have, many times, had observations made to myself, implying that the stimulants to my own professional effort must be small in retired country places, and came to their culminating point only in the great centres of society. The implication always pains, and if I must say the truth, somewhat angers me. It is a total misconception, to say the least. A true man will preach as well in the Isle of Shoals as in Boston or New York; nay *better*, I am inclined to think; for he will not have *there* the miserable envelopment of city criticism or eclat to disturb him. This is the reason why men seldom speak so well *on extraordinary occasions*, as when left undisturbed, to the free and natural force of their minds and flow of their feelings, in their ordinary professional walk. If I were to offer an artist a million of dollars to paint me a picture, unless his were one of the greatest and deepest minds, which *nothing* could divert from its idea, I should not expect as good a picture from him as I should if he painted it for nothing.

No, believe me, the effluence of genius can no more be bought or sold, than the light that streams from the fountain of day. It is the light of the world; and it is not man's purchase, but God's gift; it is God's light shining through the soul. Raphael or Michael Angelo may be employed by Pope Julius or Pope Sixtus—patronized by them, as the phrase is; Shakspeare may be honored by Queen Elizabeth, or Dante protected by the Lord of Ravenna; but all that pontiff, monarch, or lord can do for genius is, to let it *alone*, simply to give it an opportunity to work; all their largesses can do no more than that. No, the light shines from a higher sphere than this world. It shines into the artist's studio and philosopher's laboratory; it falls upon the still places of deep meditation; the pen that writes immortal song, immortal thought in any form, is a rod that conveys the lightning from heaven to earth; and the breath of eloquent speech is an afflatus that comes from far above windy currents of human applause.

It concerns my purpose in this lecture, to insist on this mission of all true intellectual labor, and to remind every worker in this field, however high or however humble, of his real vocation. "I am not distinguished," one may say; "the world, Europe, England, does not know me—will never know me." What then? Do what thou canst. Somebody will know it. No true word or work is ever lost. Stand thou in thy lot; do thy work; for the great Being that framed the world assuredly meant that somebody should do it—that men and women of various gifts should do it, as they are able. Or one may say, "My part in this good vocation is not held by the world in due appreciation and honor; I sing the music, or speak the dramas, that others have written; and my calling is profaned in the common parlance of the day; the church anathematizes it, and society enjoys without respecting it." I admit the injustice; and for this special reason, that these callings are naturally good, and for the evil in them, society and the church are much to blame. Naturally good, I say; for the world would not know or feel what Beethoven and Handel have composed, or Shakspeare or Calderon have written, if there had not been those who studied them, and, inspired by kindred genius, learned to breathe out their thoughts in song and dramatic speech.

Why can we not look at the goodly band of human occupations and arts as it is; and depreciate no *trade* that is necessary, no *art* that is useful, no ministration that springs from the bosom of nature, and is thus clearly ordained of Heaven? If there be abuses of such ministration, let them be remedied; but rejection and scorn of any one thing that God has made to be or to be done, is not lawful, nor reverent to Heaven.*

* I have always thought, however, that this fair and reasonable appreciation of all the lawful and necessary vocations in society, could never be the result, but

Let this whole system of nature and life appear as it is; as it stands in the great order and design of Providence. Let nature, let the solid world, be more than a material world—even the area on which a grand moral structure is to be built up; itself helping the ultimate design in many ways. Let the works of man take their proper place—the place assigned them in the plan of Heaven. Let agriculture lay the basis of the world-building. Let mechanism and manufacture rear and adorn the vast abode of life. Let trade and commerce replenish it with their treasures. Let the liberal and learned professions stand as stately pillars in the edifice of society. But when all this is done, still there are wants to be supplied. There is a thought in the bosom of humanity that longs to be uttered. The heart of the world would break, if there were no voice to give it relief—to give it utterance. There is, too, a slumber upon the world which needs that voice. There are dim corners and dark caverns, that want light. There is weariness to be cheered, and pain to be soothed, and the dull routine of toil to be relieved, and the dry, dead matter of fact to be invested with hues of imagination, and the mystery of life to be cleared up, and a great, dread, blank destitution that needs resource and refreshment—needs inspiring beauty and melody to breathe life into it.

Then let the artist men come and do their work. Let statues stand in many a niche and recess, and pictures hang upon the wall, that shall fill the surrounding air with their sublimity and loveliness. Let essays and histories, let written speech and printed books, be ranged in unending al-

of the highest and most reflective civilization. It was with surprise, therefore, that I read the following passage in Bossuet upon the Egyptian system of society: "Il falloit qu'il y eût des emplois et des personnes plus considérables, comme il faut qu'il y ait des yeux dans le corps. Leur éclat ne fait pas mépriser les pieds ni les parties les plus basses. Ainsi, parmi les Egyptiens, les prêtres et les soldats avaient des marques d'honneur particulières; mais tous les métiers, jusqu'aux moindres, étaient en estime; et on ne croyoit pas pouvoir sans crime mépriser les citoyens dont les travaux, quels qu'ils fussent, contribuoient au bien public."—*L'Histoire Universelle, troisième partie, chapitre premier.*

coves, to pour instruction upon the world. Let poetry and fiction lift up the heavy curtains of sense and materialism, and unfold visions of beauty, like the flushes of morning, or of parting day behind the dark mountains. Let music wave its wings of light and air through the world, and sweep the chords that are strung in the human heart with its entrancing melodies. Let lofty and commanding eloquence thunder in the ears of men the words of truth and justice,

> Or, in strains as sweet
> As angels use, . . . whisper peace.

Let majestic philosophy touch the dark secret of life, and turn its bright side as a living light upon the paths of men.

Come, other Platos and Bacons!—do we not exclaim? come, other Newtons and Laplaces!—other Beethovens and Handels!—come, other Homers and Dantes, Miltons and Shakspeares!—other Demostheneses and Ciceros, and Massillons!—and fill the long track of future ages with your glorious train, and lead on the world through ever-brightening ages to knowledge, to virtue, and to immortal life!

Under such auspices, my friends, visions of better days to come, rise before me. I look upon a company of people, a plantation, a district, or a township among us; and, compared with a Hottentot village or the tents of Alaric, there is great progress *now*—order, comfort, and a certain amount of culture. But, alas! there is destitution, ignorance, crime, weariness, heart-heaviness enough still. Cold and chill is the day of life to many within the protected pale of our modern civilization; and the bright sky is of a leaden hue to them; and the eyes are dim and the spirit is sad and heavy, that should sympathize with the fair and lovely picture of the world around them. God be thanked that it is no worse—that ours *is* a protected civilization, protected from the tortures of old superstition, and from the blows of feudal oppression; ay, that it is free; that no baron's arm *here* can strike and scatter youth and innocence into street dust for him to travel on to his accursed ends, nor cast down the noblest hearts to sigh in his dungeons. But there is uncivilized misery enough among us still; misery that comes from want of knowledge, refinement, culture, and the gracious influence of the beautiful arts and virtues. There are blows of domestic tyranny. There are cruel words spoken, fit only for barbarians. There is hard and bitter and grinding toil for many. There is the life-long struggle for culture and comfort; struggle with painful conditions of need, and uncongenial and ill-requited taskwork; struggle in schoolrooms and factories and perhaps homes; struggle in all the callings and all the liberal professions of life—for I hear voices of complaint from them all. Sad isolation, secret and untold griefs, disappointed hopes, aims, and affections, wearying mental strifes and questionings, brood far and wide upon the heart of modern society.

But I believe in a better day that is coming. Improved agriculture, manufacture and mechanism, less labor and more result, more leisure, better culture, high philosophy, beautiful art, inspiring music, resources that will not need the base appliances of sense, will come; and with them truth, purity, and virtue; reverent piety building its altar in all human abodes; and the worship that is gentleness and disinterestedness, and holy love, hallowing all the scene; and human life will go forth, amidst the beautiful earth and beneath the blessed heavens, in harmony with their spirit, in fulfilment of their high teaching and intent, and in communion with the all-surrounding light and loveliness.

LECTURE VIII.

AGAINST DESPONDENCY.—HELPS AND HINDRANCES, OR A CONSIDERATION OF THE MORAL TRIALS OR EMERGENCIES THAT ATTEND THE WORKING OUT OF OUR HUMAN PROBLEM.

We are now penetrating deeper into the world-problem—the great problem of our humanity; and we are to consider this evening some of the interior, the mental and moral conditions, on which it is to be wrought out.

I have been sensible at every step that the subject upon which I am engaged in these lectures, requires a far larger discussion than I am able here to give it. It is indeed a subject for a great work, rather than for a few lectures; I am tempted to say, for the greatest work in the domain of philosophy; and for a work, too, that is yet to be written. My conviction is, so far as my reading has extended, that only a few fragments worthy of a place in it have yet appeared in the literature of the world. And it is a work which, when it is accomplished by the united powers of genius, learning, and piety exhausted upon a life of study, and concentrated in a book of wisdom, will be of only less value than the Bible itself. Happy and crowned with blessings shall he be who can achieve it. I can but express my sense of the value and grandeur of the undertaking. I but see in future time, when thought shall be more cosmopolitan and comprehensive than it is now—I can but prophesy that then some gifted nature shall appear, which, embued and informed with the German lore, penetration and spirituality, with the French clearness and vivacity, and the solid English sense and feeling, shall so unfold the problem of human Destiny, as to become a second Plato—and a greater—the greatest uninspired teacher of men.

Let us, however, pursue our task as we can, in these lectures, and consider this evening some of the interior conditions, trials and emergencies, which attend the working out of our human problem, the helps and hindrances to it as a practical work, and the courage and cheerfulness which ought to attend it, instead of the depression and despondency which too commonly darken the way. For, in particular, I wish it to be considered whether there is anything arbitrary or unnecessarily distressing, or whether there is, to the extent usually supposed, anything peculiar or strange, in the conditions of *human* attainment.

We are apt to imagine that there *is* something *very* peculiar in man's case. Probation, for instance, is thought to be peculiar to him. The problem of the Origin of Evil is commonly regarded as pertaining to humanity alone, as darkening no world but this. The very constitution as well as physical condition of human nature, is supposed to stand in direct contrast with that of other beings in other worlds. It is very easy to see how this idea arose. For, ages, the only beings beside men who were imagined to exist in the universe, were angels, seraphs—superhuman natures, dwellers in the empyrean heaven. It was not suspected that the surrounding worlds were inhabited. And when that conception arose, it very naturally peopled those worlds with the same beings, *i. e.*, with angels. All other beings than men, before supposed to exist, were angels; therefore these were angels. The very contrary might have been more justly inferred; since those worlds are of the same nature, order, and company with our own. But the more irrational notion very naturally prevailed for a time; though I think it is now beginning to give way to the reasonable idea, that those dwellers on high—dwellers on high to *us*, but no more than we are to *them*—are indeed our brethren.*

But let us now proceed to that further consideration of the interior and trying conditions of human culture, which I have proposed as the design of this lecture.

The fundamental condition I have already discussed; that is to say, freedom, free will; and the consequent liability to error and to evil. This fact of freedom I took for granted. The necessity of it to virtue, I took for granted. I started from these points, as the very intuitions of experience. I *know* that, under the limitations of course imposed by a finite and moral nature, I am free; and that I cannot be virtuous unless I am so. I *know*, that is to say, that I possess a rational and modified freedom—that I am free—not indeed to do everything possible—but to *do* and to *be* all that is involved in virtue and a virtuous happiness. I am not free to disregard motives; but I am free to yield to good or bad ones at my pleasure—free to cherish the good and to resist the bad—free, at any rate, to turn my thoughts to which I will, and thus to give them weight and power. I am not free to be indifferent to happiness, but I am free to determine what kind of happiness I will seek for. And this freedom, it is plain, is, in its very nature, a restless and perilous element. A mechanical or irrational creation might have perfect security, and *undisturbed* enjoyment. A free creation, a virtuous, improving, advancing creation, must be liable to sin and pain and trouble.

But there are other conditions—imperfection, effort and struggle; penitence or regret for failure; illusion, fluctuation, indefiniteness in the process; and the clogs and the obstructions which flesh is heir to: let us examine them. The question naturally arises: Is not this an unattractive way? Is not imperfection undesirable; and effort toilsome; and penitence sad? And are not illusion, fluctuation, indefiniteness, obstruction, undesirable? And is not the path to good, therefore, an overshadowed and mournful path?

* Oersted's "Soul in Nature" has some interesting discussions upon this point.

Grant that it is so, to a certain extent; yet surely it would be a sufficient vindication to show that it is the only possible path. This vindication I offer; but I think that in thus considering the conditions of progress, we shall come to be convinced that they are not altogether dark nor repulsive.

1. First, imperfection is to be considered. I should hardly touch upon this point, with a view to explain or defend it, so clearly inevitable is it; but I wish to expand this element of the problem into its due place and proportions. I say imperfection. In all the ranks and orders of being, in the seraph as in the child, there must be imperfection. The grades may be different, but the thing is the same; and whatever objection lies against our degree of imperfection, in principle lies against every other. The thing, I say, is alike inevitable and unobjectionable. Our grade is human; others may be superhuman, angelic, we know not what; thrones, princedoms, principalities of heaven. Nay, what if it were true that they had started from *infancy*, as we do? What supposition, indeed, so reasonable? Is it not, in fact, inevitable, in some sense of the word infancy? We speak of imperfection; we say *that* is inevitable; must not the first steps of imperfection be infancy; if not of the body, yet of the mind? If every created existence had a beginning; if it had nothing of experience at the first; if all its knowledge and virtue were to be acquired; if the highest dweller among the stars of light must remember the time when he began to be, began to learn, began to choose the right and to adore the infinite perfection, and if his whole being has been a progress, must not his beginning have been an infancy?

And is it not reasonable, nay, is it not inevitable to suppose that the first steps were attended with more or less of mistake, of erring? What is imperfection? It is limited capacity, knowledge, virtue. It implies that there are truths not yet seen, propositions not yet solved, points of light, heights of attainment not yet reached. It is so with us; must it not be so with the highest finite natures? They may have gone far beyond all voluntary erring; they may be in this sense sinless. But in the vast breadth of their activity there must be things for them to try, questions for them to solve, as truly as in our humble daily walk there are for us. It must be so. If not, then they have learned all, and have stopped in the career of progress. A gloomy pause! For if there is no progress, there can be no activity; if no activity, no happiness.

2. This brings us to the second point—effort. And in general, I say, is it not a good condition? Is it not a favored, a fortunate condition? All experience testifies that the highest happiness is found in action, bodily, mental, moral. Any of them, all of them are good. So persuaded am I of this, that no prospect for a month or a year seems to me so attractive as a *plenum*, a crowded fulness, of healthful and wise activity. And one of the highest benefactions of which I can conceive, in the better world which we hope for, would be the privilege, the power of incessant, never-wearying, glorious activity—no more dulness, no more sleep; no stupor of disease nor sluggishness of the overwrought brain; no heavy head nor fainting heart; but action, travel, growth, increasing knowledge, expanding visions of God, amidst the bright and boundless spheres that roll around us. No soft, bland region do I see above, lulled to repose, curtained with moveless clouds, and basking beneath a tranquil sky: that heaven of the Hindoo, of the Turk, ay, and of our Christian childhood, too, is giving place to manlier and maturer thoughts of ever-unfolding life and joy.

But now if I substitute for effort, the word struggle, immediately the problem assumes a darker aspect. "I am weary," says one; "I would rest; why must I still fight this battle? Why could I not win the prize on easier terms?" I answer, *What* prize? Enjoyment, pleasure, outward abundance? That you might have had on easier terms. Mountains might have been coined into gold for you, and the rivers have flowed with milk and honey, and the trees have dropped manna and distilled wine; and all this you might have had as cheap as the grass which the innocent sheep crops in the summer field. But the heights of virtue, the sweep of expanding knowledge, the pathway of immortal joy—with other thoughts, on other terms, are these things to be achieved. Is it hard to achieve them? Nay, what if you were to learn that they are never *to be* achieved as things laid up, like gold, in a secure coffer; that they are never to be achieved or kept, but as they are held in the free and immortal grasp of beings who prize them above the universe beside? Such, I believe, is the everlasting tenure by which wisdom and virtue are held.

3. But this is not all. With wavering and wayward steps, stumbling and sometimes falling, we press on to the great end of our being—true virtue—true blessedness. Repenting, regret for failure, is an essential condition of all true moral life.

The keenness of this regret is really a remarkable thing in our moral constitution; and nothing indeed can account for its sharpness but its high mission; which is to cut the bonds of evil. Even in his sports, a man cannot shoot and miss the mark, cannot strike the ball and lose the game, without a gesture of disappointment and vexation. But in the game of life, how often and how seriously do we miss and fail! Passion crosses the track, and sways us from the mark. The lawful senses, the innocent affections, often go too far; and their erring is discovered only through experiment and by the result. And so it is in our social relations. How often does a man say, after having tried, and, it may be, honestly tried a thing, two or three times—some measure with his child, some interference with the affections of others, or some principle with the public—"I shall never do that again!" The whole history of the world, of government, of society, of philanthropy, of charity to the poor and suffering, is but a history of experimenting; of errors corrected by their consequences, of truths shaken and sifted from the chaff of falsehood, amidst the mighty winnowings of social and national convulsion.

But not to be led away from the individual reference—this private regret, this sorrow for erring and wrong-doing—what just mind will complain of it as a grievance and hardship? "*Let* me repent," such an one would say—"*let* me sorrow for my faults and follies; it is balm to my wound; God in pity has made it, not a scathing fire, but as the gentle dew of mercy to my nature." This emotion occupies so large a place in the actual working out of our problem, that I must dwell upon it a moment longer; not indeed with a view to the duty—which should be urged in another place—but to the philosophy of the matter. A man thinks, for instance, that wealth will satisfy him, that sensitive pleasure will satisfy him, or that knowledge will fill the measure of his capacity. He does not accurately distinguish, at first, between the boundaries of right and wrong; his reason, perhaps, is not clear in its discriminations, but his passions, alas! are clear in their demand; he knows what he wants, but he does not know what is best for him; he wants this, and he wants that. Well, he gets it—the knowledge, the wealth, the pleasure, the eclat—he gets it; he tries it, and he finds that it will not do. With Solomon and with many another seeker, he says, it is all vanity. Disappointed, grieved, sorrowful, he turns back; and whither must he turn? To deeper, purer, more spiritual resources. He finds, if he finds anything true, that nothing but virtue, sanctity, God, will satisfy him. He wonders that he did not see this before; he reproaches himself; he repents. The sense of his folly is keen and bitter; but it is salutary. He has learned now, by experience, the hatefulness of evil, and the preciousness of good; and only by such experience, perhaps, could he learn. This inward conflict has made the only true theory of welfare, a thousand times more true to him. *Now* he knows what is best for him, and nothing can tear from him that conviction. To all allurements he can say, "Ah! I know you; I know where ye lead; I know your false, accursed, blighting charms." Thus his repentings have been the steps of progress. Thus his errors have taught him to cease from the way that causeth to err. And I cannot but think that a more humble and tender, a nobler and more beautiful virtue may come out of erring, than would have ever been otherwise attained.

But besides imperfection, struggle and sorrow in the practical working out of the human problem, there are other things to be considered; things which at first sight seem to be hindrances in the moral course, but which, I think, as man is constituted, will be found, on examination, to be helps and not hindrances. How talk you, it may be said, of a sublime destiny for man, when we see him baffled by illusions, subject to perpetual fluctuations, bewildered by a painful indefiniteness in all his moral relations, and chained to physical conditions full of difficulty and obstruction, rather than furnished with wings to try the courses of a heavenly virtue?

4. Illusion, then—the fourth point to be considered.

We cannot see things as they are. We mistake form for substance. We mistake semblances for realities. All things are veiled and muffled to us, as if to keep us from the sharpest contact. We live in a universe of symbols, and but slowly grasp the sense. It is the hardest thing in the world to get at the very truth—at the inmost reality; and nothing, perhaps, more distinctly marks the progress of a *mind*, than the gradual disenchantment by which the shows of life dissolve—not into nothing, as they do with the idle and worldly—but dissolve away into the truths that lie within or behind them. But illusion—is it, as is commonly supposed, the antagonist of truth? Rather it is often the envelopment; the husk that protects the corn; the flower that is preparing for fruit.

Such a flower is youthful enthusiasm. The experienced eye looks gravely upon it; wisdom sits aloft and sees clearly its mistakes. But wisdom would not crush that flower. It hath the beauty of its time, and will produce fruit. It is like the flowery style of a youthful and imaginative writer. "Too much efflorescence," we say; but there is promise in it.

Illusion is often a glare that dazzles and bewilders; but it also draws and fixes the eye that will yet penetrate through it. Is it not childish and foolish in barbarous tribes, to be attracted as they are, by the mere gewgaws and trinkets of civilization, without looking at its actual superiority? But they cannot at once see that; and in the mean time, the glitter and show draw them to intercourse—the only means of improvement.

In a manner not very unlike this, it seems necessary that the whole youthful world should look with admiration upon the splendor and glare of life, for they cannot at once attain to sage and profound spirituality. They must be interested in something, that their faculties may be kept awake and active. They must have rattles in childhood; they must have dresses and gayeties in youth; they must have exclusive friendships and passionate regards; they must marry and be given in marriage, though they are hereafter to be, in expansive affection, as the angels of heaven. And when this childhood of life seems, as it does with many, to run into their maturity, and they live upon the outside of things and do not know what the things mean; still I say, better to live so, than not at all; better *this* action, than death: it may nurture strength and faculty for something higher. Better the school of worldliness than no school. That a man should not see the deep foundations of his strength and sufficiency; that he should not feel a possession in all things, higher than ownership, and enjoy a use more sacred than mere property, is a sad thing; but the Master of life hath patience with it, and will perhaps conduct it to something better.

This whole tremendous illusion about wealth—I say not about the means of livelihood; for that is a reasonable care—but about accumulation, mere accumulation, and the means of outward splendor, with no care for the treasure or the light within; we complain of it much at this day, and with good reason. But I have seen a man who was *educated* by the splendid things that his wealth brought around him; educated by his pictures, by his furniture, by his rich mansion. He was not, to be sure, so much the master of his house, as his house was master of him; and it taught him some things. The elegancies around him did something to cultivate, polish, and refine his manners and thoughts. He felt that he must do something to raise himself up to such a style of living. A certain consistency demanded it of him; demanded, at any rate, that his children should be educated for such a splendid lot.

No error, no mistake, perhaps, is a dead mass of obstruction in the mind; it is often the very scaffolding of truth, or the shore that props up a weaker part, till a firm buttress can be placed beneath. Thus, to many minds, there is hardly any greater stumbling-block than the differences of faith. "So *many* creeds, so *many* religions," it is said; "they cannot all be true." No, nor any of them altogether true, perhaps; *i. e.*, as men modify them. But what is not true, may be a temporary outwork to the true. And every honest builder may have unconsciously constructed such as he needed. Ages build so; and, I think, individual men. It is very plain to me that rude and dark ages could not have done without their superstition; and every mind may be a reduced picture of those ages. But what, now, if I were to say, in view of the differences of faith, that I would not believe in anything? It would be a startling declaration. And yet if it were even so with me—yet the error of such absurd and universal scepticism, might be a temporary shield against the edge of particular errors; infidelity might not harm me so much as some creeds would; atheism itself might shield me for a time, from some Moloch worship; and thus I might be led by a way that I knew not, to an end that I did not think of.

In fine, we complain of illusion; we ask for reality; but

it may be that we ask for more than can be wisely given. Who knows whether he be able yet to grapple with the naked spirituality of truth? Let reality be fully unveiled—all semblances dissipated, all interposing clouds swept away—and I know not but the world would go mad. We talk about the absolute in truth—seek for it. Very likely, success would be fatal. Very possibly, the human mind could not bear it. Here is this solemn vesture of mystery upon us and upon all about us. Perhaps it is only so, that we "sit, clothed and in our right mind." Give us the piercing, "microscopic eye," and nature, we are told, disrobed of its soft veil of beauty, would appear like a ghastly skeleton. And so it might be with life, if our wish could be indulged to pierce all its secrets and mysteries. And so, to see the *future* life—that which we so long for—might be more than we could bear.

5. The thing to be next considered, is *fluctuation*. Is it an evil? Life might be stagnant without it, as the sea without its waves.

In the whole system of things, no law seems to be more universal than fluctuation. I have often thought that if, after the manner of the most ancient philosophers, I were to form any generalizing theory concerning the constitution or the primordial element of things, it would not be water with Thales, nor numbers with Pythagoras; it would not be the atomic nor the dynamic theory that I should adopt—not the theory of changing atoms nor of permanent forces, not the theory that makes all loose or all fast—but the theory of eternal swaying to and fro—the theory of eternal fluctuation. Of the original nature, the essence of things, we know nothing; but we know that all things are in a state of change, of conflict, of balancing to and fro. We see it in winds and tides, in times and seasons, in action and reaction, growth and decay, day and night, and the going and coming of the heavenly spheres. Nay, light itself is now found to be but a vibration. And when, as the sun images its great daily revolution in my apartment, by the light that steals along the wall, I have observed how the line of light sways slightly, almost imperceptibly, to and fro as it advances, it has seemed to me a silent type of the infinite mutation.

Now that which seems to appertain to everything else, belongs also to the motions and moods of the human mind —constant fluctuation. Especially where the mind's experience is very strong, definite, and marked, is this observable. As the wailings over the dead in Oriental countries rise from time to time, so in all affliction does wave succeed to wave. And in states of mental anxiety and distress, I have often remarked it, and have been able to anticipate with great confidence in what state I should find such a mind, on any approaching interview.

Now all this may be thought to be very discouraging— this swaying backward and forward, this gaining and losing; but how would you have it? One perpetual strain upon the faculties; we could not bear it. One unshadowed vision; it would make life monotonous. One unvarying state of mind; how much that is of priceless worth would it cut off from our experience? After toil, how sweet is rest! After pain and danger, ease is elysium; and safety, a blessed thanksgiving. Besides, in darkness and need, lessons are learned that never would be learned in light and gladness; lessons of humility, of conscious weakness, of self-despairing, Heaven-trusting prayer. That feeling which, from time to time, comes over us, that we are nothing and know nothing, how powerful a stimulus is it! Even in languor the mind is nursing up the strength that will soon be put forth in new efforts. But moral depression is often very different from languor—is the very reverse of languor. It is when most discouraged and cast down, that the mind is often making the most rapid progress. When the waves are highest, ay, and the storm is darkest, is the ship often sailing fastest; and the bold voyager says, "Give me *that*, rather than everlasting calm and sunshine." We are cradled on an ocean, whose tides are sweeping on to eternity:

not on the bosom of a summer lake, can we be borne to that far, unseen, and shadowy land.

In short, the great trouble is, that we are moral beings at all. If we were machines, we might be put on a smooth and even course. If we were animals, we might have walked in the way of unerring instinct. But we are moral beings, and imperfection, effort, regret, illusion, fluctuation, are our discipline. We are moral beings, and are to work out our own problem, under an administration of reasonable motives, inducements, fears, and hopes.

And that we may do so, a *certain indefiniteness* in our moral relations is necessary. I have touched upon this topic in a former lecture; but there are so many persons who halt at this point; who do not feel as if there were any clear, strong, controlling moral order in this world; who misunderstand this condition of progress which we call moral indefiniteness, that I wish to say a word or two further upon the subject. If—such is their feeling—if penalty more directly and clearly followed transgression; if the bad intent never succeeded; if deceit, lying, knavery never prospered; if remorse immediately followed wrong; or if disease, for instance, struck the first excess with an instant blow, or the all-powerful hand hurled its swift thunderbolt upon injustice, a moral providence would be more manifest. And then, too, if our good endeavors were more immediately rewarded by success, the system would seem to be more encouraging.

But, in the first place, let not this indefiniteness be overrated. The results do follow both good and evil conduct very soon; and the consequences are often more certain than manifest. The bad man may seem to get along very comfortably; he is guilty of atrocious deeds, but he has no conscience, you say, no remorse; he seems very happy for the time. But he is *not*, even for the time. There is a secret, dull pain, and a pitiable impoverishment in the soul, of which he is himself, perhaps, but half conscious. And then the good man is not so happy or so successful as he might be, because he is but half good. It is the misery of our better purposes, that they are not so thorough and decided as they ought to be. We do not know what we might be, if we threw away all reserves, and gave ourselves up wholly to rectitude and purity.

But, in the next place, let us observe how the moral indefiniteness complained of, such as it is, conduces to the training of man. If Providence were to follow every dereliction with an instant blow, the mind might be overwhelmed by that close-pursuing retribution. It would have no liberty or leisure to work out its solemn, moral problem. Startled by the impending peril, it would leap from side to side, or rush through life, as from an executioner. Or it would hold itself in one cowering endeavor to preserve a negative rectitude, rather than tempt the heights of lofty and perilous virtue. Something, we see, is left to man's sagacity, to his reflection, to his reasonings from experience. A field is opened on earth for his generosity, his fearlessness and freedom. Under a system as rigid and exact as the objector seems to demand, I do not see much place or chance for self-moved, noble, and disinterested virtue.

6. But, "No," it may be said, "no, the great trouble is *not* that we are moral beings at all, but that the moral is so darkened, obstructed, burdened by the *physical* nature." The soul, says one, is a noble thing in itself; it has high aspirations, and seems at times to have the wings of an angel; but how fearfully is it chained to sense, to sensual passion, and to sensual infirmity! How many a man who is striving to be virtuous, is thrown almost into despair at times, under the awful relapses of his mind into sense—which lays hold upon him like a lion in its strength! And then when he would fight on through life, how does the darkness of sleep come over him, and bury him in its shadow! When he should be doing his great work, and *is* doing it, that leaden sceptre is stretched over him, and he is vanquished; nay, perhaps "wicked dreams abuse the curtained sleep," and he awakes feeling as if he were a dishonored being.

But if you will carefully examine all these matters, you will find, in the first place, that there is not one of the forms of sensation but is essential to human virtue or to human existence. I have not time to go into detail here, and indeed have discussed the subject before; but if you will examine the appetites and passions of a man, one by one, and survey them in all their relations, you will find that there is not one that can be spared from that complex moral constitution of human life, from that whole sum of influences, by which humanity is trained to industry, to domestic affection, to social order, and spiritual sanctity.

And in the next place, how do physical need and infirmity contribute to the same end? I have said in a former lecture, "if I could see that eating and drinking, and sleeping and waking, are ordinances," it would clear up one large part of the picture of human life. Well, I do see it. I see that physical wants are the first great bonds to labor, care, foresight, prudence. I see, too, that physical infirmities—weariness and sleep—have their moral uses. Sleep, for instance. For a being that often errs and fails, it is well that he should often begin anew; that the chain of evil associations should be broken; that he should begin a new day and turn over a new leaf; that the pure morning influences, and his freshly wakened powers, should incline and enable him to start anew in his moral career. I confess that I am glad to be sometimes delivered from myself—from my own thoughts, from their weariness and perplexity. I am not always good company enough, to wish to be always with myself. Let me sleep; let me escape: as one says to an importunate creditor, hard to account with, "I will see you to-morrow."

And then again, to evil at large, what a direct, peremptory, and powerful *check*, is sleep! What would become of the world if wickedness never slept; if revenge, if intrigue, if guilty revelling never slept; if tyranny, scorn, and hate never slept! Thus is the activity of man for evil, bounded by the mighty barriers of in-walling darkness and iron slumber. The oppressor's busy brain, teeming with mischief, loses its fearful energy, and for a while can devise no more mischief; the tyrant's arm sinks nerveless by his side, and is as harmless as an infant's; brutal intemperance, which otherwise would destroy the man, ends in stupor and insensibility—the man sleeps, and awakes sober—sober, which but for God's interposition, he might never have been; wickedness sleeps its awful sleep, which, however awful, is less so than the dread energy of its waking life. Meanwhile the victims of oppression and wrong sleep, and forget for awhile the blows and burdens that are laid upon them.

Nor is this all. It is a blessing that misery from *whatever* cause, finds that temporary refuge. What should we do if sorrow never slept; if the broken heart were never lulled to rest by its own moanings? Well for us that sleep comes to our rescue—

> Sleep, that knits up the ravell'd sleeve of care,
> The death of each day's life, sore labor's bath,
> Balm of hurt minds, great nature's second course;—

well for us that it comes, and lays its hand upon the burdened heart and aching brow. God "giveth his beloved sleep."

But while I have been thus discoursing on these trials of the human lot and heart, I can fancy some one saying to me—"Ah! smoothly you discourse upon these matters, sir! easily you seem to settle the points one after another; but here am I, after all, weak, struggling, sorrowful: here am I, bewildered, tossed to and fro, and fighting a hard battle: here am I," perhaps one may say, "poor, ay, poor in natural ability, poor in fortune, poor in the respect of society; nay more, impoverished by my honesty, a martyr to conscience, with *no* fair chance; depressed, forsaken, and forlorn: and yet you tell me that the laws of my being are wise, that Providence is kind, that all is well. *Well?*—God forgive my thought!—how is it well, when I am such an one, and so hard bested? Oh! why could I not have been perfectly innocent and perfectly happy? Fair domain of life and light and joy!—it is not mine! Why, in the realm of infinite power, could not such have been appointed to me?"

I do not cast reproach upon the solemn and painful question. I do not blame the cry of human sorrow that asks for light: it is my own. I do not believe that it is displeasing to the great Being who made us, that we should humbly ask why His goodness has dealt thus with us. I cannot but believe that just as a good father on earth would be pleased with that fearless but modest question from his sensitive child, so the Infinite Parent is better pleased with such question than with the usual stolid or cowering acquiescence; and that the time will come when filial piety will understand this freedom.

And I freely *say*, that if any needless but fatal and crushing weight were laid upon the world; if any law like that of Malthus on population, now sufficiently refuted—if any such law were to be discovered, proving that population must increase much faster than food, and therefore that famine or war, or some other catastrophe, is the irreversible doom of human society; if any such crack, or flaw, or jar were found in the frame of the world, which was destined to split or break it in pieces, that then I should be dumb, and have nothing to answer. But I see none such; I see nothing in the constitution of the world that is designed to ruin it; nothing that is destined, in the long run, to be prejudicial to the cause of human virtue and happiness.

It may be thought that in the complaint just now stated, there *is one* difficulty alluded to which requires attention; that is to say, that an ascendency is given to *intellect* which is not fair to virtue and conscience; that in the affairs of life, in the necessary business of life, honesty is not a match for cleverness and cunning. It is even maintained by some, that *trade*, and also that *legal practice*, cannot be carried on with a good conscience—that, at any rate, an honest man cannot succeed in them, unless it be by some immense ascendency of talent. *This* I do not believe. If it be true, what means the maxim universally received, that "honesty is the best policy?" Still I admit that, in the action of life, a rather startling ascendency is given to intellect. Doubtless it is hard for one to feel that he lacks talent, wit, capability. But the feeling, however, does not prove the fact. I have often observed that such complainant ill makes out his case. Modesty certainly is no proof of inferiority. I am inclined to think, if you begin with idiocy and go up to the highest genius, that self-complacency will be found to be in an inverse ratio. Still, as I said before, I admit, of course, that there is actual inferiority, whether a man knows it or not, and that it tells very seriously upon the fortunes of life. What then? Would you have all men made and kept equal? Surely not. Would you have keener wits precluded from gaining any, even any temporary advantage? I think that, on reflection, you would say, no. I think, indeed, that in a free system, it would be impossible.

If, indeed, there were created a class of beings on earth, of such superiority that, by mere dint of talent or cunning, they swept the board clean of all life's prizes, then a staggering problem would be presented. But it is not so. Still you say, "The case is very hard. Conscience is a hindrance to success." I insist that you mistake here, *on the whole.* I say, you are mistaken. But so far as you are *not*, *this* I say: life was given not to gain fortunes and honors, but to gain a fortune *within*, and an honor *within*, of an infinitely nobler kind.

7. In short, the discipline of this life involves trial and difficulty. Must it not—I come now to this point last—must it not be essentially the discipline of *all* moral life? Lift your eyes to the stars. Can it be essentially otherwise there? I draw no unwarranted analogies. I say nothing about circumstances. But must not the constituent elements of which we have spoken—freedom, imperfection, mistake, learning, progress—enter into all moral life? Does the Bible oppose this analogy? Certainly not; because it says nothing about the inhabitants of those worlds; nothing

of their being inhabited. We believe that they *are* inhabited—but on other grounds. Millions of creatures dwell in a drop of water; can those vast spheres be void? We cannot believe it. But we are *taught* absolutely *nothing* about the condition of their inhabitants. We are left to reason about it as wisely as we can. They may be higher than we; they may be lower; we know nothing about it. But we know this; we know that we cannot conceive of a free, moral nature, as learning, without some mistakes and some regrets. Possibly, ours may not be the lowest rank in the order of creation. One of the propositions of the celebrated Erasmus, that was brought into question before the university of Paris, was, "that he was not sure that an *angel* was more excellent than a man." If he had said he was not sure that an inhabitant of Mars or Saturn was more excellent, *i. e.*, of a higher order, than man, it would have been a pregnant doubt; and one that would receive better entertainment in this age than it did in his.

Now it is very obvious that the general tendency in men's minds, to discouragement and despondency in all their higher, their religious contemplations, must be immensely increased by this idea that they are placed in a dark, dismal, blighted world—cut off from the great fellowship of worlds. Under the common depreciation of this world, we do not see the significance, the grandeur and beauty of its discipline. We are impatient with many things, we are indifferent to more, because we do not see that our life, that all moral life, is meant to be everywhere and in every act, a moral experimenting; and thus, that nothing is mean, nothing is low in its intent. As we walk through the dusty street or the thronged mart, through the busy manufactory or the ploughed furrow, or amidst the homes of humble care or splendid opulence, we are apt to think of nothing but the present and pressing engagement. We do not see in this, a part of the great and solemn training of the worlds to wisdom and virtue. The true spiritual philosophy would dart a ray into this dusty cloud of life, which would make every particle of it brighter than gold. I say that there is not a care, nor a toil, nor a trial—not an act of business—not a cry of childhood nor a cut finger, nor a lost key, nor a threaded needle but it has its place in this training of imperfect creatures to prudence, wisdom, and sanctity.

But looking at this world alone, as many do—looking upon it as a sad and lonely world—looking upon it as invested with a cloud of low and mean cares and trials, there is, in not a few minds, a prevailing dejection every way injurious and greatly to be regretted. There is dejection especially in their religion, and naturally so. Sad and low and heavy beat the pulses of spiritual life, because we do not feel that they throb with the great moral harmonies of the universe. Sorrowful is our cry for help, because it seems to us to be solitary and alone. As outcasts and deserted, we feel as if there could be no sympathy for us in all the surrounding worlds. If we saw the same—as to its principles—the same great moral discipline in those bright spheres as in our own, and saw it to be the best possible, would it not give us courage and strength? But why should it not be so? Is not the supposition favored by all reasonable analogies?

For me, I shall venture to say, the universe is not parcelled out *thus:* here, a dark prison house; there, a city of sapphire and gold; beneath, a gulf of fire, where sink the groaning nations; and far around, heavenly heights, on whose battlements stand the shining ones;—this universe of Milton's poetry is not the universe to *me;* but lo! through worlds unnumbered and unbounded, rise the myriad ranks of being; each having its own sphere; each moral creation advancing; and all holding on their sublime career, from knowledge to knowledge, and from glory to glory, through the bright, the everlasting ages.

Such is the view of universal life—such, I mean, as I have given it at length in this discourse, is the view which commends itself to me, as the most just and reasonable, as most accordant with the infinite wisdom and goodness. I do not know how it will appear to you, my friends, but to me it is an inexpressible satisfaction. With it I can be resolute, I can be cheerful, I can be happy, amidst all the trials and difficulties of this tried life. I do not know how it will appear to you; but if I have lifted one unnecessary cloud from the face of the world, I shall not have spoken in vain.

LECTURE IX.

PROBLEMS IN MAN'S INDIVIDUAL LIFE: PHYSICAL PAIN; HEREDITARY EVIL; DEATH.

I now wish to take up some of the vexed questions in the philosophy of human life and history; some of those facts in the human condition, which are usually thought to be the most mysterious and unaccountable, the most irreconcilable with creative wisdom and goodness; such as pain, hereditary evil, death—such as polytheism and idolatry, despotism, war, slavery, and the prevalence of error. These facts naturally divide themselves into two classes: those which come home to man's individual life; and those which spread themselves over his social life. We have therefore to consider (so to speak) private problems, and social or historic problems. The first will occupy our attention in the present lecture; that is to say, pain, hereditary evil, and death.

Let us distinctly keep in mind the end which we are considering throughout these discussions. The end is human culture; not pleasure merely, not immediate enjoyment, but joy of a higher kind, the ultimate strength and nobleness of the human character; not an unconditional happiness, to be given to man as it may be given to an animal, but the higher happiness which, by the very nature of it, he is obliged to work out for himself. And the question is: Do the conditions of our being, just referred to, promote the great end? It is true that this is not the only question; for we are bound to show that these conditions are either inevitable in the constitution of things or necessary to human culture, and also that the severity of the means is not disproportioned to the value of the end.

To proceed then—with these statements in view,—here is this terrible fact of pain. And I mean now physical pain. That which is mental we have considered in a former lecture—under the head of imperfection, struggle, penitence, illusion, fluctuation, moral indefiniteness, etc. And the pain of bereavement will naturally come under our view when we speak of death. The point now before us is physical pain. And a sharp point it is. I confess for myself an exceeding dread of pain. Montaigne reckons it the one comprehensive calamity of our being—*le pire accident de notre être*—reducing all others to that. What we fear in *death*, he says, is pain; and in *poverty*, it is pain—*i. e.*, want, anxiety, hunger, thirst, cold. Be this as it may, the evil, no doubt, is sufficiently felt. There is no need to dwell upon it, in the aggregate or in the detail. It is the detail indeed, it is the individual suffering, that presses upon us as a problem to be solved, rather than the aggregate. The aggregate *affects* us, it is true, through *sympathy*, but not directly as *pain*. The illness of thousands does not make me more ill. Pain is a solitary thing. It does not require, like the misery of war, an army to produce it; nor can an army, though vast as that of Xerxes, fight off from its commander, for one minute, the pang of a toothache. It is the sharp puncture of pain in my own flesh; it is yet more, the suffering of years or of a life, that moves us to deep questioning. The *first*—bare pain—is the law, which we are to explain; the *last*—in its unusual degree or continuance—is an exception which, it may be, we cannot explain; unless indeed it shall be found to come under some one of the categories of the law.

The law is that of pain; of pain, not usually severe nor perpetual, but general, moderate, occasional. And the main question is: Is it useful?

Now, in general, we find no difficulty in answering this

question in the affirmative. Pain is a sentinel that warns us of danger. And therefore it stands upon the outposts of this citadel, the body; for pain is keenest, the surgeon's knife is felt keenest, *on the surface*. Now, be it granted, that pain does us some harm: but it saves us from worse harm. If fire did not pain, it might burn us up. If cold did not pain us, it might freeze us to death. If disease did not pain us, we might die before we knew that we were sick. If contacts, of all sorts, with surrounding objects—the woodman's axe, the carpenter's saw, the farmer's harrow—did not hurt us, they might cut and tear us all to pieces. Think of it. A knife, held by a careless hand, approaches us; it touches the skin. We start back. Why? Because there is pain. But for this, it might have entered the body, and cut some vital organ. An old Greek verse says, "The gods *sell* us the blessings they bestow." These are the best terms for *us*. They make us careful and prudent. Unconditional giving might lead to reckless squandering. Pain, then, is a teacher of prudence, of self-care. Nay, and if happiness alone were considered, it might be argued that an occasional bitter drop gives a zest to the cup of enjoyment; as hunger does to the feast, or sharp cold to the winter's fire. But in moral relations, the argument is still stronger. Here is a human soul clothed with a body, to be trained to virtue, to self-command, to spiritual strength and nobleness. Would perpetual ease and pleasure, a perpetual luxury of sensation, best do that? We know that it would not. Every wise and thoughtful man at least, knows that some pain, some sickness, some rebuke of the senses, is good for him. Such a man often feels, in long-continued states of ease and comfort, that it is time something should come to try, to discipline, to inure and ennoble his nature. He is afraid of uninterrupted enjoyment. Pain, patiently and nobly endured, peculiarly strengthens and spiritualizes the soul. Heinrich Heine says, "Only the man who has known bodily sufferings, is truly a *man*." The loftiest states of mind, and, compared with mere sensual indulgence, the happiest, are those of courageous endurance; and the martyr is often happier than the voluptuary. Cicero says, speaking of the sacrifice of Regulus, and after describing his happy fortunes—he had carried on great wars, had been twice consul, had had triumphal honors decreed to him—"nothing was so great as his death"; when, to fulfil his word, he went back to Carthage to suffer all that could be inflicted on him. "To us hearing of it," says Cicero, "it is sad; to him suffering it, it was a joy, it was a pleasure;" *erat voluptarius*. "For," he adds, "not the light and gay in their jollity, nor their wantonness, nor their laughter or jesting—companion of dissoluteness—but the serious and resolved in their endurance and constancy, are happy." * This is the general statement to be made with regard to pain. It is general *indeed*, and does not propose to cover every case.

But now, it may be asked, could not the same end have been gained, the same nobleness, the same constancy have been achieved, without pain? Which is, I think, as if one should ask, whether the wood could not have been cut into shape without the axe, or the marble without the chisel, or the gold purified without the furnace. But let us answer; and we say, not in any way that we can conceive of. First, it may have been *absolutety* inevitable in the nature of things, that a frame sensitive to pleasure should be liable to pain. This may be the explanation of that long-continued and severe pain, which presents the hardest problem in our physical life. With such causes foregoing, such a train of influences, mental, moral, or physical, as produced this terrible suffering, it may have been impossible, without a miracle, to prevent it. Ordinarily, indeed, such pain is not long continued. It destroys life, or life destroys it. *Si gravis, brevis; si longus, levis,* "if severe, brief—if long, light," is the old adage; and it is true. But if it fail, and the terrible case of protracted anguish is before us, we may be obliged to leave it under some great law of the human constitution, which makes prevention impossible. I may be

* De Finibus, ii. 20.

told that such pain does *no* good; that it breaks down mind and body together; and therefore that it *cannot*, in any way, be useful. But we do not know that. In the great cycle of eternity, all may come right. How much happier the sufferer may be forever, for this present pain, we know not. All experience, all known analogies, favor the idea of that immense remuneration.

The word remuneration, may startle some; and they may ask, if the sufferer does not deserve all this pain; not indeed, as meaning that he in particular, but that all men deserve as much. I answer, that it is very easy to talk about ill-deserving in the general and in the abstract. Do you think that you deserve to have a tooth extracted or a finger chopped off every day—or any pain as great as that, every day, for ten years in succession? But there are sufferers who endure far more than that amount of pain daily. Some pains *are* doubtless punitive; such, for instance, as follow sensual excess or gross negligence; that is very plain. Authors of a certain religious school—like McCosh on the Method of the Divine Government—sometimes write as if they had found out a great secret, unknown to philosophy, when they discover that pain is punitive; that the world is wicked, and needs and deserves chastisement. This, however, is no mystery, nor matter of doubt. But it will not do to bring *all* pain under this category; to resort, with Leibnitz, to the "evil of sin" as the sole "reason for the evil of pain." Some pain in a sensitive organization, and sometimes great pain, may be inevitable. If it is not, let some one answer me this question: why do *animals* suffer? *They* have not sinned.

But, secondly, if pain be not absolutely inevitable, it is relatively inevitable; it is necessary, that is to say, to the intellectual and moral training of humanity.

To see this, it is necessary to observe two things. One is, that every physical organism as it befits a higher nature is endowed with a more susceptible nervous constitution. We see this gradation in fishes, bugs, birds, and quadrupeds.

In man the highest point is attained. *He* is clothed all over with a network of nervous tissues. These minister to a higher than animal culture. Do you wish that your watch was a stone, that it might not get out of order? To escape neuralgia, would you be a fish or an ostrich?

The other thing to be noted is, that for moral purposes, this exposure to pain is still more manifestly inevitable. It is a less evil, preferred to a greater; one of which *is unavoidable.* It is only necessary to state the case, to see the conclusion. Give a finite and free nature; give a body for its training; fill that body with perpetual enjoyment; let no amount of negligence or recklessness hurt it; let no excess, no intemperance nor debauchery, no indulgence, bring retributive and disciplinary suffering into it; and the ruin of this being would be as certain as his existence. Is there too *much* of this restraint and counteraction in the world? We know there is not. I may struggle against this conclusion; but I do not see how I can get rid of it. I would have man moral and free, and I cannot have him infinite; I would have him win the prize of immortal virtue; I would have the hostile tendencies of his ignorance and wilfulness checked, controlled: I see that pain is such a restraint; I must confess it to be good.

Nor does the immortal prize cost too dear. We are in an unfair situation for the argument *now.* We are in the midst of the discipline, and have not yet experienced the full result. We are in the battle, and have not won the day. But if ever the day come when we shall rise to the height of the immortal victory, well shall we know that it is worth all that it costs; ay, and infinitely more. Nay, many feel that now, and bless their adversity as a greater benefactor to them, than ever was their prosperity.

But let us come to that form of evil—be it suffering, sickness, mental disease, or unhappy temperament—that is *hereditary.* This, it may be thought, is far harder to account for. It may be said that it is an injustice; "the fathers have eaten sour grapes, and the *children's* teeth are set on edge." Is not *that* hard? And can it be expected to be useful? No; not if all pain must be regarded as punitive, in order to be profitable; for this plainly is not. But suppose that in the best possible system of things, the best for all, the best for the sufferer, this pain, this thread of suffering in the great and useful bond of hereditary transmission, is a thing that could not be extricated, without tearing the system all to pieces; would not that alter the case? And what, after all, is there that is so peculiar or strange in the case? An incendiary sets fire to the city, and my house is burned. A flood pours down the valley, and sweeps away my mill. In either case, I am an innocent sufferer. What then? Would I destroy the quality of fire, or stop the spring freshet? I belong to a general system. If everything in it conspired for my benefit, it would not be general. It is impossible that general laws, those, for instance, of heat, cold, wind, rain, should work no inconvenience nor ill to anybody. I want rain when my neighbor wants the sun. I want a wind when he wants a calm. The law that is good for all, must expose some to harm. Why should exemption be demanded from the law of hereditary transmission—provided it be a good law? What harm or wrong does it, more than any other general law?

But now consider, that it *is*, in fact, a law of immense utility. First, it lies, I think, at the foundation of *nationality*. What is it that makes the Frenchman so different from the Italian or German, or Englishman? It is not climate; it is not situation alone; it is not the train of historic events. Back and beyond all these, we must go to something in the blood, in the temperament, that makes a Frenchman a Frenchman; something which is propagated from age to age; and which thus creates those separate schools of culture, called nations. It is well that they are separate; that they have separate governments, institutions, literature; that they should be working out experiments by themselves, free from foreign influences, sentiments, vices; experiments which may ultimately inure to the benefit of the whole. This may be the final cause of the difference of languages—to keep people separate. I am sure I am glad that the French literature cannot pour its unobstructed tide into the channels of common reading in this country. The better things—science, philosophy, do come, through the investigations of learned men; the worse things, the dregs of popular literature, are mainly kept out.

Next to the bond of nationality, and stronger, and more necessary and useful, is the family bond; and this, I think, is created by the law of hereditary transmission. I say, not the family, but the family *bond*—that mysterious affinity, which is involved in the relation of kindred. I shall have occasion in another connection to speak of the descent of property, and may fairly add the weight of that consideration to what I am now saying; but I speak now of the descent of character; of that congruity, that sympathy, that union, that oneness, which is made by affinity. It is a bond, not only of indescribable interest, but of incalculable utility; the very heart's hold in this world, upon unpurchased affection, assured confidence, comfort, and happiness. The words parent, child, brother, sister—there are no words like these. And even if the word friend, is a higher and more awful word, yet to how few, in its highest sense, can it be applied! There doubtless are some persons, of singularly attractive and attaching natures, or of certain cosmopolitan habitudes, who can do better than others, without the family bond. But how many, amidst the coldness and indifference of the world, would wander through life in sad isolation, feeling that they had none to care for them, if they could not return and lean upon the bosom of domestic affection! Amidst the wide-flowing fibres of human feeling, amidst the wilfulness and recklessness of men's passions and regards, are set these fast knots, these ties of kindred, to hold the social world together; nay, and they link together family after family in succession, and thus become the binding ties of generation to generation, and of age to age.

Now I suppose it is obvious, that if anything is heredi

tary; if influence, temperament, character, the very life-blood, flows down from sire to son; if good or bad name descends, then some evil must pass on along with the good. The one cannot be separated from the other. Nay, and observe that the general influence of all this must be good. The very thought of this transmission must be salutary. What a premium upon good conduct is it, and what a tremendous admonition to bad conduct! Many a tempted man has been startled and struck to the heart with that thought—that his children may inherit his passions, his vices, his diseases. Nature within us, keeps a stricter account with us than we think. It expects us to do right; and so exquisitely is everything adjusted within us and around us, that we can never do wrong with impunity. In all these awful depths of humanity and life, there is no hiding place where evil can be buried forever. It may be cloaked in secrecy or decency all our lives, and yet break out in misleading and misery to our children, and to our children's children; ay, "unto the third and fourth generation."

But the subject to which I intended to devote the principal part of this lecture, is the end of earthly pains and of the human generations—the solemn departure from this life.

Three great facts, says the Italian Vico, are everywhere found, embedded in the foundations of human society: "worship, marriage and burial." Among all nations, in all ages, exist these solemn usages; and without them, human society could not exist. They are not mere facts, and universal facts; but their significance is manifest; they are essential ministrations to the moral culture of the human race.

The rites of sepulture are as peculiar to man as those of worship or marriage. Man is the only being on earth that buries his dead. This usage is the expression of a sentiment, far beyond the reach of animal instinct. It is not mere convenience that suggests the practice. It is a sentiment; it is a sense of fitness; it is a dictate of respect for the venerable form of humanity; it is to garner up its sacred dust as reverently as if it were laid in a royal mausoleum, where,

> "Nor steel, nor poison,
> Malice domestic, foreign levy, nothing,
> Can touch it further."

Man marks as holy the spot where he lays down the frame of the spirit's life to its "dread repose;" and over those holy remains he builds the sepulchre, the tomb, the pyramid. He builds them as monuments of veneration and affection; as testimonials to the solemn import of death, and to the hope of immortality.

It is in this light that I am now to contemplate death; not as a bare fact, not as the simple ceasing of life—for animals too die—but as clothed with moral sentiments, and as ministering to the moral improvement of mankind.

By the unreflecting mass of men, death is regarded simply as the greatest of evils. They survey its ravages with dread and horror. They see no beneficent agencies in the appointment; they scarcely see it as an appointment at all. The behold its approach to their own dwelling, not in the spirit of calm philosophy or resignation, but simply with a desire to resist its entrance. To "deliver those who all their lifetime are in bondage through fear of death," was one express design of Christianity; but only in a few minds has this design been fulfilled. Death is still regarded, not as an ordinance, but as a catastrophe. It is like the earthquake to the material world; that which whelms all. It is the one calamity; that which strikes a deeper shaft into the world than any other. It is the fixed doom, which makes all other calamity light and phenomenal. The world trembles at it, grows pale before it, as it trembles and grows pale before nothing else. Nay, and with reflecting persons, I think, the feeling that they *must die*, is usually the feeling as of some stern necessity. "Now let me depart: it is good for me to go hence," is a language sometimes heard; but it is rare. That dark veil, at the termination of the view, there forever suspended, casts a shade over the whole of life.

Can it have been meant, is it reasonable, that an event so necessary, so universal, and appointed doubtless in wisdom and goodness, should be thus regarded? For death, it is evident, in fact, if not in form, is a part of the original world-plan. I know that it is commonly looked upon as the consequence of sin, the consequence of the fall. But observe the language in which this doom, supposed to be consequent upon the fall of man, is pronounced. It is in the third chapter of Genesis. It is a doom, in general, of toil and pain and sorrow; and when death is mentioned, it is in these terms: "In the sweat of thy face shalt thou eat bread, *till* thou return unto the ground; *for* out of it wast thou taken; for *dust thou art, and* unto dust shalt thou return." "*Till* thou return to the ground." This then is represented as a part of the already appointed ordination of nature. "*For* out of it wast thou taken." The reason assigned has no reference to the fall, but to the constitution of human nature. "For dust thou art, and unto dust shalt thou return." That is, thou shalt die, for thou art naturally mortal; earth has part in thee, and shall reclaim her own.

I have no wish to strain this language to the support of any theory; and perhaps it *does* imply that if Adam had stood in innocence, the doom, or rather the present form of that doom, might have been averted; but then it certainly *does* imply also that it was the natural consequence of the human conformation. Saint Paul indeed says, that "death came into the world by sin;" but he may mean, death figuratively, *i. e.*, misery; as where he says, "the commandment which was ordained to life, I found to be to *death, i. e.*, to misery, to despair. Some able commentators have been of this opinion.* But whether it be so or not, is not material to the view I take; which is this—that there is a wide distinction to be made between death, as a gloomy, fearful, distressful event, *and* simple departure from this life. "That

* See Koppe on Romans v. 12.

death," says Jeremy Taylor, "which God threatened to Adam, and which passed upon his posterity, is not the going out of this world, but the manner of going." Grant, then, that death as a mode of departure were the consequence of sin, yet the simple exit from this life, the return of the body to the dust, is evidently a part of the original plan. It belongs to the constitution of man and of the world.

Dissolution, death, is that to which the human body tends by its essential constitution. It is as much in the natural course of things as childhood, youth, manhood, age. The earth too was evidently made for transition, not for permanent abode to its inhabitants. If successive generations enter it, generations in succession must leave it. Its supplies of *food* are limited. Its accumulating generations could not even *stand* upon it. One therefore must give place to another. If not, there would have been no place for *us*, at any rate; *we* should not have been here to discuss the matter, anyway.

All this is but saying that each generation must die. In this sense, therefore, death was a part of the original plan; the departure from this world, that is to say, was a part of it; even as that most ancient, Scripture record of it implies. But still, doubtless, this departure may have assumed a particular character in consequence of sin. It may be, I repeat, a *death*, dark and fearful—distressful both to body and mind. Vice, for instance, brings on disease; and disease produces death: and this death, thus premature and agonizing, is the fruit of sin. And doubtless in many ways and in every way, departure from this world must be a more afflictive event, both to the sufferer and to survivors, in consequence of our moral darkness, wandering, and weakness.

Nevertheless—for I must insist upon this point—the departure, in *some* way, is inevitable. The over-crowded dwelling must dismiss some of its inmates; the over-populous nation must send out colonies. Thus must the world, so to speak, colonize its inhabitants, translate them to another country. Else death would come amidst horrors now unknown ; amidst the agonies of famine and the suffocation of fulness.

I do not know whether I succeed in the attempt; but I wish to impress upon your minds the conviction, that man's life on earth could not have been meant to be immortal; that death, considered as a simple exit from this world, must have been as certainly a part of the original plan, as birth; that, if the system of the world is capable of defence, this inevitable part of it must be; in fine, that if God is good, this ordination must be a good, and not an evil. For, so long as this natural and wise limitation of the period of life is looked upon as an unnatural and dreadful catastrophe—as wreck and ruin to the genuine, all-comprehending order of nature, and not a legitimate and beneficent part of it—it is in vain that we speak of it, and urge the grounds for placing it among the wise and good ordinances of our being.

Let us now consider this event, first, in its circumstances, and then, in its direct ministration to the great ends of our being. The circumstances to which I refer are the isolation that attends it, and the disease and suffering that usually conduct to it; and the question may arise—why these arrangements, so full of pain and affliction?

First, the event is isolated. "Alas!" one may say, "earth does *not* colonize its inhabitants; it does not dismiss them in tribes and families; then were we spared the sorrows of bereavement; one by one men depart for the spirit land." But let us see how important *this* arrangement is, not only to human culture, but to the general intent and economy of the human condition. What would become of the cultivation of the earth, where would be the transmitted fruits of experience, and in what state would be the whole training of the human race, if men departed for the other life in companies, in families? Take away that one bond from the world—inheritance, inheritance of property and experience; and the world could not stand in its present order; it would fall to pieces. Houses, estates would decay, if none, neither friends nor children, none for whom we had any regard, were to take them from our hands; all forecast, prudence, industry would die out of the world; like the animal tribes, each generation would have to take up the lesson anew. It is only upon the plan of single, isolated departures from the world, that its instruction can be kept up, or its progress carried forward. If nations, generations died off at once, all the labors of humanity would only weave its winding sheet. But now, throughout the mighty frame of society, unnumbered hands sink from the loom at every moment, and unnumbered new ones rise, to ply the great task; and thus is woven the unbroken web of ever-progressive human fortunes.

Next, let us consider the illness that is usually the precursor of death. Why, it may be said, the pains of mortal disease? Why so much suffering that is apparently useless, *i. e.*, morally useless? I might answer, holding to the strict coherence and continuity of the present and future life, that it is no more useless than any disciplinary pain. But I am looking now only at the general economy of the human condition; the advantage or disadvantage for this life. And in this view, it may be assumed, without regard to the moral issue, that it is desirable, almost necessary, that men should have some premonition of their departure from this world; that they should not drop instantly from the scene. They wish to give directions and make arrangements for the future. Endless difficulty and confusion would arise with regard to property, to trusts, to important matters involving the welfare and comfort of survivors, without this final disposition. And then with regard to the pain of a last illness, simply considered; suppose the premonition were to be distinctly given in some other way, and long enough previous to the event; suppose there were something in the human system that gave the note of preparation, like the clock before it strikes the hour: does not the illness that slowly breaks the tie to life and makes the sufferer willing, and perhaps desirous to depart, cause less *pain* than would be felt in one week passed in health, under the doom of that fearful certainty? For one, in the midst of health and enjoyment, in the fresh and vivid sense of what life is, and of all its ties, to be told that he shall die next Monday; what a dread interval would it be—at least to most men! I cannot doubt that the present mode of our dismission from life is more *merciful* than that would be. "No escape!" says Egmont in Goethe's drama—(he was doomed to the scaffold by the cruel Duke of Alva)—"no escape! Sweet life! beautiful, kindly wont of being and action!—from *thee* shall I part—so quietly part? Not in the tumult of battle, nor amidst the noise of arms, dost thou give thy swift farewell; thou takest no hasty leave—cuttest not short the moment of parting. I shall take thy hand—look yet awhile into thine eyes—feel all lovingly thy beauty, thy preciousness—then tear myself away—and say, farewell!" More merciful, I repeat, than this, is God's ordinance of sickness and pain as the pathway to the grave.

I will venture to add that death sometimes brings specific relief—from evils for which there is no other remedy; from sickness and pain which nothing else can end; from painful relations, from mental difficulties, from embarrassing crises in life, of which nothing else can break the knot, the bondage and sorrow. It is not always hard to die. There are those, and more of them perhaps than we think, who *desire* to die. I have looked upon those, in sad relations to one another, or to the world, of whom I have said, "Nothing that I see but death can help you." And there are persons, involved in such *moral* emergencies—so desperate and irremediable—that they are fain to say, "Let me die; let death deliver me; I would begin anew; I would try again." There may be more of them, I repeat, than we think.

But let us now proceed to the main and final question—the moral question, to be examined: whether the highest culture, the safety and happiness of this life, do not make the appointed departure from it, however naturally unwelcome, actually necessary, and even desirable. In this view, I am to speak of death, not merely as the end of this life, but as the passage to another.

The learned Bishop Warburton, assuming, though, as I think, erroneously assuming, that the Hebrews had no knowledge of a future life, has gone into a very elaborate argument to show that Moses must have had a divine Legation, attested by miracles. For he maintained that without the expectation of future rewards and punishments, nothing *but* a special and miraculous interposition could hold a people in the bonds of moral order. Doubtless the argument is just, whatever may be thought of the premises. What could keep in any bounds the swellings of ambition, pride, cruelty, luxury, and licentiousness, did not death interpose its dread barrier? It is commonly called "the king of terrors;" as if in that character it were to be deprecated. But its terrors are for those who most need them. And well is it, that that shadowy king stands in the path, and says to self-indulgence, "remember!" and to oppression, "beware!"—else were not the earth habitable.

But I wish to speak of this event in its widest relations to human improvement; not merely as a terror, but as every way a wisely appointed and good discipline.

Death is an epoch in our moral course. A youth at school is far more likely to be affected by the prospect of an approaching examination, than by his general responsibility. *Then* he is to answer for himself. *Then* his learning is to be brought to the test. *Then* his fidelity or neglect is distinctly to appear. Such is the coming hour of death to the moral learner. It brings the sense of obligation to a point, from which there is no escape. It brings the great moral trial of life to a solemn issue. Doubtless there is a higher thought, a larger view, for the manhood of reason; but in this respect, most men are yet children, and need the discipline of children. Doubtless the moment that lies in the distance of a thousand years, is to answer for the moment that is now passing; the whole vast future is bound to the present hour, by the indissoluble chain of cause and effect;

but for creatures of our limited capacity, that prospect is too general; and it seems expedient that there should be distinct steps in our progress; that manhood, for instance, should distinctly answer for youth, and age for manhood; and in like manner, the immediate future life, for the life that now is.

Again, the nearness of the event has its purpose. If any one should ask why the allotted term of man's existence on earth should be so brief, I still answer, that I see in this a wise ordination. The advancement of the world depends on the earlier vigor and flexibility of life. I say not upon young men and women—for that seems to me one of the follies of our time—but upon the age between twenty-five and sixty-five. After that, opinions usually become settled, habits fixed; and the world may not look for new ideas, innovating enterprises, nor the enthusiasm to prosecute them. Inventions, reforms are seldom to be seen in old age. Age has indeed its part to act; to guide the zeal and restrain the rashness of the young. Its experience and wisdom are to be respected; far more, I think, than they are at this day; but old men, generally, are not the working men of the world. What then is the ordinance that is to meet this condition of humanity? The scythe of death mows down the generations, that it may provide for a more vigorous growth. The axe, that "is laid at the root," cuts away the aged trees, that younger and fairer ones may shoot up in their stead. The builder removes fixtures, that he may prepare for improvements. Thus the world is continually recruited with fresh strength, and is pervaded with an imaginative and flexible enterprise; and thus its arts are advanced; its fields are cultivated with increasing skill; its houses are built on improved plans; its science and literature are constantly rising; and its religious systems are advancing to higher truths and wider ranges of vision. Death, then, grim and fearful as it is accounted, is, like decay in nature, the constant improver, enricher, and beautifier of the world.

Yet further, the inevitableness of the coming change is

a weighty element of its moral power. The certainty of it; the feeling that *nothing* can stay the event; that no hoard of gold, nor crown of honor, nor crowd of cares, nor pressure of engagements, nor thronging visions of coming prosperity, nor momentous crisis in affairs, can ward off the inevitable hour—how does that feeling penetrate through the whole of life, and sober, at times, the wildest levity, and subdue the haughtiest ambition! The Grecian Epaminondas, when told that a distinguished general had died while the battle was raging, exclaimed, "Ye gods! how can a man find time to die, at a moment like this!" But every man must find time to die! Ay, the man of blood, whose ruthless sword has cut down its thousands and ten thousands; who was deaf to the groans and pleadings of human misery; who has crushed ten thousand human hearts beneath his blood-stained car—Tamerlane or Alaric, Cæsar or Napoleon—he has, in God's dread forbearance, found a time to kill; but he has also, in God's awful justice, found a time to die! And the private man, the man who dwells in the deepest seclusion; who lives hidden and shrouded from the public eye; who draws the veil of midnight around his deeds; that man still feels that an eye is upon him; he is obliged to confront the awful image of death; he cannot escape. "But I must die!" is a thought that steals upon many a worldly dream, and many a silent rumination. He feels it, though no solemn message, as in the Egyptian feasts, take up the admonition and say, "Remember! thou must die!"

Yet not with terror only, but with tenderness does death touch the human heart—touches it with a gracious sympathy and sorrow. One may know the house, where death has set his mark, long after the time. Traces are left in its affections, that are never worn out. Traces are left *in memoriam*, in poetry, in all human sentiment. Death is not the sundering, but the consecration of friendship. It strengthens that holy bond. It makes the departed dearer. It gives new power and sanctity to their example. It in vests their virtues with the radiance of angel beauty. It canonizes them as patron saints and guardian angels of the household.

Nor could it fulfil its high mission, if men departed from the world in families, in tribes, in generations. Then indeed were we spared the sorrows of bereavement; but at the expense of much that is most sacred in life. If families were dismissed from life together, they would inevitably become selfish; contracting their thoughts and affections within those domestic spheres, in which all their destinies were bound up. If generations were mowed down at once, like the ripened harvests, then had there been no history of public deeds nor record of private worth. The invisible presence of virtue that now pervades and hallows the earth, that consecrates our dwellings, and makes them far more than the abodes of life, would be withdrawn from the fellowship of men; and the signal lights of heroic example that are now shining through the ages, would all go out in utter darkness. A working-day world, a utilitarian world, we should have; shut up to the cares and interests of the generation that is passing over it; not as now a world that is overspread with the mounds of departed nations, with the dust of buried empire—the theatre of majestic history, the heritage of genius, the altar of holy martyrdom. The earth is no longer the mere material globe that, at the beginning, rolled round its parent sun: it is the tomb of generations, the monument of ages. From out of its hollow recesses and echoing caverns, what oracles come! Upon its majestic brow, what names are written—Assyria, Egypt, Phœnicia, Greece, Rome; the Goth, the Gaul, the Saxon, the Slavonic race, and races of the old, the dateless American time! The very dwellings, the cities of the world have become monumental. *Not* present convenience, *not* bustling activity alone, but the sanctity of death makes them what they are. Their walls have echoed to joys and sorrows that have passed away. High, heroic hearts have throbbed within them, that beat no more; pain and patience have built altars in them, to lowly resignation and prayer; the last sigh has ascended from them, and, as holy incense, consecrated them for ever. Oh! not the *present* alone is here; but the image of the majestic past stalks through the world, and casts its solemn mantle over the life of to-day. We live, that we may garner up the treasures of humanity, and, adding to them the little that we can, transmit them to those that come after. We survive, with whatever pain to ourselves, that virtue may not die. We guard the holy bequest. See we to it, that it waste not, nor dwindle in our hands!

Nay, in another respect, the grandeur of death imparts a reflected dignity to life. God puts honor on the being to whom He says, "Thou shalt die!"—to whom He does not veil the event, as He does to animal natures, but unfolds the clear prospect. He, to whom the grandest achievement of courage and heroism should be proposed, could not be a mean creature. But every man is to meet the grandeur of death. In these mortal lists he stands—ay, the youth, the child, the frailest spirit that ever was clothed with the habiliments of mortality; and he knows that he is to meet a crisis more sublime and mysterious than any other, that ever challenged mortal courage. The meanest man lives with that prospect before him. More than that which makes heroism sublime, it is his to encounter.

Yes, and in the bosom of death are powers greater than itself. I have *seen* them; I have seen them triumph, when death was nearest and mightiest; and I believe in them—I *believe* in those inborn powers of life and immortality, more than I believe in death. They will bear me up more than death will weigh me down. I live; and this living, conscious being which I am to-day, is a greater wonder to me than it is that I should go on and on. How I *came to be*, astonishes me far more, than how I should *continue* to be. And if I am to continue, if I am to live for ever, I must have a realm fitted for such life. Eternity of being must have infinitude of space for its range. I would visit other worlds; and especially does the desire grow intenser, as the boundless splendors of the starry heavens are unfolded wider and wider. But I cannot go to them—I cannot skirt the coasts of Sirius and the Pleiades, *with this body*. Then—some time—in God's good time—let it drop. Let my spirit wander free. Let this body drop; as when one leaves the vehicle that had borne him on a journey—to ascend some lofty mountain—to lift his gaze to wider heavens and a vaster horizon. So let my spirit wander free—and far. Let it wander through the realm of infinite good; its range as unconfined as its nature; its faith, the faith of Christ; its hope, a hope full of immortality!

LECTURE X.

HISTORIC PROBLEMS: POLYTHEISM—DESPOTISM—WAR—SLAVERY—THE PREVALENCE AND MINISTRY OF ERROR, IN THE SYSTEM OF THE WORLD.

I MUST now take up the great social problems to which I referred in my last lecture—Polytheism, Despotism, War, Slavery, and that problem which embraces them all: the Prevalence and Ministry of Error.

"A grim and fearful host of ills," it may be said, "to preside over the destiny of the human race; or if not to preside, to prevail—to have darkened the world with fear, to have bound it in chains, to have torn it with violence, from the beginning; to have led the generations of men in mazes of darkness and wandering through all ages! How can such things have been ordained, or permitted? How in any way could such things have been the agencies of a good and wise Providence?"

Now, in dealing with these questions, we must take along with us what has been already said upon the very grounds and principles of the human problem. Man, as a moral being, must of necessity be free; as a created being, he must be imperfect and ignorant; as a being whose destiny it is to improve, he must *begin* somewhere; nay, as a being, all whose knowledge and virtue are to be acquired, he must begin at a point where he has *no* virtue or knowledge; *i. e.*, he must begin in infancy. Look, then, at this being, and consider what must be the inevitable laws of his development, and what the probable course of it. Do not ask why this or that could not have been hindered; but see that the *principle* of hindrance would be fatal to the system; that the demand for divine interference made by millions, irretrievably complicates, and, if listened to, ruins all. See man, then, as he is and must be. Imperfect, ignorant, infantile—yet endowed with powerful energies and impulses, without which he would be nothing—he is placed upon the earth to *do what he pleases.* Deprive him of the *liberty* to do so, and you unmake the man. Deprive him of his imperfection, his ignorance, his exposure to error, and you make him God. Or yet once more: interfere with his free development, by incessant miracles to ward off the evils into which he falls, and you break up the whole regular training on which that development depends. Take the case of any evil, any wrong, any misery that ever was inflicted, and consider it. The assassin's arm is raised to murder. Almighty power could arrest it; but then the agent would not be free. Two armies are about to rush into battle. Almighty power could in an instant chain these hosts like statues to the earth; but then they would not be free—would not be men.

I must desire you further to take it into the account, not only that *some* evils were likely to flow from such a constitution of things, but that *these very evils* which we are to consider were the natural, if not inevitable, developments of human ignorance and weakness; nay, and of the higher human sentiments too: of the feelings of *right* and of *religion.* Not from some dark cavern are they let loose, like avenging furies; not from some fabled Pandora's box have they issued, but from the bosom of humanity; nor from any constitutional badness of nature, but from passions, from errors, from mistakes, from collisions, from circumstances necessarily attaching to this nature. I pray you to look more nearly into these evils than you do when you generalize and sum them up into one portentous and crushing mass of gratuitous calamity and wrong. Thus, error, for instance—religious error, superstition in many forms—*could* man escape it? Thus, again, in rude and lawless times, was not the governing hand likely to hold things with a strong grasp—to be despotic and oppressive? And when questions arose between nations, was it not natural that they should resort to physical force—*i. e.*, to war? Could rude barbarians stand still to argue? Could they settle, could they understand any code of international law? Was it not almost inevitable that they should fight? If the question was about a piece of land, or a fishery, was there anything else for them to do but to endeavor to push one another from the disputed possession? Supposing the parties to be honest—supposing that each believed the thing in question to belong to him—supposing there was no umpire to which they could appeal; must not a natural sense of *justice* have led them to strive for their right? War is ordinarily the clash of opinions. "You have got that which is mine," one says; "you will not give it to me; you will not listen to my just claims for it: then I must take it from you." In fact, must not this, where the case arises, be the language of to-day? But certainly, where neither right nor reason would be listened to, must not the party wronged, or conceiving himself to be wronged, enforce his claim with the strong arm—or else sit down, abused, crushed, robbed, and despoiled on every hand?

Doubtless there has been violence enough in the world which has had no such plea. I only wished to show that it is not *all* blank malignity nor wilful error which has filled the world with darkness and sorrow. And do you not suppose, let me ask, that He who made the world foresaw all this? And are sin and pain agreeable to Infinite Benevolence? Must you not believe that God would have prevented them, had there not been obstacles to prevention in the very nature of things and in the welfare of the beings he made?

It is of some such intrinsic obstacle, I think, that Plato speaks, under the name of "necessity,"—a something inevitably and inextricably interwoven with the constitution of things, and preventing the exclusion of evil and misery from the world. He appears to me obscurely to intimate in a passage of the Timæus, that view of the origin of evil which I have endeavored plainly to set forth in these lectures as the true and only solution of that dark problem. His mind evidently had not *settled* upon any theory. Sometimes he speaks of a malignant *being*, next in power to God, as having introduced evil into the creation; sometimes of dark, intractable, obstinate *matter*, as the source of evil; for these old ideas of Zoroaster seem to have pervaded all antiquity. But in the Timæus we find him speaking of "*necessity*" as some strong and apparently opposing power, "on which," to use the language of a learned commentator,* "on which the divine energy was constantly exercised, not so much in directly overcoming as in controlling and directing it to the accomplishment of the Divine purposes." "But since," says Plato, "mind (*i. e.*, the Supreme Mind) rules necessity by persuading her to bring to the best results the most of things as they are generated (or made); thus in this way, through necessity overcome by rational persuasion, this universe received its construction;" or was fashioned into its present order.

"By rational persuasion," says Plato, *i. e.*, not by irresistible coercion, but by a wise urging and turning of things that are unavoidably liable to evil, to good account. This is the light, in fact, in which I am about to speak of the special problems which are now before us.

Indeed, our Holy Scriptures teach a doctrine not dissimilar to this; as when they say that "God causes the wrath of man to praise him, and the remainder of wrath he restrains;" as when they say that he permitted certain things to the Hebrew people "because of the hardness of their hearts," *i. e.*, because they could bear no better; as when they say, "I gave them statutes that were not good," *i. e.*, not absolutely good—not in themselves desirable, but tolerated, and turned to good account.

I know there are those who regard human superstition,

* Prof. Tayler Lewis on "Plato against the Atheists," p. 217.

oppression and strife, simply and only as the results of a depraved nature; who see no farther into the great problem of human fortunes; who, as they look back upon the history of the world, only exclaim, "See what a wicked race!" But the philosophy of human life and history, and, as I conceive, a just reverence for the Divine Providence, demand another consideration of things. It would be deplorable for us to leave the world-story in that blank abstraction. It would quench all good faith in the past, and all good hope of the future. It would be strange, also—nay, incredible, that human nature and history should want all those evidences of wise and good design of which the material world is full.

I say, then, and lay down these three propositions: First, that the bad institutions and usages of the world, whether religious, political, or warlike, have been better than none; secondly, that they have been the only ones in every age that the world could then receive; and thirdly, that they have ministered to human energy and improvement, and ultimately to human happiness.

First, they have been better than none. Idolatry has been better than no religion; superstition than no restraint; despotism than no government. War itself has been better than no activity—better than savage stupor and indolence, or stupid submission to wrong. It has developed more strength, more heroism, more virtue, than absolute languor or moral indifference would have done. The strife of man with man in the assertion of rights, or what were deemed to be rights, was better than a total disregard of all right. For suppose that one man or nation does another man or nation a gross wrong; taking away with the strong hand lands, goods, property, rights—nay, wife and children. The invading nation carries them off! Would you have the wrong quietly acquiesced in—submitted to in dull stupidity? It would be to deny our humanity. No, we would have every man feel the right, and fairly assert and defend it. We would have *force* applied for that end where it is necessary. And this force, intervening in national questions, is war. Some wars have been right, though many have been wrong. We must not, for the abuses of a principle, however enormous, discard the principle. It is right to assert our rights, and to compel others, if we cannot persuade them, to abstain from wrong. This appertains to our humanity. A *sense* of right must so assert itself; and if rights could be violated, and no resistance, no contention followed, humanity itself would be dead.

Secondly, the institutions and usages of every age have been the only ones it could receive. The mind of every age has been bodied forth in its religious systems, in its political forms, in its activity, whatever that activity has been. Its action, its idea of right, and its mode of righting itself, would have been better if its mind had been more improved. Each form of development has been that which the spirit of the time gave to it.

Let us state this point, however, with proper care and qualification. In one respect, the rudest age is susceptible of *high teaching*—is capable of receiving the very highest ideals. There are certain innate ideas of right, of justice, of religion—eternal intuitions—to which appeal may always be made. To these, prophets and wise men *have* ever appealed, and met an unhesitating response. But institutions, usages, are different things. These must be in general accordance with the culture of a people. Yet even here there is still room for the reformer: because the institutions are ever falling behind the culture, and need to be reformed. Nevertheless, the reform in any given period, could not proceed beyond a certain point.

In ages of darkness and ignorance and materialism, superstition was inevitable; oppression was inevitable; war was inevitable. Men could not arrive at once, at refined and spiritual ideas of God, or at those ideas of moral justice that should banish oppression and war. They could not comprehend, they could not agree upon, those principles that should supersede coercion and strife with the strong hand. Alas! the world does not comprehend them yet. But to the *infant* world it had been as impossible to teach the highest ideas of religion, of law, and of the right social relationships, as it would be to instruct one of our infant schools in the mathematics, in astronomy, and moral philosophy.

Thirdly, the defective religion, polity, and intercourse of the nations have ministered to their energy, improvement, and happiness. They have not only been better than none; they have not only been, in general, as good as the general mind could receive; but they have done good. This observation opens the whole field of our present discussion.

But in entering upon it, I wish carefully to state the ground upon which I proceed. I said in my opening lecture, that in the prosecution of the subject, I had nothing more at heart than to show how this system of human free action, while necessarily free, in order to *be* a *moral* system, is nevertheless governed and controlled so as to bring about good ends. But I seek now, in this connection, to make the distinction between *freedom* and *control*—between the erring of the human will and the overruling of it for good—perfectly explicit and clear. In man as a free agent, there is, of necessity, the power and liability to err, to go wrong. Acting freely, he runs into polytheism and idolatry; he builds up despotic governments; he wages cruel war; he oppresses his fellow. Now in this mass of error and evil, there are two elements. There was *mistake*, incident to the infancy and ignorance of the world. Or, there was *theoretical imperfection*—as, for instance, in idolatry and despotism—and yet, withal, a certain fitness for the time. And there was downright and wicked *hate*, and *cruelty*. Now *this* I am not to defend. I do not say, with some, that evil is good; that there is no evil in the universe. I say and feel that hate and cruelty are evil and wrong and odious. But I maintain that out of this whole system—out of mistake and imperfection, and in spite of hate and wrong, good has come; and *this* it is my simple and sole business to show. It is not to defend human erring; not to lessen my own or *your* sense of it; but to show the guardianship over it of a divine and guiding Providence.

There is one point, especially, on which I admit all that can be charged upon human erring; and that is, the abuse of power; of power in religion, of power in government; of power military, feudal, social, individual. Power of *every kind* has been abused, beyond anything else that man has possessed. There is nothing that distresses me in the contemplation of past ages or of the present age, like the *inhumanity* of power. That which furnishes the noblest opportunity for doing good, has been turned into the most frightful instrument of cruelty and oppression. "Man's inhumanity to man"—whether it be a doom to the prison, to the rack, or the fire, or whether it be the scornful word of the superior to the inferior—I have nothing to say for it; I give it up to the righteous indignation of all just men. Let that indignation rise higher and higher; let it accumulate in mountain masses, to crush and drive the accursed thing out of the world.

What then am I to say to all this? *This*, first of all: that to a free nature, even *that hateful abuse* could not be forbidden. Man must do what he will. Here, now, to-day, *you* have power to strike down an inferior in strength or station. God does not miraculously interpose to wither the lifted arm, or to palsy the proud and scornful tongue. And then, next, I must resist the impression that all this abuse of power is a mass of unmitigated evil. I must not leave it to be supposed that this has been a godless and forsaken world. Amidst the strugglings of man with man, I must endeavor to show that all has not been intentional wrong; that there have been unavoidable mistakes; that there have been insuperable difficulties; and that there has been good amidst evil. I must endeavor also to correct our own mistakes in looking at these things; and to present the great institutions that have presided over the world, in the justest light that I can.

In the first place, then, we are to speak of polytheism

and Idolatry. And here we find immediate occasion for applying the observation just made to the *old religion*. There are mistaken views with which we have grown up from our childhood, that need to be reconsidered. For instance, beast worship, among the Egyptians, the worship of dogs, cats, and even of meaner creatures; looking at it as we have, it has, of course, always seemed to us an unspeakable degradation. In the view we have been accustomed to take of it, it might well have seemed to us, as partly it has, an *incredible* degradation. It passes belief, that any human beings should be so stupid as literally to worship the meanest reptiles. Yet more is this incredible of a cultivated people, like the Egyptians; who had carried the practical arts to a point hardly surpassed by ourselves; who had a learned priesthood, to which the Grecian sages resorted for instruction; upon one of whose temples, at Sais, was recorded that sublime inscription, expressive of the Divine nature—the sublimest of all heathen antiquity—"I am all that has been, all that is, and all that shall be. No mortal has ever raised the veil that conceals me!" *

What then, was this mysterious Existence? It was that great Life of Nature, which all the East worshipped. And no doubt, it was this great Life of Nature that the Egyptians worshipped under animal forms. In this view, Hegel maintains that the worship of animals is noway less respectable than the worship of the sun and stars.† He remarks, indeed, that there is something peculiarly incomprehensible and mysterious in the animal spirit—dumb and shut up—never articulating its thought. If we compare it with the spirit in ourselves, he says, it is clear that we less understand it; for we know ourselves by consciousness. But what is passing in the horse, the ox, or the dog, we do not know; and the idea and the observation must be familiar to us all, that "we should like to know what they think." "A black cat stealing by us in the twilight," says Hegel,

* Proclus adds, "and the fruit I have produced is the *sun!*"

† Philosophie der Geschichte, p. 258, 259.

"brings over our minds an impression as of something preternatural."

Then again, with regard to idolatry, the worship of images: the idea that these images of wood and stone were literally worshipped as the all-powerful deities who presided over the world, is utterly inadmissible. They were worshipped, doubtless, as representatives, symbols of the gods. This worship, however, became so gross that it was vehemently denounced by the Hebrew prophets; though there is reason to believe that there was a time when a species of images, called Teraphim, were recognized in the Hebrew worship.*

And with regard, in fine, to polytheism itself, great as the error was, yet it was natural, and perhaps unavoidable. The rude mind, in the infancy of the world, first awaking to the conception of unseen, stupendous, creative agencies around it, would not, perhaps *could* not, immediately learn that all these agencies centred in one Being.

But I must desire you to observe, that great as the error and the evil of polytheism were, it was not powerless, nor altogether useless. What a keen and quickened sense of religion must it have nourished! We have no *devotees* to compare with those of India and Thibet. In Lassa, the metropolis of Bhuddism, says the traveller, M. Huc, the whole population gathers at nightfall into little circles for prayer; the sound goes up from the whole city. But look at the ancient polytheism. Erring as it was, yet how strong it must have been, and intense, and ever awake! A local deity, instead of one far off; a god of the field and the stream and the grove, and of the house, and of the very hearthstone; how must it have struck the every-day and hourly thought of men! In the later ages of Grecian and Roman refinement, this religion was dying out, and so making way for another; men did not believe in the religion of their fathers, and the Christian apologists might well speak, as they did speak, of its inefficacy; but in its pristine strength, it was far from deserving that charge. Then, again, the idol, the

* See Hosea iii. 4, 5, and Newman's Hebrew Monarchy, p. 28.

visible symbol of the present deity in every household; how must it have appealed to the imagination, and the very sense! Its wooden or stony eye; how must it have seemed at times to look into the very misdeeds of men! The Catholics feel a similar influence now, and their sense of religion, whatever may be thought of it in other views, is stronger and more frequently awakened, I have no doubt, than that of many Protestants. Nay, I should doubt whether the Protestant world has not swung too far toward the limit of bare and naked spiritualism. Some sense of this I mark in that extraordinary movement some years ago, known as Puseyism, in the Church of England; in which if there were some things that I could not sympathize with, yet this tendency to reconsider and reassume some elements of the past, were it wisely controlled, I cannot help regarding as healthy and good. Then, again, and once more, the sacrifices of the old religion, the victim on the altar, the daily rising incense —all that direct and visible appeal to Heaven; how impressive must it have been to the worshipper! And every head of a household too, was a consecrated priest: now few men comparatively are priests in their families, in any sense. And when the parent took his child from its mother's bosom and sent it through the fire, a victim to Moloch—dreadful god—that offering was not hypocritical, but terribly sincere; it was not a mere form, but religion awfully in earnest; it was not mere cruelty, but the shuddering homage of religious fear—of a fear strong enough to tear the very life-cords from the palpitating heart! In all this there was much error; but in all this there was a tremendous power to bind the rude mind to religion of some sort, and to restrain its wildest excesses. The bond of religion, the dread of Divine displeasure, I am inclined to think, was *stronger* then than it is now. Men *now*, in courts of justice and in national quarrels, appeal against bad faith, to Heaven; but not perhaps with such positive impression and effect, as when they said in old time, "The gods will punish you! Neptune will awake his storms, Jupiter will launch his thunder against you! the god of the rooftree will desolate your dwelling; the god of the field will sweep down your harvests, or will send disease among your flocks!" Other things are indeed to be desired in religion besides strength, and no one would bring back the old superstition; but here, I say, was strength; here was a power over the infant world, the highest that it could receive, which guided and controlled its steps, and was leading them on to something better.

Turn now, in the second place, to the political relations of men. A hard and grinding despotism weighed upon the ancient world. Equal laws, the just rights of men, were unknown. The chieftain—patriarch, priest, or king—reigned with absolute authority. Here and there, democracies, republics sprang up, but died away as soon, and were, in fact, despotic while they lasted. And throughout the ancient world, there was no just *conception* of the equal rights of men. The many bowed down to the few with absolute, slavish, superstitious allegiance. The *people*, even in feudal Europe, says Guizot, were as timid as sheep. We see the injustice and falsity of all this. We have better theories. But what would our theories of equal rights have done, if they had been cast into the bosom of the old Asiatic nations; ay, or into the communes and kingdoms of the middle ages? Torn them all to pieces. Society could not have lived a day with these theories. The single, strong arm was necessary to bind and hold together the wild elements of the primeval world. The deep and lowly submission to it was necessary. It was more than merely necessary; it was beneficial. Absolute rule was the best thing possible; and it was attended with the *then* best possible results.

This instinct, the blind instinct of obedience, natural to rude and savage life, worked usefully in two ways. First it was a good guidance for those whose minds could not yet rise to any high or reverential obedience to *law*, or to a *political constitution*. It was well that something should attach them to the chieftain, to the king, to the head of the State.

And then the sentiment was saved from the meanness and degradation that would otherwise have belonged to it, by its being so reverential, affectionate, and disinterested. There was something affecting and beautiful, as well as fit for its time, in these old homages to superior rank. The attachment of the Scottish clansman to his chief, of the feudal retainer to his lord, was often of the most touching character. It is good to reverence *something;* and even the excess of the homage is better than the opposite extreme. I had rather pay it, than always to stand up stiffly for my rights. I like the story of the son of Ivan IV. of Russia, better than some with which our theories of equal rights might furnish us. The armies of the emperor, says the annalist, had been worsted in one or two engagements. His favorite son said, "Let *me* go and take the command." The brutal father, stung with self-reproach, jealousy and anger, felled him to the ground, with a blow, that, it was evident, must prove mortal. Struck with horror at what he had done, the emperor rolled in agony upon the floor, and offered millions to his physicians if they would save his child. The dying son, as he lay upon his couch, strove to reassure his father. "You did right," he said, "to strike me. I ought not to have asked you that question. I have offended against the laws of the empire and against you; and I deserve to die."

All power, alas! is liable to abuse, and to the grossest; but protestants against despotism as we Americans are, we are prone perhaps to do it some injustice. Certain it is, that it has often been paternal and protective, in proportion as the homage to it has been filial and affectionate. Hegel says that there was more personal freedom in the old Assyrian Empire than in Rome. In those soft Eastern climes especially, the government was paternal, the people as children, compared with the stern Roman rule and the stalwart Roman men. The Oriental despotism, compared with the Roman, was as a flowery girdle to an iron band. The Persian monarch was a sort of teacher and sage to the people;

attendant scribes, in court and camp, were ever at hand to write down his sayings; and these were deposited in the state archives, as the annals of his reign *—a tremendous environment for a man, and it must have made him thoughtful, and his speech the wiser. In the earliest times of the East, the patriarchal king sat in the gate. The Persian royal palace was *called* the Porte or Gate †—and hence the phrase Sublime Porte, to describe the Ottoman sovereignty —the patriarchal king sat in the gate, to hear complaints and award justice; and although, in later times and in crowded empires, this was, of course, impossible, yet always there was a right of personal appeal, as of children to a parent, unknown to our more complicated systems of administration. The court was a scene of magnificent hospitality: Ctesias, a Greek historian of Artaxerxes' time, says that fifteen thousand persons sat down daily at the king's table; seemingly an incredible number; according to Xenophon, it took—I know not *how* many persons to make Cambyses' bed.‡ In short, more ease, freedom, and happiness existed under these old despotisms, than we are apt to think—bad as they undoubtedly were.

But I must now turn, in the third place, to a more awful element in the world-problem; and that is war.

I have already said that it has been, and is, inevitable. In fact, unless we give up the right of self-preservation; unless we go the length of saying that any man who pleases, may take what he will of ours, or may break our limbs, or beat us to death, *without resistance from us*, we admit the principle that lies at the bottom of war. But let us consider further, whether it has not a providential place in the world, among the means of its discipline and culture.

There certainly have been worse things in the world than war. There have been states and conditions of human society, worse than that of martial conflict, and which that

* Heeren, Asiatic Nations, vol. i. p. 55, Bohn's ed.

† Ibid. p. 260.

‡ Heeren's Researches, Asiatic Nations, vol. i. p. 254.

conflict has broken up: deep-seated injustice, which nothing but a violent shock could overturn; intolerable oppression, universal corruption and licentiousness, universal effeminacy and stupor. Better that the cause of justice and right be pleaded with the sword, than not pleaded at all. I had rather see the moral sentiments, or the material interests of men, in fierce collision, than in a state of palsy and death; it is more hopeful, if not more agreeable.

Then, again, war is a means of intercourse, communication of knowledge, interfusion of ideas, between nations. In some cases, there seems no other way to lift a people out of its stupor and degradation. By means of isolation alone, China has remained the same for ages. But in times when there was no printing, and little travel, nations lay side by side, more ignorant of each other than people now are in opposite hemispheres. What, then, did a war effect? It brought nations into the presence of each other's homes, institutions, usages, arts. Thus the Northern barbarians were brought to look upon the Roman civilization. Imagine the Roman Empire to have gone on undisturbed, sinking deeper and deeper into lethargy, luxury, and corruption; and the Goths and Vandals to have remained in their rock fastnesses and woody deserts, the same brutish people. Instead of this, the invasions have given us—cultivated Europe.

But we must go to a question more radical, with regard to the influence of war upon the human character and condition. Could the world, or can it, go on nobly—go on improving—go on safely even, without this dread discipline of war? The elder Bonaparte is reported to have said, "The conscription is the everlasting root of a nation, its moral purification, the real foundation of its habits." I do not know precisely what he meant by that; but I should interpret it thus: Lay upon every family in a nation the bond of that dread liability—that one of its members may be called forth to fight and die for his country; and you put a principle of sobriety, of manliness, of sacrifice, of obedience to the law, of consecration to the common weal, into that family, which nothing else perhaps could impart to it. Who does not feel that such an inquisition coming to the household, for son, brother, or father, must search out and stir to the very heart everything loyal, heroic, ay, and religious, in it? And how many have felt this in the present solemn crisis in our country! How many have found life, with them, to be more earnest, high hearted, meditative, and prayerful than it ever was before!

Suppose, on the contrary—in this nation or any other—war never to come. Days, years, centuries pass on, and in all the households of a people there is nothing but toil, accumulation, multiplication of comforts and luxuries, care for themselves and their children. Can human nature be trusted thus to go on, in profound and unbroken peace and prosperity? In its present state, I must doubt whether it can. We have been wont, in former days, to bless ourselves, that, separated by the ocean from Europe and European complications, we had the prospect of going on for ages, undisturbed by the alarms and horrors of war. That dream is broken by intestine discord, and by the levelling of the ocean barrier through steam communication; and for my part, I believe it is best for us that we are to take our share in the solemn experience and discipline of nations.

But at the same time, while I see and admit the inevitableness and the moral uses of war, I believe that the war time is a transition state in the world, and that a better time is to come. I look upon war as being to the body politic what disease is to the individual. When men learn to live more wisely, simply, and innocently, there will be less disease: ultimately there may be little or none. But till then, disease is not only inevitable in the constitution, but is a moral element bound up with it and essential to its welfare. So with war: human society will outgrow it, when it outgrows its vices, its angry passions, its injustice, selfishness, and ambition. Till then, the world must suffer, and I believe it is best that it should suffer, from this fearful scourge.*

The last specific problem to be considered is slavery; the subjection of man to man; the subjection, not of man to the Government, but of man to man—of the serf to his feudal lord, of the slave to his master. It is a fact, in the history of past ages, too universal to be overlooked; too deep founded in the order of the world, to be passed by. I am acquainted with no such fact among animals—except the ant—as one making a servant, serf, or slave of another; or one species, of another and inferior species. *Everywhere* in the history of the human race, we are met with this stupendous problem: how is it, or why is it, that man has thus been subject to man; that a condition, directly opposite to every free tendency of humanity, should have been as universal almost, as if it had been an ordinance of nature?

I desire you to dismiss from your thoughts all those questions connected with this subject, which are so warmly debated at the present moment: I am looking at the course of ages, and not at the controversy of to-day. Keep your own opinions, whatever they be; for the present I controvert none of them. Nay, let a man entertain the worst opinion possible of the system; all the more reason is there, it seems to me, why he should desire to see, in the calm survey of God's government over the world, all the good he can see, coming out of it; and all the more, the *worse* he thinks of it.

Montesquieu observes, in his Spirit of Laws, that slavery, cruel as it seems, and unjust as it certainly is in the form of chattel slavery, had its origin in comparative mercy. That

* I have been led to some modification of my views of war, by M. Prudhon's "*La Guerre et la Paix*" (War and Peace). I have been led to see it, that is to say, more as a Providential fact; to be accepted with patience, instead of being regarded simply as horrible. M. Cousin led the way, in the same course of thought, in his Lectures Introductory to the Philosophy of History; see lec. ix. latter part. With regard to the New Testament protest against fighting, I regard it as a protest, not against war absolutely, but against the ordinary war spirit.

is to say, it succeeded, in the morality of nations, the barbarous practice of putting to death all captives made in war. But I was about to observe, that there was another step which society had to take, that involved greater difficulty. It passed from the slaughter to the slavery of captives; that perhaps was not difficult; and it certainly was beneficial. But how was it to pass from its nomadic state, from the wild and wandering habits of the hunter and shepherd, to settled abode, and the tillage of the soil? It has been contended by an able French writer, M. Auguste Comte, that fixed occupation must have been originally enforced; that the necessary industry could not have been obtained but by compulsion. He maintains that the natural indolence of mankind, and especially in warm climates, could, in no other way, have been overcome. We, stirring Anglo-Saxon men, cannot understand it perhaps; and there may be more truth in it than we suspect. If it *be* so, then look at it. Here are men doomed to death, saved alive; that is something. Then here is a soil which, in the ruder ages, nobody will cultivate without compulsion; and these men are put to work upon it. I have said in former lectures, that hunger was a spur to activity. To *regular* activity, to *industry*, other inducements may have been neces sary. And although they may have been wrongfully or cruelly applied, yet it cannot but be grateful—looking away from man's injustice to God's wisdom and goodness —to see any good that has come out of evil.

In the next place, this translation of men from states of barbarism and ignorance into more civilized communities, has been a means sometimes—has opened a school, however unintentionally, for their improvement. Civilization has thus taken the wilder natures into its bosom, and, with however much imperfection and error, has performed the office of education. The Thracian and German tribes experienced that effect in the old Roman school: and there is one instance on record where the civilizing influence came from the other side; for Herodotus tells us that the Lydians did that service to their Persian conquerors and masters. But look at Africa. Surrounded by a wall of darkness, and filled with cruelty and blood; with no civilizing influence in herself, as the story of ages has proved; what now do we see? Britain sends to her borders the man stealer, to tear her children from her bosom, and transport them to the American colonies. It was a deed of unmingled atrocity; compared with which, capture in war was generous and honorable: the African king of Dahomey grows white by the side of the Saxon slave-trader. But what follows? The African people in this country improve, and are now far advanced beyond their kindred at home. And now they begin to return; they are building a state on their native borders, which promises to stop the slave trade with Africa, and to spread light and civilization through her dark solitudes. Was this the *best* means conceivable, to such an end? No, but it was a means; and the best means possible —man being left free to act his pleasure. Was it *his* design to civilize Africa? No, but God may overrule his action to bring about that result.*

We have now examined the four great historic problems: Polytheism and Idolatry, Despotism, War, and Servitude. But these are all wrapped up and comprehended in another, which is yet to be considered; and that is the prevalence of error. The place and part which error has had in the world, and in the working out of the world's problem—this more precisely is what we have to consider.

Some place and part it must necessarily have had. For although men *might* have just ideas of certain *absolute truths*, and *have* had them—as of the beauty and rectitude of justice and benevolence—yet when they came to apply these ideas to practice, to *institutions* in religion, in government;

*I cannot leave this subject without lifting up my hands and heart to the great hope, that the way is now opened for purging our American soil from the stain of slavery. Many of us have long been asking how this was ever to be done. At length we see the way. The slave system is destroying itself. The madness of the slavemaster is breaking the chains of the slave.

to *usages* in war, or to the *relations* of *man to man*, it was inevitable that they should err. What place, then, has this erring?

Now to some, the problem may present itself in this way—that things should have been so ordered in Divine Providence, that error should seem to have been better than truth, polytheism than pure theism, despotism than equal rule, servitude than freedom, war than peace. That error should seem to have *worked* better than truth, wrong than right—does it not appear to be a contradiction in ideas? Does it not stamp the charge of essential falsity upon human nature itself?

To this I reply, in the first place, that it is mainly a *mis-statement* of the problem. The case is too *broadly* stated, and only requires some analysis, to be relieved of its main difficulty. In all the instances referred to, there has been a mixture of truth and error. And it is the truth, and not the error, in every case, that has been useful. Thus in religion; the belief in an all-creating Power; the feeling that that power was present in all nature and life; and the attempt simply to express or body it forth in visible forms—all this was right, and it was useful. Even the giving to this Power "a local habitation and a name" for every place it occupied, was, to a certain extent, right; it conveyed a juster idea, I am tempted to say, than that extreme abstraction of thought, which sees God nowhere. The *excesses* to which all this went, the low and degrading forms of idolatry, the *errors*, in short, were the things that were not useful. The essential strength of polytheism lay in the truths, and not in the falsehoods it involved. So also with regard to superstition—that men should *fear* God, should feel that He is displeased with evil; that He would punish evil—this was right: and it was useful. When it went too far, when it created an *irrational* terror; in so far, that is to say, as it was false, it was not useful. Then again that *government* should be strong, and controlling, and, simply as a form of government, despotic, was necessary and beneficial. That political form is the best, the nearest to right, which is best suited to the people to be governed. And for a rude, ignorant, lawless people, a strong, central controlling power is best. But the selfishness, injustice, and cruelty with which it is often exercised, are *not* good, nor do they work any good. The ideas of *divine right* in a government, and of the duty of religious obedience to it, could they be justly construed, are right and useful; and they have worked usefully in all ages. It is evident that God meant that nations should have some kind of government; for they cannot *be* nations, cannot be moral, peaceful, well-ordered communities, without it. Government, therefore, in a certain sense, is of God. What, then, has been the error? That of investing government with irresponsible, unlimited power—that of consecrating its abuses, worshipping its very tyranny, enthroning its very corruption. That part of absolute sovereignty has not been the useful part. The truth has been good, but not the error. Then, once more, with regard to *war* and *servitude*—in considering which, the question is about usages rather than theories—certainly I do not say that evil has worked better than good would have done. A war may be right—a battle to defend homes and households, to resist overwhelming wrong, to achieve a lawful freedom. Such a war does good. It sets up and sanctifies with blood the great and everlasting claim of right. Human blood is not too dear to pour out for such cause. The names of Thermopylæ and Salamis, of Bunker Hill and Yorktown and Fort Moultrie, are watchwords to honor, to patriotic vigilance and self-sacrifice in all time. But wars of mere ambition and desire of conquest, have another account to settle; the worse they have been, the worse has been their influence; and any good that has sprung from them has been incidental, and has arisen in spite of them. And so in the subjection of man to man—not the bad elements, but the good, have done good; not injustice or cruelty, but kindness and care—the superiority that has been humane and gentle. If you could suppose that, not by human violence and injustice, but by the simple fiat of Providence, a rude, ignorant, nomadic people was taken and transferred to the presence of a cultivated people, to be trained to regular industry and social and spiritual improvement, you would say *that* was a good.

Thus I think that I see a great, a solemn, a Divine Providence extracting good out of all the conditions upon which humanity has fallen. I think that it becomes me to be patient with what God has permitted. I look with awe upon the sphere in which an Infinite Providence is working. I think it is but reverent to seek for the *good* that is evolved from the dark and mysterious ways of Heaven, rather than to look upon anything that Heaven permits, as *altogether* dark and evil. I understand well enough what indignation at evil and wrong, is; but I doubt whether that is the last and best state of any thoughtful mind. I might rail at the world, and heap wrath and scorn upon it; but I believe that philosophy is better than satire. With a brotherly consideration and sympathy and sorrow, must I take into my heart the struggling fortunes of my kind. What mistakes, what errors, what crimes, what sufferings, what overwhelming floods of disaster, what a mournful train of evils, filling the long track of ages! I must see something besides this—something beside evil or the Evil One in the world. I must see God in history; or I must not look at it at all.

But far be it from me, at the same time, to spread the shield of this philosophy over any mistakes that now demand to be corrected, over any evils that now can be remedied.

That evil has been overruled for good in certain circumstances, is no argument for abetting or perpetuating it, but the very contrary. In the calm and philosophic consideration of the past, I can have patience with its errors and abuses; but patience with *present* evil and wrong, though possibly to some impetuous spirits it may need to be recommended, is a virtue scarce likely to need any general inculcation or enforcement. On the contrary, we are far too liable to acquiesce in established wrong, far too slow to apprehend the high point after which we should be reaching and striving. Custom, habitude, even prejudice has its uses; there would be no stability without it; but it would be death, if it were not mixed up with the element of progress. Therefore we need ever to hear the stirring words of the reformer. The human mind must not stand still. It cannot indeed forsake entirely "the old paths," nor ought it to do so. But it must not stand still. Therefore, I say, must the great word, *Reform*, be sounded out through the world. It has been sounded out through all past ages. It has been the trumpet call that has led on that grand march of progress, whose steps are centuries; whose history is the history of all time; whose forces are every day sweeping on with accelerated movement; and whose final victory must be the redemption of the world from Idolatry and Despotism, and War and Bondage and Error.

To trace this great movement in the world, will be the object of the two remaining lectures.

LECTURE XI.

HISTORIC VIEW OF HUMANITY: HUMAN PROGRESS—THE AGENCIES EMPLOYED IN IT; THE HISTORY OF THOUGHT —OF INSTITUTIONS—AND OF ACTIONS OR EVENTS.

We have hitherto surveyed humanity in its fixed and permanent conditions. We are now to contemplate it in its grand movement. Hitherto, that is to say, our studies have been occupied with man simply as a being, subject to certain principles and influences; and subject to them in all ages; subject to them alike, though not in the same degree, at the beginning as now. We have considered, first, the ultimate end evidently proposed in the creation around us and within us, human culture; secondly, the fundamental principle on which the end is to be achieved, moral freedom. Then, in five following lectures, we considered the ministration to this end, first, of the physical creation, of nature; secondly, of man's physical organization; thirdly, of his mental and moral constitution; fourthly, of his complex nature, including the periods of life, society, sex, &c.; and fifthly, of the occupation and arts of life—agriculture, manufactures, trade, and the learned professions; and of architecture, sculpture, painting, music, poetry, and literature. In three more lectures we have considered certain circumstances pertaining to the human condition and culture; and circumstances which are thought to involve peculiar difficulty; as first, imperfection, effort, and penitence; illusion, fluctuation, indefiniteness of moral attainment, and bondage to the physical infirmities and appetites;

secondly, pain, hereditary evil, death ; and thirdly, polytheism, despotism, war, servitude, and error.

These are the subjects in which I have endeavored to interest you, in the ten previous lectures. In the two that remain of the course, I wish to invite your attention to the historic view of the human race; to single out some of the leading traits that have marked its successive developments; to contemplate—of course it must be in the most general way—the story of the world from the beginning.

What was that beginning? What, may we suppose, was the condition and character of the first inhabitants of the earth? With the purpose which I have in view, I have no occasion to discuss the question whether the various races of men had their origin in distinct stocks, created in different parts of the world, or in the one pair in Eden. Were the first created *men*, whether many or few, brought into existence in a state of high development—incarnate angels in wisdom, knowledge, virtue; or in a state of infancy, ignorance, and weakness? The question is enveloped in thick darkness; and with regard to it, we are left mainly to inference. Proceeding upon this ground, I adopt, for my part, the theory of an infancy for mankind: I mean, of an intellectual and moral infancy. There is no evidence in the Scripture record, whatever value or validity may be ascribed to it, that Adam was advanced beyond that condition. We are told that he was innocent at first—which he might be in a moral infancy; and I find no mental act ascribed to him but that of naming the animals—which is the first and humblest step of thought. And I say that the natural inference from all we *know*, is, that the human race, like the human individual, began its career in infancy. When I see a tree growing through successive years, I naturally trace it back to the sapling. When I see a river gradually enlarging as it flows, I justly conclude, not that it burst forth from the earth at first a noble and majestic stream, but that it began as a little rill. From the earliest recorded history of the human race, we see a constant progress; and as we follow it back, step by step, we naturally trace it to a beginning—to an infancy.

From this beginning, I say, to the present day, there has been a progress; a gradual advancement in human culture, character, knowledge; institutions, government, state of society; religion, virtue, and happiness. I shall take this for granted. I suppose that nobody denies it. It will be the ground idea of these two lectures. It will not be, therefore, by analysis that I shall proceed; *i. e.*, by taking the multifarious facts of history and life, and tracing them up to the one principle of progress, but by synthesis rather; *i. e.*, *assuming* the principle of progress as lying at the root of humanity, I shall speak of its actions and fortunes in successive ages, as the natural unfoldings of that principle. The fact of progress will be equally made out on either plan.

But I shall not attempt, after the manner of the German philosophers, to construct the world out of an idea. Fichte, proceeding on Plato's doctrine of innate, seminal, world-producing ideas—a doctrine often reproduced in the later German philosophy—undertakes to deduce the epochs of human development and history, in their necessary order, from a certain principle. He conceives that things *must have unfolded themselves*, according to a certain plan, which he has wrought out in his own abstract contemplations. He tells his auditors, that, as a philosopher, he is not concerned with the facts, but only with his theory. He plainly says: "If the philosopher must deduce from the unity of his presupposed principle, all the possible phenomena of experience, it is obvious that in the fulfilment of this purpose, he does not require the aid of experience," and that "he pays no respect whatever to experience." * He says to his hearers, in substance: "I see, I know, from the very nature of humanity, and from the very nature of things, that the human race must pass through certain epochs. Two principles lie at the bottom, reason and freedom. The end

* Fichte's Characteristics of the Present Age, p. 3.

is free self-culture. The epochs must be these: the first, when reason is obeyed as an instinct; the second, when despotic authority fastens itself upon the neck of this obedient reason; the third, when the human mind struggles to free itself from this yoke—which is the present age; the fourth, when reason shall reign as speculative truth; and the fifth, when it shall reign as moral wisdom. Now I shall draw out these epochs from the one principle of free self-culture, as a matter of abstract reasoning; *you* will see whether the facts correspond; that is not *my* concern."

I have thus referred to this work of Fichte—it is that on "The Characteristics of the Present Age"—not only as very curious and interesting, but as pursuing a method in direct contrast to that which I propose. For while I recognize the law of progress as self-evident and certain—it being the very nature of the mind and of all its faculties to expand and advance, as much as it is of a tree to grow, or of a stream to flow onward—I shall not attempt to deduce the *necessary* results of this law, but to point out the *actual* results.

It has been made to appear, I trust, in our previous lectures, that all the great laws of nature, of life, and of humanity, tend to promote, as their end, human culture. As the proper complement of this representation, which has thus far been mostly applied to individual life, I wish now to show how the whole course of history, the collective life of the race, falls into accordance with it. For this purpose I propose to take a cursory view of the leading processes, circumstances, and agencies which have contributed to this result.

With the task I have before me, it is time that I should have done with preliminary observations; but there are yet two points which I must impress on your minds, even at the risk of repetition; because in this matter they are the opposite poles of thought, upon which everything turns.

Two principles, then, I say, preside over the world-devel opment; human *spontaneity* and Divine *control*. When you look back upon past ages, upon past races, upon the heaving elements of the world's life, what impression do they convey to you? Do they not appear to you in disconnected fragments, in stupendous revolution, in wild and almost fortuitous disorder? Do not the fortunes of men, in this larger view, appear like a chaotic mass of accidents? Bear in mind, then, on the one hand—do not merely *say*, but see clearly, and fully admit, that in the working out of the human problem, men *must* act their part freely—ay, foolishly, madly, distractedly, if you please; any way, so it be freely done. In vain shall we look for any exact system of arrangements by which everything can be said to have helped on the race in the most direct way, to the most rapid advancement. No: it *could* not be so: the race must find, and make, and work out its own way. Cruelties, butcheries, battles, murders, crushing oppressions, conflagrations kindled by incendiary hands, the whelming of cities and nations in fire and blood; these things could not be helped, if man was to be free. Nay, free thought by its *natural expansion*, has burst asunder, age after age, the very frames and fixtures in which it grew—the idolatries, despotisms, false systems, cramping institutions; and much to the general advantage, though to much temporary harm.

But recollect, on the other hand, that things have never been left to run their own wild course, free from Divine control. In the very bosom of humanity are many checks, placed there by a Divine hand. There is what M. Guizot calls the "natural morality of man, which," as he truly says, "never abandons him in any condition, in any age of society, and mixes itself with the most brutal empire of ignorance or passion." * Men grow weary of wickedness, and ashamed of degradation. One wonders sometimes that human passion stops anywhere, but it does stop. One wonders that communities and nations, sinking lower and lower into dissoluteness, do not sink to utter perdition; but there are powers put forth to arrest their career. Powerful as

* Histoire de la Civilization en France, tome i., p. 262.

evil is, there are antagonist powers still stronger. There is the WOE that evil brings; a flaming sword, set upon the heaven-erected barriers and battlements of all times, for the protection of the human race. And other messengers, too, are sent forth; yet more distinct interpreters of the Great Will above. Through ages of declension from virtue and piety, ever from time to time, has rung out the stern and solemn voice of the reformer. Some Moses, some Menes or Confucius, some Zoroaster, some Socrates has arisen to call back the forgetful world from its wanderings. As Christians, we believe, also, in special interpositions for the rescue of the world from evil and misery.

But this leads me to speak, as I propose to do in the present lecture, of the agencies which have been employed for the world's advancement. In considering these agencies, I shall not confine myself to any one precise order in which they have appeared, but shall be governed by that of time or affiliation or natural precedence, as I may find convenient.

Thus the *history of thought*, in the first place, would take the natural precedence over every other topic; because thought lies behind all other agencies, and is the cause of them. This great subject would naturally divide itself into a history of philosophy and a history of public sentiment. The first would embrace the theories of the few profound, speculative thinkers; from Thales and Pythagoras down to the present day. The second would occupy itself with the pervading, the popular ideas, sentiments, and aims that have prevailed in successive ages. The first has been the subject of many treatises. The second has not, that I am aware, been attempted in any work distinctly and exclusively devoted to it. It may be that the history of popular opinion would be too multifarious and too vague for any such definite treatment. But if the successive phases of public sentiment, like the theories of philosophy, *could* be traced; if the dominant thoughts that stirred in the bosom of the old Assyrian civilization, of the Egyptian, the Phœnician, the Hebrew, the Grecian, Roman, feudal, and modern civiliza-

tion, could be unfolded to me, I should better understand the world and the problem of the world's life, than by any other means whatever.

This history of human thought, both philosophic and popular—you must see at once, how impossible it is that I should deal with it here, except by the most general suggestions, even if I were ever so much qualified to do it. But consider, in this matter of mental development, how natural it is, and we may say certain, that every man's individual life is a picture of the world's life. Look at the natural traits of individual life. In *childhood*, docility—receiving impressions with little questioning of them, wilfulness and waywardness controlled by authority; timidity, also—fears, natural or superstitious: in *early manhood*, the forming of opinions, the struggling with questions, the liability to be misled by false theories; premature judgments, and presumption and confidence, in the same proportion: in *later manhood*, a correction of those errors, a larger knowledge and experience, a settling down upon more simple and certain bases of thought; more caution, more modesty, more wisdom: in short, impressions for the *first* period, assumptions for the *second*, solid results for the *third;* these are the natural steps of individual progress. They have been the steps of the *world's* progress. These are the steps, indeed, which Auguste Comte has so laboriously traced out, under the denominations, of what he calls, the theologic era, the metaphysic era, and the era of the positive philosophy; *i. e.*, in other words, the ages of superstition, of theory or assumption, and of the observation of facts; for, I think, his terms are new, rather than his ideas of progress.

But let us look at the *world's* periods. The first was that of superstitious *obedience*, to whatever was taught or established. It embraces the oldest Asiatic nations, together with the Egyptians, and, indeed, all the rudest tribes of men everywhere. Its grand characteristic is that of childlike and implicit acquiescence in the existing system, in the political or social order, as a Divine enactment. Whether that order was *caste*, or subjection to a priesthood, or to a patriarchal head, or to the king, it was never questioned. Kings were often slain by their *rivals*, but the people, in those earliest days, seldom rose against them. We can hardly comprehend, at this day, that absolute obedience. And we must not confound it with rational obedience, which is one of the latest fruits of the highest culture. It was unreasoning, instinctive obedience. And the lessons to be obeyed, extended to everything; to the daily action of life as well as to political relations. Men took their trade, their occupation, from their fathers. In India and Egypt, it was assigned to them by the law of caste; but among all rude people, the same principle has prevailed, though not to the same extent. Then, in political relations, the chieftain, the king was priest also; and in that double character was regarded with unbounded awe, and had unbounded power. This was the childhood of the world.

The next period begins with Greece, and embraces Rome and the whole of semi-civilized Europe in the middle ages. It is the period in which thought began to be free. It is the period of struggling theories; about philosophy, politics, law, and the social relationships. Thales and Pythagoras—both of Phœnician origin, though born and brought up (about six centuries before the Christian era) in the great cities of Miletus and Samos—were the harbingers of this second period in the history of human thought; but it burst forth in morning splendor in the schools of Socrates and Plato, and of Aristotle. Now one of the darkest problems in the history of thought, is the apparent declension in philosophy from the time of Plato and Aristotle to the time of Bacon; a period of about twenty centuries. Platonism in the new Platonic schools of Rome and Alexandria, in the second and third centuries, died out into mysticism and pantheism. Aristotle's system arose and flourished in the eighth century, under the culture of Arabian philosophers; and partly through the Arabian schools in Spain, and the fostering care of Charlemagne and Alfred, it attained, under the name of the *scholastic philosophy*, to a firm lodgment in the culture of Europe. It was less spiritual, less elevating than that of Plato; yet it prevailed. It was full of irrational hypotheses, and barren syllogisms and subtilties; more fitted to exercise human thought, than to lead it to any true knowledge. Why then did it prevail? May we not fairly suggest, that it may have been better and safer for the human mind in that stage of its culture, than the philosophy of Plato? Plato's philosophy, we see, was abused; it declined into mysticism and pantheism! Aristotle's, more formal and mechanical, held its place more firmly. And do we not see a type of this phase of the world-development, in our own individual progress? Is there not a time in our mind's life, between youth and later manhood, when we are struggling, rather than attaining; when the faculties, the tools of thought, are sharpening, rather than building; or when their building is experimental rather than final; when we are trying many things, many theories, and do not yet find the track to clear and settled conclusions. In politics, however, in the science of law, in ideas of social justice, there *was*, at the same time, a great progress. And in this connection we must not forget that grand achievement—the separation of the temporal and spiritual powers.* The union of political and spiritual authority in the same hands, formed and established in the ancient world the most solid and impregnable despotism. Christianity set up a new thought in the world, that was to reign over kings and emperors. It was the power, not of an idol god, but of an omnipresent Divinity; not of a ceremonial function, but of a God-obeying conscience. In the persons of the Christian priesthood, it separated itself from the temporal power, struggled with it, and at length gained the ascendency. When Pope Hildebrand, in 1077, summoned the Emperor of Germany, Henry VI., to Canossa, in the Apennines, and made him do penance on the cold mountain side for three days, before he would admit him to his

* Comte, Philosophie Positive, 54th lecture.

presence or give him absolution, the battle was fought and won. Doubtless the religious power in its separate form was enough abused, but its separation was a great step onward.

The third great period in the history of human thought commenced with the sixteenth century. The revival of learning, the protest of Luther, the invention of printing, the discovery of America, nearly simultaneous, gave a new spring to men's minds, and philosophy partook of the general movement. Under the guidance of Bacon, Leibnitz, and their successors, it turned away from subtilties and the ories, to real knowledge, and to its foundation principles. For the last three centuries, then, the human mind, having struggled out from the cloud-land of the middle ages, has been advancing on firmer ground and in clearer light, and to more decided and substantial results. It is the manhood of the world.

I am sensible that this discoursing is too abstract and cursory to be profitably pursued. But it may serve to convince you that there has been a progress in the highest regions of thought; in that search for truth which touches the vital springs of all human welfare.

Let me add a word on the progress of thought, as it appears in the form of public sentiment. And let it be considered that public, like individual opinion, will always be working itself out into expression, into action. Now the progress of public sentiment through ages, has manifested itself in a constantly increasing respect for freedom, for justice, for humanity. Let us dwell upon this last point for a moment; for it covers the whole ground.

Civilization, says M. Guizot, embraces two elements, the improvement of society, and the improvement of the man; and the question, he says, which is to be put to all events, is—What have they done for the one or the other? Of these two developments, he further asks, which is the end; and which, the means? Was the individual made to advance society, or society the individual? * And he quotes

* Histoire de la Civilization en Europe, tome ii. p. 23, 24.

Royer Collard in favor of the latter view. Can there be any doubt about it? Of course the actual tendencies are reciprocal; general culture helps individual; the individual, in turn, helps society. But if any one asks which is the ultimate end, I say the culture of the individual soul. Indeed, what is the development, improvement, perfection, happiness of society, when analyzed, but that of individuals? Society, like humanity, is a mere abstraction; only individuals have any actual being or fortune, weal or woe. Society is only a relation; man is the substance. Society passes away; man is immortal. The family, tribe, commune, nation, state, is instrumental; man, final. Society can do nothing greater than to make noble and happy men. But men can do something greater than to make noble institutions—to make themselves noble. It is beautiful to die for one's country; but it is more beautiful, it is majestic, to die for the right—for the sense of right in the lonely and private heart.

Now the progress of the world, of society, of freedom, of education, intelligence, literature, religion, has witnessed a gradual development of conscious individuality, of the worth of man, of the individual man. It may be traced down through successive institutions and ages.* Under the ancient despotisms, Assyrian and Egyptian, still more in China and India, the man was nothing. Society was strong; but the man was nothing. Armies of hundreds of thousands of men, with terrible unity, cohesion and force, swept over the world; still the individual man was nothing but a particle of that destroying cloud. In the Roman time, man was nothing but for the state. The sole thought of parental affection, yea, of the tenderest maternity, was, to rear children for the state. Christianity gave birth to individuality. Feudalism permitted the great idea to grow. Man became free, and learned more and more that he was a man. The consciousness of one's self has gone on developing ever since, till, in these days, it is tending in some instances to

* To do this, was the favorite thought of Hegel in his Philosophy of History.

isolation, to a sort of intellectual monachism, to fastidious peculiarities of thought and modes of speech, and almost to self-apotheosis. Its creed is a very short one: "I believe—in myself;" and its practice equally brief: "I will live, in, by, and for myself."

From the History of Thought, the next step naturally is to the History of Institutions; though they are closely connected, and cannot, in our consideration of them, be entirely separated.

And here, religion, by every right, claims the first place; by its dignity, its priority in time, and the extent of its influence.

This grand impress upon the world is a sublime testimony to human nature. Religion was the dominant thought of all the early ages. The sceptic, nay the atheist philosopher of history and humanity, has been obliged to take it into the very heart of his theory; for no account can be given of the world, without it. But in the ancient world especially, religion reigned supreme. It was the shadow in every grove, the wind upon every shore, the waving harvest in every field; the sunlit mountains were its burning altars; the deep-sunken glens and caverns its haunted chambers; its idols were in every house, its signet was upon every hearthstone; birth and burial, feast and fight it claimed for its own; it was the consecration of marriage, the strength of government, the sanctitude of kingship; it was the seal upon everything sacred; upon every oath and covenant and bond in the world. Nay, and concerning the more modern ages, the ablest judge on the subject, M. Guizot, says, that "until the fifteenth century, we see in Europe no general and powerful ideas, really acting upon the masses, but religious ideas."* "Yea," says Plutarch, who stood a little this side of the dividing line between the pagan and the Christian ages,† and thus belonged to our Christian era in *time*, though not in faith—"Yea, shouldst thou wander through the earth, thou mayest find cities

* Civilization in Europe, p. 307.

† Died about A. D. 120.

without walls, without a king, without houses, without coin, without theatre or gymnasium; but never wilt thou behold a city without a god, without prayer, without oracle, without sacrifice. Sooner might a city stand without ground, than a state sustain itself without religion. This is the cement of all society, and the support of all legislation." *

In religious ideas and institutions, it is hardly necessary to show that there has been a constant progress from the earliest ages; but its steps have been more marked than is likely to be comprehended by the common and vague impression of the fact. The first form—I except, of course, from this account of the natural progress, the Hebrew system—the first form of religion that prevailed over the world was Fetichism; a word derived from the Portuguese *fetisso*, meaning a block, worshipped as an idol. It prevailed over all Asia and in Egypt; and was substantially the worship of nature. It was the worship of nature, or of idols, the monstrous births of nature; for the idolatry of these countries is widely to be distinguished from that of Greece. So gross were the Oriental ideas, that the idol was sometimes chained by the leg to his place in the temple, lest he should leave it, and desert his worshippers. The idols were ugly and misshapen, often huge and monstrous; like the statue of Nebuchadnezzar, fifty cubits (about one hundred feet) high, or like the colossal Sphinx at Gizè in Egypt, one hundred and fifty feet long, and sixty-three feet high. The Sphinx, you know, was in the form of a human head on the body of a lion—humanity, as one has said, looking out from animalism. Indeed, the Egyptian, as a worship of animal life, was an advance upon the mere worship of material nature; and was an approach—was a "looking out," perhaps we may say—to the Grecian development. This, the Grecian development, was the second step, and was the worship of deified human attributes; the worship, that is to say, of the *gods under these representations*; for we are always to understand *this* by the worship, as it is called, of

* Quoted from the Biblical Repository, vol. ii. p. 259.

outward forms. The Greek worship formed its symbols of the Divinity, by an idealizing, not of nature, but of humanity. That is to say, it was distinctively this; for much, doubtless, of the old Oriental worship was left; it is always to be remembered that much of the spirit of every previous, flows into the succeeding age. The Greeks, then, deified humanity; the most illustrious men they had known, represented their idea of God; and they made their idols in the most beautiful human forms. It was a step onward. Next, the Romans abjured idolatry entirely. This trait the better prepared them for the further and last great religious step in the world, the introduction of Christianity. Christianity has presided over all the best culture in the world, since its advent. It has itself passed through successive stages of development and improvement. That is to say, its principles have been better and better understood.

But before speaking more particularly of Christianity, let us turn a moment to consider the place which the Hebrew religion has held in the world.

There is scarcely anything that is so urgently demanded in our literature, as a work which will justly discriminate and fairly present the claims of the Hebrew system to our attention and veneration. The Bible is regarded by a part of the world, as a literal record of the words of God—a theory which precludes all free appreciation; and by another part, as a book of old and useless stories, and formal and antiquated writings—a presumption that altogether overlooks its true character. For here is a book that stands out, amidst the darkness of antiquity, in bold relief and unchallenged superiority, to everything around it. Here, in the first place, is the most valid history of the earliest known period of the world; of the time before the flood. Here, in the second place, is a record of the most liberal polity of ancient times. There was nothing among surrounding nations to compare with the freedom of the Hebrew State. Here, in the third place, is the sublimest poetry of the ancient, if not, indeed, of any time. Some of the ablest critics have agreed to assign to the Book of Job and the writings of Isaiah, a place, not only above the Indian Mahabarat, but above the Iliad itself. And in the fourth place, here are writings, of such lofty spiritualism and devotion, that they not only leave all contemporary records far behind, but have been the food of piety and the language of prayer, among the most enlightened nations, to the present day. Compare the prayers in the Zend-Avesta and the Iliad with those of David—and they are all nearly contemporaneous—and you must feel that David soared far above them all.

Such a system of lofty spiritualism, moral wisdom, and civil polity could not fail to have some effect upon the surrounding nations. Indeed, M. Auguste Comte himself, though far enough from recognizing any element of supernaturalism in the Hebrew system, is disposed to ascribe to it, the initiative and leading part in the great transition of the world from polytheism to the worship of one God.* The position of the Hebrew State favored such an influence. It stood in the centre of the most ancient civilizations; with Assyria on the one hand, and Phœnicia and Egypt on the other. At a later day, it was a central province of the Roman Empire. And, as if its office were meant to be diffusion, the Hebrew State was never at any time, a locked-up and impregnable kingdom. It was frequently overrun by the armies of Egypt and Assyria and Rome; many times they desolated and despoiled the Holy Temple; yet they found there no idol nor idol-worship, but only a simple altar to the one, invisible God. They dashed it in pieces, indeed, with idolatrous rage; but they must have felt the sublimity of the symbol and the worship. So little, in truth, did the Hebrew theocracy exist for its own sake; so much for the lifting up of a standard of pure theism to the nations, as the Hebrews themselves were often told, that they were *reared* as a *people* in Egypt, and were more than once carried into captivity into Assyria. Not for national aggran-

* Philosophie Positive, vol. v., p. 290, 291.

dizement did the Hebrew State exist, but for the diffusion of higher truths than the world had elsewhere attained, and thus to prepare the way for a still higher and purer religion.

This was Christianity. The crisis of its advent and the consequences must occupy some attention, even in the most cursory notice of the world's progress.

The old religions were worn out. The Asiatic and Egyptian worship of nature had given place to the Grecian mythology, and to this had succeeded the Roman latitudinarianism, and indifference. Though abjuring idolatry, Rome admitted the gods of all nations indifferently into her pantheon, and her philosophers believed in none. The observation of Cicero is familiar to you, that the very priests could not help laughing in one another's faces, as they celebrated the sacred rites. All faith was fast dying out of the world, and where faith is dead, nothing lives.

Then it was that Christianity came, as we may say, to the world's rescue: and many circumstances favored its introduction. I do not choose to say, as most writers do, that Providence especially prepared these circumstances; they arose in a natural way; the facilities of communication opened by the extent of the Roman Empire, language and law, the prevalence of peace, the failure of polytheism, and the despondency of philosophy, all favored the new religion. Occasion was taken from these circumstances, we may doubtless say: it was "the fulness of time." But what I wish especially to mark is the crisis in civilization. Civilized society, to which the rescue came, was about to sink under the weight of its own inherent vices. The life of the world had been gathered up in Rome, to one central point; the limbs had been drained to fill the heart to repletion; and now that destruction threatened it from very plethora and consequent gangrene and corruption; now, too, that the Goth and the Vandal were coming to pierce it, that mighty heart was about to burst in deluges of blood. It had been an awful problem for any philosopher of those days, any Cicero or Plotinus, to consider, *how*, from that dark and mysterious abyss into which humanity was descending, it should emerge—how, and in what form and character. But there was a power coming to help and to rescue, of which the philosophers knew nothing. Christianity descended with the world into that awful abyss, where the wild torrents and stormy winds of human passion were struggling together in the night-brooding chaos; and that heavenly Guardian and Restorer brought it up again to stand on a firm basis. For then it was that the spiritual powers, the dread sanctions, and the imposing ceremonies of the Christian religion, awed the rude invader. Then it was, that its mitred bishops clothed themselves with the office of the civil magistrate, to restrain the lawless. Then it was, that its monasteries preserved the treasures of the ancient learning. Then it was, above all, that the *one great idea* arose in the world, to reign over all after ages—the Christ, the divinest being that ever appeared in the world, and the most human; divine to inspire reverence, human to win confidence; and suffering, in such wise, as to touch the springs of love and pity through all time. And it did touch the hearts of men. It transformed many from earthly baseness, into confessors, saints, and martyrs. And it is a circumstance to which I wish to call your particular attention, that the lives of these holy men became the popular literature of the world, from the sixth to the eighth century. The profane literature had disappeared; and these Lives of the Saints took its place. The Collection of Bolland, a Belgian Jesuit, with its continuation, consists of fifty-three volumes of these Lives. I wish I had time to recite to you some of these legends of the early Christian saints. They were often extravagant; but they contained some of the most beautiful pictures of heroism, self-sacrifice, and saintly pity and care for the poor and suffering, that can be found in any literature of any age. And these, amidst the wild license and cruelty of barons and robbers, were the good Christian legends that circulated among the people.*

* Guizot, Histoire de la Civilization en France, 16e et 17e leçons.

And thus, amidst the corruptions and vices of succeeding times, Christianity has ever stood forth as the image of purity and goodness. It has not been, as in the ancient heathen time, when the religion was no better than the morals of the people. Ever in the Christian ages, there has been an ideal, drawing on to something better. And thus Christianity has ever been impressing itself more and more, upon Governments, upon social institutions, and upon art. It has made Governments more just and tolerant. It has built hospitals and asylums on the sites of voluptuous baths and bloody amphitheatres. It has formed worshipping congregations, built for them temples for meditative thought, for instruction—a thing unknown to other religions; an institution, indeed, of almost inappreciable value. And what but the Christian idea, has been imaged forth in the architecture of Europe; in its solemn temples, its majestic cathedrals, its time-hallowed universities? And what is it, that is spread in forms of living beauty upon the walls of Italy? It is the great Christian idea. The moving incidents of the Christian story, and the sublime virtues of Christian confessors and martyrs, are there portrayed before the passing generations.

I cannot dwell longer upon the institutions that have advanced the world, and must come, in the third place, to actions and events. Ideas, institutions, actions—this is the order of my discourse; and I am obliged to content myself with the mention of only some instances under each head.

As I shall pass from the agencies employed in the world's progress, to consider in my next and last lecture, the actual steps of it, I shall reserve several points under the head of action, for the places into which they naturally and chronologically fall; and I shall take up in this lecture, only some of those movements of a general character which have occurred occasionally and indifferently in all ages.

The first is Colonization. The great, peaceful colonizers of the world—for the military colonization practised by

Rome and Russia does not come under our present view— have been Phœnicia and Greece, England and Holland: Phœnicia having had colonies in Spain and Northern Africa; Greece, in Asia Minor and Southern Italy; and England and Holland, in the East Indies and in America. This swarming of the hives of men, has always been attended with certain advantages to the cause of civilization and progress. Heeren says, "it is from the bosom of colonies that civil liberty, nearly in all ages, has set forth." * It is easy to see that colonization is likely to be an emancipation from many prejudices and many inconvenient usages at home. Men, in a long-established order of society, become weary of burdensome and cramping institutions, long before they can get rid of them. They have improved ideas which they desire to put in practice; and when founding new communities, they are certain to do it. Our own forefathers, indeed, came to this country with that distinct purpose; and in consequence, they abolished all state religion, all orders of nobility, and all irresponsible government.

The next great movement which I shall mention, is invasion. By this I do not mean international war, to settle some temporary quarrel, but those immense tides in human affairs, by which either barbarism has poured itself down upon the seats of civilization to settle itself there, or civilization has invaded barbarism to uproot and supplant it. Of the first kind, was the invasion of India and Persia from the central mountain land of Asia, and of the Roman Empire from Northern Europe and Tartary. Of the second, are the remarkable movements of the present day—of Russia upon Tartary and Circassia, of France upon Northern Africa, and of England upon Southern Asia.

Here opens an awful page in human affairs, written in blood and blackened with many atrocities and miseries, and we must pause to consider it. And everything depends upon our standpoint. If we demand some *artificial*, *best culture* for the human race; if we permit ourselves to say

* Historial Researches—Asiatic Nations, vol. i., p. 303.

—why was it not carried forward in civilization, with the fewest blunders, troubles, and sufferings, and all according to some factitious ideal of our own?—we shall meet with a confounding problem. But let us say, here is a race made as it is made, and, as we are bound to think, wisely made, and of necessity left mainly to work out its own way; and from this standpoint, what do we see? Nations, in fertile realms, like Persia and Italy, grow in wealth, comfort and luxury, and sink into indulgence, licentiousness, baseness of every sort. Every tendency is downward, and there is no internal power or life to bring them up. Injustice, cruelty, and corruption cry to heaven for their destruction; and moral debility, waste, and woe have left no argument on earth for their continuance. The cup of iniquity and misery is full; and the rudest barbarism is better and happier, than this effete, worn-out, blighted civilization.

Then, from the founts of primeval nature, are collected the mountain streams, that pour a new life through the corrupted channels of the old society. The streams are turbid and violent indeed; but after the first rush is over, and they have swept the choking filth from the old channels, they become in time calmer and purer. The elements that compose the new civilization, are better than the old. In fact, the better part of the old are retained. For the barbarian cannot understand the effeminacy, the sloth, the luxury, the artificial vices into whose presence he comes; but the visible improvements, the comfortable dwellings, the useful arts, and even the institutions and laws, he, in a measure, comprehends and partly adopts.

He is improved. But now at length, he too sinks into debility and corruption, and is prepared to share the fate of his predecessors. And certainly, if this terrible revolution in the wheel of fate, by which another invasion is to cast *him* out and sweep him away—if this, I say, were but mere repetition, without any progress, the problem of all human history would be as dark as ever. But the contrary is the undoubted fact. The experiment is not in vain. The new civilizations that arise are ever better, and have been growing better through all ages.

Let us now turn to the counter movement of civilization upon barbarism. The most remarkable instance of this is the establishment of the British power in India. It is the most stupendous spectacle of an age, full of wonders. Within a century past, more than a hundred millions of barbarous people—the number is now said to amount to 150,000-000—a population greater than that of the Roman Empire in the time of Claudius—spreading over twenty-seven degrees of latitude,* and almost as many of longitude, from Cape Comorin to the Himalaya Mountains, and from Persia to the Ganges—has come under the ascendency of the highest civilization in Europe. Commenced by a company of merchants, and carried on by a people from the other side of the world, nothing could have been more unintentional or improbable than the result of this movement. That in this stupendous march of events, great suffering, great wrong has been inflicted; that princes and nations have been trampled under foot, cannot be denied. And yet it has not been a course of mere reckless and ruthless conquest. Many of the Indian princes have been taken under British protection at their own instance; many others have met with subjugation as the reward of unjust aggressions on their part. And the English are not a people to let oppression in their name, go unchallenged; as the trial of Warren Hastings, Mr. Fox's East India Bill, and many other parliamentary interpositions, show. They have labored, at the same time, to suppress many abuses and to spread education among the people.

The effects must be immense, must be incalculable; and they must be good. For two thousand years India has made hardly a step forward; bound in the chains of political despotism, of a religion at once dreamy, cruel, and degrading, and the fatal institution of caste. All this is destined to give place to Christian order, law, religion, and

*From 8° to 35°.

society. Where Alexander with his armies, and Mohammedan conquerors, and Tamerlane with his Mongol hosts, swept like a destroying cloud, leaving behind them the same sterile immobility and death which they found—in that land a new realm is rising, with the seeds of a new life in it.

Meanwhile England is spreading her influence far, both to the east and west of India. Already she meditates a land route by railroad from the Mediterranean to Hindoostan, through the plains of the Euphrates and Tigris; and that fallow ground of the old Assyrian Empires, which has lain waste for ages, is to be turned into a fruitful field, busy with thronging life, by the ploughshare of modern civilization. England seems destined to regenerate entire Southern Asia, from the Mediterranean to the China Sea. What a magnificent mission for that Island Queen!

There is one further topic, to which, but for fear of exhausting your patience, I should give some space in this lecture: and that is political Revolutions, or more exactly, popular resistance to arbitrary power. Insurrections of the people against the government are seldom aroused without a cause; when successful, they are usually followed by beneficial changes; and even when they fail, they often do good service to the cause of liberty and justice. It is to this last point, as the darkest in the case, that I shall direct your attention in close.

The burden of the case, so to speak, usually rests, as we survey it in history, upon the sad fate of conspicuous individuals; for they are ordinarily the victims. Ever since history began the record of human struggles for justice and for progress, we see that the rack and the scaffold, the market place and the battle field, have been stained with the blood of the free and strong hearted, of patriots and martyrs, of men who died nobly, because they could not live ignobly. To any high and heroic sensibility, it is the saddest and most agonizing spectacle in the world.

But the moving story, that stirs our blood with indignation and pity when we read it, does not end *here.* No, there is another account to be made of deeds like these. Haughty power has its day, and martyred heroism has its day—ay, and it sets in darkness and blood; but, that day past, and they change places forever. Forever hallowed and dear to all mankind is that martyred heroism. Every drop of innocent blood that ever tyranny and injustice have shed, has been sprinkled upon the heart of the world, as upon an altar, to cause the flame of indignant virtue to mount higher. No such weapon was ever formed on earth to sustain the right, no such weapon to beat down the wrong, as the battered sword of martyred patriotism. Separated from all earthly dross in the furnace of tyranny, forged on the anvil of hard injustice and oppression, and tempered in holy blood, it is lifted up as a standard before the eyes of all mankind.

Nor let it be thought that things like these, are buried in obscurity; as the tyrant *would* have the names of his victims. Some of *us* perhaps, never heard of the Duke of Alva and of the Count Egmont—the one, the brutal Spanish commander in the Low Countries; whose cruelties were such, that he drove a hundred thousand people from their country, and *boasted* that he had caused the public *execution* of eighteen thousand persons; and the other, a young nobleman—the Count Egmont—otherwise to have been unknown in history, whom he sent to the scaffold: but all Germany, all Europe has heard of them; of the one for execration, of the other for pity; the pen of genius has written their names on everlasting tablets; in history, in ballads, in dramatic story, they are known, and will be, to the end of the world.

But we all have heard of the heroic Wallace of Scotland. From indignant resistance to the English soldiery stationed in his country, he was led to armed assertion of her rights; and after many daring actions, he was defeated through the jealousy of the Scottish nobles, and by the command of Edward I. was beheaded and quartered in the English capital. With grief and indignation we read the story. We sympathize with the lonely sufferer, torn from his country and his home, and sinking to his doom amidst exulting crowds of enemies. But there is another award—far other than that of the English court and the London of that day. Suppose that behind that hostile crowd had risen an amphitheatre, on which were seated a hundred thousand spectators, all execrating the deed, and lauding and glorifying the victim of arbitrary power. *He*, alas! saw no such majestic amphitheatre, but only murderous foes around him. Yet how feebly would that crowded theatre represent the verdict of posterity! How do the ranks of ages on ages rise, to take the victim's part; ay, to the end of time—to celebrate, through all time, with song and pæan and dramatic scene and historic story, his nobleness and heroism! Yes, it is such, in their melancholy but glorious fate, that fire the hearts of millions, with new indignation at wrong, with new enthusiasm for the right. It is such, in their melancholy but glorious fate, that are the noblest teachers of all mankind. Chairs of philosophy, pulpits, forums, thrones, sink to the dust before them.

The difference between the faint approval which contemporaries give to virtue, and the decisive and loud award of posterity, is strikingly evinced by a passage in Herodotus, concerning Aristides. Herodotus was born in the very year of the banishment of Aristides from Athens—*i. e.*, 484 years before the Christian era. Speaking of that event, Herodotus uses this language: "He was banished by a vote of the people, although my information induces me to consider him as the most upright and excellent of his fellow citizens." * "My information induces me to consider him"—is the cautious language of the time: while the ages have rung with the title of the "Just," appropriated without doubt or hesitation to the name of Aristides; while every language, every literature, every writing of human speech, from the schoolboy's theme to the sage's thesis, has repeated the eulogium; and while, moreover, the name of Themis-

* Book viii., sec. 79.

tocles, the adversary of Aristides, the most successful man of his day—proclaimed by all Greece the greatest general at the battle of Salamis, but worldly wise, wily, and unprincipled —while that name, I say, wins no good verdict from posterity. There stands the little day's vote of Athens, on one side; and the verdict of sixty generations of mankind on the other.

It has been thought wrong, to desire martyrdom; but I can think of no death so much to be coveted, as, after having lived a heroic life, to consummate all in one bright example, which, at no more cost than an hour's pain, shall send light and power through the world. This is heaven's commission to suffering innocence. This is heaven's vindication of its bitter pain. The lowliest sigh from the valleys of Piedmont, is echoed from distant continents. One glance from the dying martyr's eye, flashes through the ages. Small cost for such stupendous purchase! Little to do and to suffer, for so much to follow! That little done, is worth the world beside. Let us not despair at the dark pictures which history spreads before us. From that darkness is the brightest flashing out of heroic virtue. In the dark cloud is embosomed a splendor, that outshines the common light of day. Ay, and but for the gathering storm, that sometimes closes around the noblest men that the world ever saw, their virtues had never been signalized nor clothed with honor and beauty for the admiration of all mankind.

LECTURE XII.

HISTORIC VIEW OF HUMANITY: HUMAN PROGRESS—THE STEPS OF IT.

I HAVE considered in my last lecture, some of the great agencies, by which human progress has been promoted. I propose now to trace the steps of this progress. A few preliminary observations may prepare us to take a juster view of it.

There are difficulties, in many minds, about the world's life, which do not press equally upon individual life. Many feel that in their personal experience and lot, moral laws are revealed, and that things are tending to moral issues; that there really *is* a high purpose in their *own* life. "But to what end," they say, "have the wild, warring, slaughtering, struggling nations lived? This wide waste and desolation which history spreads before us—this confused turmoil of follies and crimes—what necessity has there been for it? What good has come of it?" Such is the view which they take of the past life of the human race, that they are almost ready to feel, in the spirit of the Manichæan philosophy, as if the domain of the world had been divided between good and evil spirits; ay, and had been given to the evil more than the good. Nay, there are those who say that man is but an animal, sprung from the ape; and stamped with animalism in his whole embryotic development

Now suppose it were true, that humanity is a development from animalism. Yet even upon *this* theory, as upon *every* view of the world, one fact is found to be involved in the whole history of humanity; and that is the *fact of progress.* Everywhere, from the beginning, through all ages, there has been progress. If, indeed, the race had been running down, or if it had stood stationary amidst its struggles and sufferings, then must we have given it up to the scorn of the satirist or of the false philosopher. Then had our problem found no solution. But progress redeems all, pays for all; shows that in all things, however dark and mysterious, there has been a good intent and tendency, a good Providence, ruling all,

> "From seeming evil still educing good,
> And better thence again, and better still,
> In infinite progression."

This, it is our present design to trace and show.

And we may observe that this order of progress has presided over successive productions and races on earth, *before* the appearance of man. There were, unknown ages ago, monstrous amphibious creatures; nameless when they lived, for there was none on earth to name them; and it has been left to the present age to classify them—the ichthyosaurus, the megatherium, the megalonyx—names that seem monstrous and fabulous like themselves; but they have lived. Then appeared more perfect animals; then man. The vegetable products, too, kept pace with the needs of animal life. When those amphibious monsters were seventy feet long, when there were such swarms and clouds of insects, that their fossil remains formed quarries and mountains of rock, then our common fern and brake shot up seventy and eighty feet high. Not till man was brought upon the scene, perhaps, were created "the grass, the herb yielding seed, and the fruit-tree, yielding fruit after his kind." And Mr. Agassiz says, that no fossil remains of roses are found, of a date prior to the advent of man. Let me add in passing, that these discoveries of modern science do not conflict with the Mosaic account of the creation; since, in a just construction, the "days" there spoken of, are not to be taken for periods of twenty-four hours; certainly not the first period, which was before the sun is represented as measuring the day; but for a term of indefinite length; during which the earth was "without form and void;" not yet prepared and beautified for the abode of man.

But the important observation is, that in all progress, the past has ever been preparing for the future; and in the progress of rational beings, that the future is ever borrowing wisdom from the past. Tradition, history, experiment, are ever spreading before mankind the facts, from which they are perpetually drawing almost unconscious conclusions. With the philosophic observer, however, they are not unconscious, but plainly traced out. The work which John Adams wrote in defence of our political Constitution and for the guidance of our Revolutionary times, was founded altogether upon the *experience* of nations. In matters of practical wisdom, it is only by experience that we truly know anything; *quantum sumus, scimus;* and only so it is, that the world knows or can know. It is striking to see, how one *political* truth after another, slowly rises out of the bosom of past ages of experience; first, that the people must share the government, to make it safe and just; and with this conviction, falls the divine right of kings: next, that the people's interest in the government, must be expressed through representation, through suffrage; and with this, sinks a hereditary nobility: then, on some experience of the representative system, that majorities may tyrannize; and the sanctity of numbers begins to be called in question, the rights of minorities to be insisted on, and the necessity asserted, of intelligence, of education; nay, more, of virtue, of mutual regard, of reverence for the Supreme Lawgiver.

Thus great principles take their place with us, as familiar truths; and we almost forget whence they have come, and what they have cost. Our commonest beliefs are the fruit of ages of experiment. They are familiar, and we imagine that they were easily acquired. We cannot look "to the rock whence they were hewn, nor to the hole of the pit whence they were digged." We think them intuitions; but the truth is, the steps of centuries have led to them; the pathway of generations has been opened, through mountains and through deserts, through flood and fire, to bring down to us the precious heritage.

Yet further, I must pray you, not to look at the material in this world alone, but at the spiritual yet more. Not as a dull, obstinate, intractable world, must we see it, but as God's ever-renewed and instant work; not as a mass of matter and sense and corruption, but as penetrated all through and forever with spiritual rays; not as darkness and gloom, chaos and night and storm, but as the theatre and story of a heavenly order; not, if I may say so, as if it were that dull, familiar place which we call the world; for which we have no respect because it is familiar; as the husbandman unwisely has none for his farm, because he has always trodden it and toiled upon it; but rather should we look upon this world, as some vast repository of life, some fair planet, rolling through the heavens, and bearing, midst light and shade, midst change and struggle, midst varying forms of development—Celtic, Saxon, Slavonic, Gothic, and African—its infinite burden of human joy and sorrow: concerning which we would know, as far as we *may* know, the divine history of God's providence over it.

But there is one further preliminary point, to which in this connection I wish more particularly to draw your attention; and that is, that the progress of the world has been a purpose and a plan above all human sagacity; inasmuch as it has been carried forward by man, while acting in total unconsciousness of any such instrumentality.

It has been justly observed, that in some views, animal instinct is a clearer proof of Divine direction, than human reason. Reason acts for itself. Within a certain sphere, it seems to act independently of the Power that made it. Instinct, on the contrary, is the mere vehicle of an intention acting through it. Unconscious tendencies in human nature, bear a similar character. And it is by these mainly that the world has been advanced. Men, nations, generations, have not purposely combined to secure its progress. No grand council, amphictyonic or ecclesiastic, Grecian or Roman, ever sat down and solemnly resolved that the world should improve. If there was such a design from the beginning, and if it has been steadily kept in view, it has come from a thought behind all, and above all; it has been God's design, and not man's. And in point of fact, it *has* been a purpose, not of man's, but of God's creation; it has been a purpose, aided, as we Christians believe, by Divine interposition; it has been, as I have said, a purpose accomplished by man while acting in total ignorance of it; and it has been a purpose, too, accomplished in spite of man.

But it was especially of human unconsciousness in this matter, that I proposed to speak. A French writer, M. Hello,* has devoted an entire work to the illustration of this point, in the history of France. He contemplates the elements of national progress, as social, territorial, and political. Thus under the first head, he says, that the gradually increasing freedom of the mass of the people, the circumstances that aided it, the pecuniary needs of kings which cast them upon the help of the people, the means provided by which the cities bought their privileges; and hence the rights of property, the value of labor, and the increasing dignity of labor—that all this did not come from any design of man, but from God. Then again, with regard to the territorial element—to hold together an immense empire like France, he says, some principle, some power was necessary, some permanent bond of union. What should it be? Perhaps there was no other possible in that country, but a metropolitan city; the centre from which should radiate the great routes to the extremity of the kingdom; to which everything should be subordinate; to which all the world should resort. Such is the great central city of that

* Philosophie de l'histoire de France.

empire; and when it is said that "Paris is France," the importance of this may be more than its import in the common speech of men. I have sometimes felt, for myself, that this relation of the imperial city was a great hardship to the provincial towns and districts; but I confess that this view of it has put a different aspect upon the matter. But what has given to the central city this preëminence? Not the intention of those who founded it, but the course of events, the force of circumstances—in other words, the providence of God. A similar course of observations conducts the writer to a like conclusion with regard to the political element, the government; which has been gradually changed and improved by struggles between the king and nobles and people, mainly of a personal character, and having little reference to the general good. "Modern Europe," says M. Guizot, "is born of the struggles of different classes of society." Society has wrought out these changes; but society did not know what it was about.

This view, which M. Hello takes of his country's history, is a good, a religious, and you will think perhaps, a somewhat remarkable view of things, for a French philosopher; and I was willing to spread it before you.

But the same view may be extended to the entire history of the world. Its progress has been carried forward by many agencies that were unconscious of their high mission.

He who discovered the mariner's compass, he who invented the art of printing, they who perfected the steam engine, little thought, perhaps, what instruments they were putting into the hands of humanity, for advancing its great end. Each one developed his own genius, followed his own taste in his individual sphere; in his privacy, he held the thread of inventive thought; in his humble workshop, he pursued his task; but the eye of Providence looked upon that work, and saw those narrow walls burst asunder, and the wide world, pervaded, illuminated, revolutionized by the ingenuity of that dreaming recluse—a Gutenberg or Faust, a Fitch or Fulton, a Watt or Arkwright!

In like manner, science has owed its triumphs mainly, to the simple love of knowledge, to single-hearted enthusiasm. But the secrets of nature which it has unfolded, the unsuspected powers which it has developed from the earth, and the wisdom which it has drawn from the skies, have united to bear the world onward, though Newton, "child-like sage," and Davy, torch bearer in the dark earth-mines, thought of but little, perhaps, besides their studies.

And so it has been with men of genius, those masters of human thought, that they have labored, not for influence, but for utterance—not for fame, but for truth. Genius is the grandest power on earth; for in its highest form it is religious as well as intellectual; and yet it has been well said, that it is as remarkable for its unconsciousness as for its energy. The eloquent thought, the epic story, the life-imaging drama, have come from depths of self-development, far beneath all calculation of results.

And why has not thought terminated in itself? Why has it not ministered only to its own improvement, died in its own bosom? Why are the noblest emanations of human genius, running on glorious errands through the earth, and to the ends of the world? Is it not evident that God has made man thus to act on man, for the general enlightening and advancement? If the imperial minds in this magnificent empire of thought, were conscious of their appointment and mission, *then* the plan and the intent were plain; but how much more striking is it, when just in proportion to their efficiency, has been their *un*consciousness of the glorious ministration for which they are raised up!

But it is time that I should proceed, as I proposed, to take a brief survey of the actual course of things, the steps of human progress.

The first two thousand years are very dark, in every sense; whether as history to be studied, or problem to be solved. A wild wandering over the earth, as far as we can judge—men nomadic—hunters, shepherds; no civilization, at least, capable of making any record of itself.

The infant school of the world had rude teachers—cold and hunger and nakedness and need and peril were its teachers. The early cosmogonies represented the earth, when it first became the abode of man, as a scene of disorder and misery. Diodorus the Sicilian speaks of the trees, plants, animals, and man himself, as springing from the mud warmed by the sun, and pictures the first men as brutish and weak. Heraclitus, according to Plutarch, imagined the original habitable earth to have been but a mass of cinders, left by volcanic fires. Plutarch himself gives his opinion in the touching picture which he draws, of a man of the earliest period, addressing those of later ages: "Oh! how are you cherished of the gods," he says, "you who live now! How fortunate is your time! The fertile earth yields you a thousand fruits; all nature is engaged but in giving you delights; but *our* birthtime was mournful and sterile; the world was so new, that we were in want of everything; the air was not pure; the sun was obscured; the rivers overflowed their banks; all was marsh and thicket and forest; the fields were not cultivated; our misery was extreme; we had neither inventions nor inventors; our hunger was never appeased; we tore the limbs of wild animals to devour them, when we could find neither moss nor bark; and if we found an acorn, we danced around the oak, chanting the praises of the earth; we had no other fêtes nor rejoicings but these; and all the rest of our life was trouble and poverty and sadness." *

But let us leave this period of the world's infancy, which is indeed, as you see it in the historic charts, covered with clouds; concerning which we can offer nothing but conjectures; and come at once to our proper starting point—the earliest period of recorded history. We can trace no proper history of the world but in the form of nationalities; and we know nothing of nations earlier than the Chinese, the

* See Boullanger—Antiquité Devoileé, tom. i., p. 195, 196.

Indians of Hindoostan, the Persians and the Egyptians; nor anything of them earlier than about the year 2000 of the Mosaic era.

In the survey which I am about to take of known epochs and of distinct nationalities, the points to which I wish to invite your attention are these: that every great step which the world has taken, has been a manifest improvement upon the past, and a manifest preparation for further progress; that at every great step, the world has paused and gained a foothold, in which it has rallied the energies of the past, to throw them into the fortunes of the future; that every great era of civilization, in other words, has presented these two remarkable facts—it has received and collected the improvements of the preceding era, its political forms, its laws, philosophies, theologies, literatures; it has carried them to the highest point it was able; and then it has cast them into the bosom of the future.* Thus improvement has passed on: from Asia and Egypt to Greece, from Greece to Rome, from Rome to the feudal forms of Central Europe, and from Central or Continental, to Western Europe, and to America.

The childhood of civilization then, was in Southern Asia. In the soft clime and fragrant bowers of the East, was man's birthplace and cradle. There indeed, was the Eden of the world, and there was its childhood nurtured. There were the earliest and simplest governments; patriarchal, despotic, but parental too—parental in their indulgence, parental in their summary discipline and instant punishment; and *there* were institutions fitted in every respect to be the leading strings of the world's childhood. Do you not see men there, seated as on school forms, in the great divisions of caste; generation after generation taking their places on those forms, with all the docility of children; finding them, to a certain extent, seats of instruction, and at any rate barriers against universal anarchy—barriers indeed,

* I state this in the most general way. I know how many exceptions and deviations there may seem to be; but such, taking the whole world into the account, I believe to be the general course of things.

without which they could receive *no* instruction. Caste, in India and Egypt, was nothing else but the extreme of a principle that has prevailed in all ages; *i. e.*, the division of society into ranks and orders. The Indian parent taught his son his own trade or pursuit; and the son could follow no other. He could not, like the German apprentice in the middle ages, wander over the country for three years as a journeyman. The German had more liberty; but *his* liberty was strictly limited. There have always been restrictions upon the freedom of occupation; till in *this* country every man is allowed, I had almost said, to do *what* he will, *where* he will. But this liberty would have been disorder and ruin in the old Indian or Egyptian life. It could no more have borne the same liberty than *literal* children could, in these days. Do you not see again, the leading traits of childhood, in the absolute and universal submission to authority, and in the unreasoning, unaspiring contentment with their lot, of Hindoostan and China? Do you not also see the people of Southern Asia and of Egypt, lapped in the bosom of a rich mother earth and of a mild embracing climate; with few wants, with few cares, with few calls to exertion? Do you not see them moreover wrapped about with material influences, pupils of matter, taking all their ideas from physical nature, and so building vast pyramids and splendid mausoleums and stupendous rock-temples, excavated from the very mountains, like those of Petra and Ellora; and estimating the forces of their armies alone by numbers; attracted by outward decorations, conceiving of power, of kingship, always as something seated upon a magnificent throne, holding out a jewelled sceptre and clothed with gorgeous habiliments? Look at Xerxes and Darius, thus seated on their thrones—the great child-kings; surrounded by the cloud of innumerable hosts; Oriental homages at their feet; silken tent-curtains swelling in the night breeze over them; music in their ears: *they* never imagined that anything of hardship or peril could approach *them*:—when lo! at Platæa and Marathon, shot the lightning of intellect into that cloud, and scattered the visions of Oriental greatness, and revolutionized the ideas of an age.

There is discrimination doubtless to be made, among these Oriental nations, in regard to progress. In China, life retires back into the *most* childish simplicity, docility and subjection. The emperor was the government, and the law, and the morality, and the religion—and the *very people;* all was absorbed into *him.* The rigor of *caste* in India —*i. e.*, recognized classes with recognized rights—was something better than this stereotyped, this solidified unity. The subjection of inferiors was such in China, that if a son complained of his father, or a younger brother of his elder, he was to be whipped with a hundred blows and banished three years, even if his complaint were just; if not, he was to be strangled. If a son lifted his hand against his father, his flesh was to be torn from his body with hot pincers. I am speaking of the past; such is the law; how often it is executed now, I do not know. In China, all was prosaic—life, learning, and philosophy alike. The earliest Chinese sage divided all knowledge into three departments—silk culture, bridge building, and the training of burden-bearing animals. The philosophy of Confucius never went beyond the simplest precepts of morality and religious veneration. No deep questions are discussed; no sense is entertained apparently that there are such questions. It is the very earliest childhood of philosophy. The Indian philosophy, with all its dreaminess and mysticism, goes far beyond this. It meditates the *deepest* questions. The secret of nature, the mystery of God, the end of being, invite its contemplation. Its system indeed was pantheism; but the Chinese could hardly be said to have any system. And although they were a purer people than those of India, it was because they were more childlike, submissive, and timid. The mendacity of the people of India is well known. The Chinese, perhaps, did not dare to lie.

The Persian was considerably advanced beyond either. The *Light* which he worshipped was not Lama, not Brah ma, not any particular existence, but the sentient *All itself.* It was not Ormuzd as the original principle, but the Zeroene Akerene—the infinite and uncreated Life. And the Persian Zend-Avesta—*i. e.*, living words—discoursed far more nobly than the old Indian mythologies. In all respects too, political and social, the Persian life was a clear step beyond the Indian. In fine, the Phœnicians, the Hebrews, and the Egyptians, it is well known, went far beyond them all; whether we consider their polity, their religion, their commerce, learning, or arts. In fact, as you advance westward from the farthest East, every step of your survey is a step of progress; and I believe the rule will hold good, as you travel on through successive nations and ages down to the present day. "Westward the star of *empire* takes its way," says Berkeley: certainly that has been the course of the empire of civilization.

We have glanced now at its first great phase; in which docility, submission, mental slavery to religion, to government, to social order, held almost absolute sway.

But Asia at length ceased to be the theatre to which the eyes of men were directed; and the great drama of the world's story passed away to the shores of Greece.

Here was a new world, a new people, a new genus of the human race. Offshoots perhaps from Oriental civilization, that took root on the shores and islands of Asia Minor, small tribes that wandered at their will along the northern boundaries of the Mediterranean, born of the sea, bred among the hills, they had escaped from Oriental passiveness and from the bondage of great empires; they were hardy, vigorous, active, and above all, free. For here especially was the birth of intellectual freedom; of a freely working and creative energy, which unfolded itself in religion, in polity, and in literature.

So situated, trained and endowed, Greece made a large step in the world's progress. She took from Asia and Egypt what they had to give, their laws, their systems of philosophy, their mythologies, their crude and gigantic forms of art; and refined them from their grossness, stripped them of their clumsy overlayings, idealized what was crude and material in them, and wrought them into delicacy and beauty—both of form and thought. She rose from sense, to idealism. The earth-gods gave place to celestial powers. The fabled war of the earthborn Titans against the heavenly divinities who overcame them, is probably the mythological expression of that fact. But all the mythology and religious art of Greece had their precursors and prototypes in Egypt and Asia. The Sun in the Persian worship, the Osiris of the Egyptians, was in Greece, the beautiful Apollo. "The gods of Greece," says Heeren, "were *moral persons;*" they were not symbolical, but ideal; and they could no longer be represented as monsters with many heads and arms.

But Greece had more to do than to make statues or to spiritualize or humanize the old mythologies. In her was developed the first free, political energy in the world. There had been singular freedom in the Hebrew land; but it was comparatively passive; and besides, it was pressed on either side, by the Assyrian and Egyptian monarchies. In Greece, freedom had a field to itself. Yet more, it was disenthralled from Oriental languor. It breathed its inspiration into the whole life of the people. It expressed itself in literature. It resolved itself into deeds. It was full of restless, of youthful activity. Yes, upon the hills of Greece went forth the struggling youth of the world; it went forth in toil, and it went forth in battle. Her soil was comparatively sterile, and her climate bracing, though pure and delicious; and hers was the hard hand, the strong sinew, and the manly nurture. Her very sports were races and wrestlings and feats of strength.

The Grecian literature was a still more remarkable stride; and may seem to bring into question our position, that she lived in the youth of time. There are indeed wonders in it that cannot be accounted for, except by an original power, a divine energy native to the human soul, and hardly yet recognized in our theories of culture. That the poems of Homer, defying all after competition in epic verse, should have burst out from the darkness of a rude and almost unknown antiquity, is a mystery, for which I confess I have no other solution. The perfection of the Greek language and style surprises me far less. For it appears to me that the whole Greek culture owed a great deal of its perfection and power to the limited channel in which it flowed, to the singleness of its aim; which was to embody nature and humanity in their simplest and grandest characteristics, without grasping the wider ranges and more complicated forms of human thought. I think I have known a youth of twenty who, in his style, approached much more nearly to the Greek simplicity and purity, than he did at forty, when he had much more complex and difficult forms of thought to grapple with. Deep philosophizing is very apt to spoil the style, or at least this kind of perfection in it. And the modern poet, who sounds the depths of the modern mind, has far more difficulty in expressing his thought with force and clearness, than had Homer and Sophocles. And I maintain that the whole literature of the Greeks was youthful, compared with that of modern times. There was nothing in their drama like that comprehension of the whole breadth of our humanity which we see in Shakspeare, or the espousal of its noblest interests and affections in Schiller. There was nothing in their poetry like the introversion, the self-communion, the subjective character of modern genius, in Wordsworth and Browning. There was nothing in Herodotus and Thucydides to compare with the philosophical insight into history, of Herder and Guizot. There was nothing in Plato and Aristotle to compare with the breadth of Bacon and Leibnitz, or the sharp and patient analysis of Locke or of Kant. Of ancient and modern *science* I need say nothing; for there is *no* comparison.

The next great step of the world was planted in Rome. But *was* it a step onward? This it may seem more difficult to prove. In philosophy, in poetry, in art, in graceful culture, certainly it was not. But there were two offices which Rome discharged for the world's culture, that were of more practical and diffusive benefit than anything done in Greece.

The first was that of lawgiver; more important to the world at that period, than philosophy or art. In this respect she went entirely beyond her predecessor. For impracticable political theories, like those of Plato, and for ill-defined rights of property and persons, she substituted a grand and elaborated Code of Law. Law has far more to do with the welfare of well-ordered society, than books or theories, orations or poems, pictures or statues. The Roman law was precisely what her barbarian invaders needed; nay, and of such permanent value is it, that it has continued, under the name of the Civil Law, to be the guide of more than half the cultivated world to this day.

The second office which Rome discharged for the world, was that of diffuser. That which was pent up within the narrow confines of Greece, was now scattered through the world. Plato and Aristotle, Homer and Herodotus, Æschylus and Sophocles, were transplanted to the banks of the Rhine, the Seine, and the Thames. Stores of cultivated wisdom there were in the world; but how should they benefit, how enlighten the Gaul, the Saxon, the rude tribes of Germany! It was for that stupendous and earth-shadowing power, that spread her wings from Britain to Parthia and India, to bear to the nations the burden of ancient lore. Her legions swept through the world; but not for evil alone; philosophy and the arts, and Christianity too, followed in their train. Gaul and Britain might have remained unchristianized for ages, if they had not come within the sweep of the Roman power.

For the part which she had to act, Rome was fitted by her character and whole training. She who was to spread herself over the earth, had no *home* character to begin with. Not from quiet patriarchal hearths did she take her origin, but from a robber's lair. Rome, at the first, was a nest of military marauders, a refuge of renegades from surrounding tribes, a *colluvies*, says Livy himself, a sink into which flowed the dregs of the Latin cities around; their very wives these Roman robbers tore from the Sabines, and the children of this violence were Ishmaels. From this origin came, not beauty nor grace, nor the liberality which commerce, friendly communication with the world, give; but simple, concentrated strength. The Roman was a man of iron nerve and firmness. In his girding arm was a power to hold in check those tendencies which, in Greece, had snapped the bonds of social order. The beautiful Grecian theories of right, with the Roman, hardened into law. Law, with him, as has been often observed, was morality, religion, the only *idea* of right. Religion—*religio*, from *religare*, to bind—it was simply a state bond. The Roman genius is not attractive, not beautiful to us; but it had its use. Cicero is its fairest representative, but for spiritual beauty he does not compare with Plato. His religion was a correct sentiment, often noble, touching sometimes from its sadness; but it does not freely and joyously well up from the deep fountains within, like Plato's. In short, the joyous and graceful Grecian boy of fifteen has become, in Rome, as we sometimes see a youth of twenty, when first touching the practical interests of life, utilitarian, selfish, grasping. It is not beautiful. An iron jar is not so beautiful as a porcelain vase; but it may be more useful; it can better hold and transmit what is deposited in it.

And when that iron jar was expanded to a mighty vase, wide as the world, and then broke in pieces, we do not lament over it; we say, it had served its purpose. Perhaps no great empire ever fell, with so little of the sympathy of the world, as this. When we learn from Tacitus, that even so early as the first century, the armies of Rome, ay, of old military Rome, were composed wholly of foreigners; when we read that, in the fourth century, in a time of famine, all the teachers of youth were banished from the city, and six thousand dancers were retained—we give up a people, who had lost all the spirit for which national existence is worth preserving.

The dissolution of the Roman Empire opens to us the next great scene in human affairs. The theatre is Central and Western Europe. The political form is feudality. The social powers are the family and individual force. The presiding genius is Christianity; sadly corrupted indeed, but still it is Christianity. To adventure upon this restless sea of the middle ages, with all its struggling elements, its crossing tides and stormy winds, is of course more than I propose; but something may be said to indicate the great current that was bearing the world onward.

The feudal system was far freer than the despotisms that preceded it. It was *not*, as I think is often supposed, a mere relation of barons and serfs; it was a general form of government, a political hierarchy; extending from the emperor or king, through successive grades, down to the lowest subject; barons, counts, lords, kings, as well as serfs, holding their power or privilege respectively of their superiors; and holding it on condition of certain services to be rendered. The tenure was a *fee;* a word from the old Teutonic, or from the Latin, *fides*—*fede* in Italian—*fe* in Spanish, *i. e.*, a trust. The idea involved in this tenure was that of a duty—of the low to the high, and of the high to the low. It is obvious then, that the feudal system undertook to define the relations of the governing and the governed. It recognized in both alike, certain rights and duties. This, if I mistake not, was a new thing in the world. The old Roman law minutely described the rights and duties of citizens toward one another, but not the reciprocal claims of the government and people. That is to say, it was law, but not a constitution. In the feudal time was first heard in the world the word *privileges.* It was the fashion of the time, so to speak, to demand them. The religious orders, as well as the civil, were constantly obtaining *privileges* from their superiors. Privileges, I repeat; it was a word of potent effect, a precedent never to be forgotten. The whole struggle in Europe, by which political freedom advanced, has been a struggle for privileges—a struggle of nobles with kings, of the people with them both.

Next, as M. Guizot has remarked,* a new *family* culture sprang from the feudal system. The feudal lords, the feudal superiors of every rank, dwelt apart and alone. They were driven by their very isolation to some culture, to some mental resources. And they were numerous enough to give some tone to public sentiment. Woman assumed a new place, a new importance in society. The romantic poetry of the period, and the spirit of chivalry, both afford sufficient proof of that.

But above all, individual force was developed in this period. Men began slowly to learn and to feel that they were men, that they had rights, that they had individual, yea, and immortal interests. Christianity inspired this feeling, but feudalism fostered it beyond all previous systems. Service to superiors was voluntary. The serf or vassal might choose his suzerain, and exact guarantees from him. A new feeling of selfhood, self-consciousness, self-reliance slowly grew up in the human breast. It grew especially in the cities. Commerce and mechanic art made men rich and strong; and they were able to buy or exact from kings and nobles, important concessions. There was much freedom in *Greece*, but little individual force. And when did there *ever* stand upon the earth such a visible representative of individual force as the armed knight?—clad, himself and his good steed, in complete steel; with his plated gauntlets, and breastplate, and shield and barred helmet; with his double-edged falchion on one side, and poniard on the other, and the axe at his saddlebow, and his long lance resting upon the stirrup—a moving tower of iron, seated upon a fire-breathing engine: our modern men dwindle into puny citizens compared with this.

And the good knight must needs wage war—must wage

* Civilization in Europe, 4th lecture.

it even to the walls of Jerusalem. And what followed? Why, he must have means—must have money. And where could he get it? Why, of the good burgesses and citizens. And did they give it for nothing? No, they bought privileges of knights and nobles and kings. Thus, the whole course of things, and especially the Crusades, helped to raise the people, to sink the rulers. The iron tower, like the image of Nebuchadnezzar, was destined to fall, and crumble in pieces, and disappear from the earth.

I have said that Christianity presided over this epoch. However imperfectly understood, it did reign with absolute sway. It was a law from which there was no appeal. The high and the powerful, though they violated, never dared formally to set it aside. They trembled before its spiritual powers and awful retributions. And it was not only a law of right, but a spirit of mercy. It not only awed, but softened the hearts of men. It was an image of suffering patience and pity that they worshipped. That one perfect life—that one great sacrifice—think, what its appeal must have been, compared with the influence of any former religion. It espoused, above all, the cause of the poor, the suffering, the wronged and crushed. The gospel was humanity, even more than it was divinity. The light that came into the world, was veiled in the softened shadow of human pity and gentleness.

Still, however, the civilization of this period was extremely immature. It was full of misdirected efforts and wild struggles. No satisfactory civil order was established, nor proper recognition of human rights obtained. The human race went on through the middle ages, like a rash and reckless youth, when approaching his majority. It pursued a wild and irregular career; now rising, now falling; now stumbling on the dark mountains of ignorance, and now wallowing in the great Roman sink of sensuality—with broken columns and fallen temples all around—now filled with the fierce, hot haste of passion, and then, with the sullen melancholy of despair. All its labors were tentative.

The whole course of things was a series of experiments, preparing for a future and brighter day.

In that brighter day, I believe, we now stand; in the great day of the world's manhood; not in the latter, however, but in the earlier part of that day; for I look upon the grand agents now in the field, as having only commenced their magnificent work.

This epoch, beginning with the sixteenth century, is crowded with events, which are alike proofs and promises of advancement—the birth, as a popular fact, of free religious thought in the Reformation in Germany; the great stand for political liberty in England, and the building up and prosperity of the American Republic; the establishment of the inductive philosophy, and the almost entire creation of the physical sciences; the rise of the fine arts in Italy, and the cultivation of music, which are almost wholly within this period; the invention of the art of printing, of the cotton gin, and of the steam engine; the introduction of the system of common schools and the diffusion of knowledge among the people; in fine, the unprecedented impulse given to the minds of men by the universal spirit of improvement.

All this, I need not insist, is progress. Neither can I dwell upon these subjects in detail; nor is it necessary, perhaps, for my purpose; they speak sufficiently for themselves. I can only refer, in general, to the indications which these agencies bear, to the sphere in which they are working, and to the encouragement, if not a more solemn feeling, which they should inspire.

Look then at this grand array of forces. Can any one of them stop? Can the spirit of freedom, political or religious, die out from the hearts of men? Have they got hold of rights, and will they ever let them go? Can philosophy or science stop? Go ask the studious and enthusiastic toilers in those enchanted fields, and they will tell you that you might as well expect them to desire the sun to go down, when its morning light is spread upon the mountains. Can genius be quenched, or the fine arts dash chisel and palette to the ground, or music, that is making the air of the world vibrate to its melodies, die out into mournful silence? Can men stop printing books, or reading them? Can they break the steam engine in pieces?—unless they find, if that be possible, a better power. But will they give up, after having found it, a power to bear their cars over the land, and their ships over the sea? Can this pestilent notion of educating the people, this universal diffusion of knowledge, by any means have a stop put to it? I am afraid not. Let Austria try. But she does *not* try. *She* is swept on by the resistless current. No, the spirit of improvement has got hold of the world; and the exorcism to drive it out, is not yet found, and never will be. No, the world has got beyond the waverings of its youth. It has come of age. It has come to the sober thought and settled purpose of manhood; and nothing can shake that thought and purpose. Look again at the theatre of this modern culture. It is Western Europe and America; not an inaccessible mountain land, fit to be the fastness of mere freedom; not a vast plain, like those of Asia, opened for the expansion of immense empires; but a tract of the earth, washed by oceans, intersected by bays and rivers, essentially commercial; having easy communication with all the world. It is the grand propagandist portion of the world. Its inhabitants, descending from races in whom the fullest measure of human energy has been developed, have become the most enlightened nations of the earth—and the most rapidly growing. The Saxon race, which two centuries ago was only 3,000,000, now numbers 53,000,000. These countries, thus advanced in civilization, filled with manufactories, with arts, with books, with inventions for human comfort and improvement, possess the very advantages which the rest of the world wants. And now, just when they are prepared for this office of diffusion, is the grand instrument of diffusion put into their hands: I mean, of course, the power of steam. Now, at length, shall they send back to Asia and the farthest

Tartary the cultivated children descended from their swarming colonies; and to Africa, the descendants of the captives once torn from her bosom. It has become just as certain that steamships and steam cars shall penetrate the solitudes of Africa and the crowded villages of populous Asia, and carry to them our arts, our sciences, our literature, and our religion, as that the light which breaks upon the eastern horizon shall spread itself through the world.

I know that dark fears are entertained by some concerning what is passing in these very countries—popular outbreaks, decline of the old reverence, signs, as they think, of social deterioration. But it seems to me, with all due respect for their opinion, that they are looking at the little eddyings on the stream of events, and not at the deep current. There are popular outbreaks, but they soon pass away. There is less respect for rank and riches—less even than there should be—the world does not easily stop at the right point; but is there less respect for talent, learning, and worth? I believe that the indications, which the alarmists constantly adduce, are the superficial ones. The movement of things is perhaps *never* direct, but in circles. Rubbish and straw are on the outside, and they are blown this way and that way; and in the wide sweep of the elements, in the vast gyrations of the slow revolutionary movement that is bearing on the civilized world, things may seem to be going backward, and may really *be* going backward in certain quarters—*i. e.*, relatively going backward, while all is *actually* going forward. Nay, and the more violent are the gusts upon the surface, the eddies upon the stream, the more rapid and strong may be the great and onward tendency.

This impression which prevails in the minds of some of the best men, that we are in a state of social deterioration, is no new thing in the world, and it is a very curious thing. I have sometimes thought that it proceeds, in part, from a natural modesty; that it results, under this influence, from a comparison very likely to be made by superior minds, and not by the body of the people. Our predecessors, the leading men, by whom as pillars, the world was borne up, are venerable to us; the places they filled, the presidencies, the magistracies; the parts they acted—of orators, judges, lawyers, clergy—were clothed with dignity and honor: they were great and noble men to us; their figures loom up majestically in the dim land of the past. *Now* these great functions—these presidencies, magistracies, forums, pulpits—have fallen into the hands of us, pigmy men; these high places have sunk down to the level of our common and every-day life; we are nothing to ourselves, compared with what *they* were to us; we cannot believe that we equal them, or anything near it; all is run down, we say; society is deteriorating; the world is growing more ignoble every day. The next generation will probably make the same reflection, when it compares itself with us.

It is no new thing in the world, as I have said; and if it were true—if the world, according to this impression, had been really ever growing worse, it must have come, by this time, to a sad pass indeed. Even the old Greek Hesiod thought that he was living in "an iron age," and that all the happy ages had gone by. Longinus, who lived in the time of Aurelian and in the court of Zenobia, compared the men of his day, to children, whose limbs were contracted and cramped by bandages.* The decadence of Rome might well justify something of this despondency. And we can sympathize with the noble Cicero in his sadness, who, writing to his friend Atticus, from his retreat in the beautiful island of Astura, says, "I retire in the morning to the thick and wild wood, and do not leave it till evening. Next to you, the dearest thing is solitude. In this, my converse is with letters; but tears often interrupt it. I restrain them, as much as I can; but as yet, am not equal to it." † More magnanimously fought his battle with discouragement a modern man, and in an hour no less dark. It was amidst

* De Sublimitate, chap. 43.

† Epist. ad Atticum, B. xii. 15.

the horrors of the French Revolution. There, in a street in Paris, in a house sought for hiding, and while the blood of the innocent and noble was flowing around him, sat a man whose quiet employment was the writing of a book. That man was the Marquis de Condorcet. And what, think you, was the subject of the book he was writing? It was *man's certain progress to liberty, virtue, and happiness.*

It *is* certain. It is certain because it is the purpose of Heaven. It is certain because of what it has already cost. It is certain because all the steps of past progress are promises. And *what* promises? Promises earned from ages of toil and sorrow; promises written on the rack and the scaffold, where patriots have died for liberty, and Christians for truth; promises pronounced over the gloomy altars where sorrowing nations have been slain; ay, and sealed in the blood of the noblest men in the world: such promises shall not go unfulfilled.

Ever solemn is the story of the world. A solemn thing it is for us, the American people, to take our place in the great procession of nations. Whence came we; and why are we here, but to do our part? The sorrowing ages call upon us to do our part. The tears and groans of long-suffering and sighing humanity call upon us to do our part. Empires crushed under the weight of hopeless bondage—millions that have wandered in the darkness of ignorance and amidst the terrors of superstition, address to us—to *us especially*—the great adjuration; and they say, O ye, a people, free, intelligent, Christian!—who know your duty and have liberty to perform it; O ye, a people, whose foot is set upon an unchartered soil; whose hands are filled with the riches of the world; whose children, partners of yourselves, are to wander down the coming ages, through the fairest domain that God ever gave to man; hear the voice of humanity; hear the voice that comes from earth—and that comes from Heaven!

THE END.

www.ingramcontent.com/pod-product-compliance
Lightning Source LLC
LaVergne TN
LVHW010228110826
845151LV00004B/1221

* 9 7 8 1 4 2 5 5 2 5 7 4 3 *